Chinese Entrepreneurship

After more than 30 years of reformations in agriculture, manufacturing, and trade and industry, China's economy has grown to become the second largest in the world. This book examines the contributions of dynamic entrepreneurs to the economic development of mainland China and Hong Kong – an analysis that is largely lacking in existing studies on China's economic stronghold. This book adopts theories of entrepreneurship and market processes as major analytical frameworks to conclude that entrepreneurship is the true engine of growth in mainland China and Hong Kong.

Chinese Entrepreneurship focuses on the knowledge drivers and systemic challenges of these businesses to examine how entrepreneurs under uncertainty identify and pursue profit opportunities, and how their efforts have enhanced China's economic dynamics.

This book offers vital insight to students, teachers, and researchers of Chinese business and economics, along with Chinese culture and expanding economies.

Fu-Lai Tony Yu is Professor at the Department of Economics and Finance, Hong Kong Shue Yan University, Hong Kong.

Diana S. Kwan is Project Coordinator at the Office of Educational Services, Chinese University of Hong Kong, Hong Kong.

Routledge Studies in the Modern World Economy

Chinese Entrepreneurship

An Austrian economics perspective

Fu-Lai Tony Yu and Diana S. Kwan

Routledge
Taylor & Francis Group

LONDON AND NEW YORK

First published 2016
by Routledge

2 Park Square, Milton Park, Abingdon, Oxfordshire OX14 4RN
711 Third Avenue, New York, NY 10017

Routledge is an imprint of the Taylor & Francis Group, an informa business

First issued in paperback 2018

Copyright © 2016 Fu-Lai Tony Yu and Diana S. Kwan

The right of Fu-Lai Tony Yu and Diana S. Kwan to be identified as authors of this work has been asserted by them in accordance with sections 77 and 78 of the Copyright, Designs and Patents Act 1988.

All rights reserved. No part of this book may be reprinted or reproduced or utilised in any form or by any electronic, mechanical, or other means, now known or hereafter invented, including photocopying and recording, or in any information storage or retrieval system, without permission in writing from the publishers.

Notice:
Product or corporate names may be trademarks or registered trademarks, and are used only for identification and explanation without intent to infringe.

British Library Cataloguing-in-Publication Data
A catalogue record for this book is available from the British Library

Library of Congress Cataloging-in-Publication Data
A catalog record for this book has been requested

ISBN: 978-1-138-88661-2 (hbk)
ISBN: 978-1-138-31702-4 (pbk)

Typeset in Times New Roman
by Apex CoVantage, LLC

Contents

Illustrations

Figures

Table

Preface

After more than 30 years of economic reform, China became the second largest economy in the world in 2010. China's dazzling economic performance is in large part attributed to dynamic entrepreneurs emerging after Deng Xiaoping implemented the market reform in 1978. On the other hand, the role of entrepreneurs in Hong Kong's economic success is well known too. The island economy has been regarded by scholars such as Jon Woronoff and W. K. Chiu as the "capitalist paradise." Economic research using neoclassical growth theories on East Asian economies in general, and mainland China and Hong Kong in particular, is not lacking. However, entrepreneurship, which is the true engine of growth in the two economies, is largely missing in mainstream economics literatures. This book adopts Austrian theories of entrepreneurship and market processes as a major analytical framework. Specifically, the book focuses on knowledge and coordination problems. It examines how entrepreneurs under uncertainty identify and pursue profit opportunities, and their efforts have enhanced economic dynamics.

Part I is the theoretical framework. Chapter 1 reviews the contributions of Austrian economists to the theories of entrepreneurship. It covers the works of Carl Menger, the founder of the Austrian school of economics, Ludwig von Mises, Friedrich A. Hayek, Ludwig M. Lachmann, and Israel M. Kirzner. This chapter also reviews the contributions of some quasi-Austrian economists to the theories of entrepreneurship. These scholars cannot be regarded as Austrian economists in the strict sense. However, their arguments are consistent with the Austrian school of economics. They are Richard Cantillon, the "founding father of modern economics," Frank Knight, a leading American economist pertaining to subjectivism, and Joseph Schumpeter, an Austria-born economist who studied under Eugen von Bohm-Bawerk. The chapter ends with a construction of a model of the entrepreneurial process in Hayekian perspective.

Part II is a collection of cases from mainland China and Hong Kong. Chapter 2 integrates the concept of entrepreneurial leadership and capabilities theories with Austrian economics to explain the growth of a manufacturing firm in mainland China. It argues that entrepreneurial leadership provides a vision to the development of a new product or an organization. The entrepreneurial leader organizes and coordinates production activities under uncertainty. In doing so, the entrepreneur becomes a systematic capital structure builder. In the production process, capital resources are combined according to entrepreneur's plans and judgment. As the market indicates that there is a need for the firm to expand, the entrepreneur will combine more capital resources with the capabilities to yield larger profit to the growing firm. Austrian theories of capital structure interpret the expansion strategies of the firm through imitation, joint ventures, and mergers and acquisitions. The growth of the Haier Group, one of the largest and most successful household appliances firms in mainland China, will be used to illustrate our arguments.

Chapter 3 introduces an Austrian perspective of international entrepreneurship and coordination. This framework will be applied to understand the economic success of the paper magnate Zhang Yin and her Nine Dragons Paper Company. Zhang started her career in Shenzhen (China), then established her paper factory in Hong Kong. Later, she ventured into the paper recycling business in the United States and eventually returned to China to deal with paper manufacturing. Zhang conducted global coordination around the world. Her international entrepreneurship has made her become one of the richest women in the world. This chapter concludes that self-interest entrepreneurs such as Zhang Yin who pursue profits for their own benefit result in global markets unintentionally linked together, with resources effectively allocated.

It is well documented that Israel M. Kirzner's theory of entrepreneurial alertness follows closely that of Mises' praxeology. Kirzner argues that the entire role of entrepreneurs lies in their alertness to profit from opportunity hitherto unnoticed in the market. In Kirzner's subjectivist theory of knowledge, alertness to opportunity is subconscious learning. Once a subconscious hunch is arrived at, it becomes a resource (knowledge) for the entrepreneur, to be utilized to exploit profit. Moreover, in Kirzner's view, entrepreneurship means profit arbitrage, and it is the continual profit exploitation in the market process that drives an economy towards a higher level of capitalist achievement. Kirzner's theories of entrepreneurship and subconscious learning will be illustrated by the case of Mama Moon, a woman entrepreneur in tourism, catering, and hotel industries in Guilin, China (see Chapter 4).

Chapter 5 integrates the contributions of Ludwig von Mises, I. M. Kirzner, and F. A. Hayek to entrepreneurship and market processes to obtain a theory of global coordination. This theory is then applied to understand Li & Fung's corporate dynamics. This chapter argues that Li & Fung, one of the largest providers of consumer goods in the world, hardly owns or hires any worker, raw material, machinery, or factory for making household products. However, by linking up and coordinating the most efficient and cheapest manufacturing processes in different parts of the world, the company is able to gain pure entrepreneurial profit. This chapter concludes that Li & Fung is a successful international coordinator that transmits, integrates, and creates knowledge around the globe. The efforts of Li & Fung and other Chinese entrepreneurs have transformed Hong Kong into an Asia's most dynamic knowledge hub.

Contemporary neoclassical economics ignores the subjective evaluation of information and therefore fails to explain the persuasive role of advertising. Chapter 6 explains the roles of advertising and promotion strategies from a subjectivist lens. In particular, it attempts to use a phenomenological approach to explain the persuasive power of advertising. It will argue that when consumers watch a piece of advertising, they will interpret the message conveyed in the content by their stock of knowledge which is accumulated from everyday life experience. If consumers fail to interpret the advertising content, we cannot expect them to accept and buy the product. In other words, the content of advertising has to make sense to consumers. Sensemaking implies subjective understanding. When consumers find that the advertising content makes sense, then consumers and the advertising agent (on behalf of the product) share 'common sense', or share the same definition of the situation, which can be made possible only through intersubjective communication. Since knowledge is obtained from everyday life experience and has history, in order to share the same biography with consumers, a successful piece of advertising requires the firm to know consumers' personal growth history, racial identity, culture, and social and economic backgrounds. The phenomenological approach to explain the persuasive power of advertising will be applied to understand the successful advertising campaign made by Vitasoy, a well-known soybean drink in Hong Kong.

Chapter 7 uses the theories of the firm to explain the Chinese family business succession in Hong Kong. More specifically, it utilizes capabilities theories, property rights economics, and Neo-Confucianism to understand management disputes and infighting among the members in a Chinese family business in Hong Kong. This chapter will argue that the founder of a Chinese business firm in Hong Kong is able to lead his or her offspring to create a dynamic enterprise via charismatic leadership and family rules embedded in traditional Chinese values. However, these two strategic assets disappear following the passing away of the founder as well as the emergence of new social values. When the founder passes on the enterprise to his or her offspring using more or less the equal inheritance system, the traditional Chinese values are unable to enforce the leader's will to consolidate the strengths of second-generation family members to maintain the founder's business. Furthermore, when the business is owned by all family members, property rights of the firm become unclear. Without effective enforcement of traditional Chinese values and with collective ownership rights, some family members will have the incentive to capture the economic rent which is shared by all members. In other words, some family members behave opportunistically or even cheat in order to capture economic gains in the public domain. High monitoring and enforcement costs in the form of court battles and endless disputes will occur. Rent dissipation occurs in the form of deterioration of the quality of the family business. This chapter will use Yung Kee, an internationally well-known roast goose restaurant in Hong Kong as an illustration. This chapter ends with policy recommendations on the succession of the Chinese family business in Hong Kong.

Chapter 8 utilizes the Austrian theory of market competition to interpret the supermarket war in Hong Kong. Unlike mainstream neoclassical economics, which assumes perfect competition with equilibrium configuration, this study focuses on the market process in which market participants are fully aware of their rivals. In the dynamic competitive process, entrepreneurs are not portrayed as passive profit maximizers but active, creative, and strategic agents. To achieve business success, entrepreneurs explore new alternatives and invent new methods with an incentive to outperform the others. The discovery process involves entrepreneurial learning, knowledge acquisition, trial and error, and experimentation. As a result of fierce competition, new ideas emerge and bring "surprises" to the market. Moreover, in the free market without any government intervention, sellers or producers have no absolute market power and cannot abuse the "monopoly" situation by charging unreasonably "high" prices for their products. If they do, new entrants or rivals can always join in and take profit away by providing better but cheaper services to customers. This Austrian perspective of market competition will be applied to understand the supermarket war in Hong Kong in general, and the confrontation between two retailing stores in Hong Kong, namely ParknShop, a well-established supermarket giant, and the 759 Store, a new entrant, in particular.

Chapter 9 attempts to examine the roles that technology and culture play in the business success of a Chinese family enterprise in Hong Kong. It argues that culture influences the adoption of new technology. Likewise, new technology changes the way people think as well as organizational culture. In the market process, business strategies are formulated according to the entrepreneurs' stocks of knowledge, which in turn are based on their everyday life experiences. Since everyday life experience is culturally embedded, culture can impede or facilitate the adoption of new technology. The ability to learn and adopt new technologies is a key factor for a latecomer firm to catch up in the global market. On the other hand, new technology changes the mindset of people in general and organizational culture in particular. New technology and novel events bring about a conflict of knowledge in entrepreneurs' minds. As a result, the entrepreneur either resists the new technology by condemning it as vice or deviance, or adapt to it by modifying his or her way of thinking. Those entrepreneurs who resist new things do not catch up with the changing world and are doomed to fail. Given new technology, most entrepreneurs learn to adopt new methods by trial and error, and experimentation. Successful strategies will be adopted and routinized as a rule of thumb, resulting in institutional change. In this chapter, we shall examine how changes in culture and technology influence the business strategies, and hence the transformation, of Lee Kum Kee, a well-known oyster sauce manufacturer in Hong Kong.

Chapter 10 illustrates the role of Hong Kong in globalization. In particular, the chapter examines the contributions of African entrepreneurs to world trade using Hong Kong as an international hub. Unlike the multinational giants which earn impressive profit through global sourcing, small African entrepreneurs survive by identifying opportunities in petty businesses and exploiting narrow profit margins. Through careful economic calculation, they buy low-end goods from one part of the globe and sell them in the other part. Their self-interest activities enhance global well-being. This chapter begins with an Austrian perspective of international entrepreneurship and global coordination. The theory is illustrated by African entrepreneurs who source Shenzhen-made mobile phones in Hong Kong and sell them in Africa. By arbitraging price differentials, they earn pure entrepreneurial profit. A detail case study of the global coordination of a Tanzanian entrepreneur will be accounted. This chapter concludes that as a result of the effort of African entrepreneurs, low-end mobile phones manufactured in Shenzhen are shipped to Hong Kong and consumed by people in Tanzania, bringing benefits to all parties concerned. The case study fully illustrates the principle of the 'invisible hand' in global markets.

This volume is a collection of papers written over the past several years. Each of the individual papers has consistently applied the Austrian subjectivist framework to explain the contributions of dynamic entrepreneurs to mainland China and Hong Kong. Since a new idea does not arise from a vacuum but builds upon previous ideas, when individual papers are gathered into a book volume, some materials/arguments will be unavoidably repeated. In preparing this volume, every effort is made to avoid repetition while at the same time ensuring that the arguments in each chapter flow smoothly without a loss of continuity. We extend our apology for some repetitions of materials, if any.

We have enjoyed and benefited from stimulating discussion with our academic friends Simon Chien-Yuan Chen, Richard Lam, Gary Moon-Cheung Shiu, Ho-Don Yan, and scholars from the Chinese Hayek Society over the past years. Of course, none of them bears any responsibility for the errors or shortcomings in this volume.

Fu-Lai Tony Yu
Diana S. Kwan

Acknowledgments

Earlier versions of some chapters in this book were presented at international conferences and/or published in academic journals. We thank conference participants for their comments and acknowledge the publishers of the following journals for permission to reproduce some materials in this volume.

Chapter 2 is modified from Fu-Lai Tony Yu (2014) "Entrepreneurial Leadership, Capital Structure and Capabilities Development of the Firm: The Case of the Haier Group," *International Journal of Economics and Business Research*, 7(2): 241–255. Special Issue on Entrepreneurship in Emerging Markets: Firm Formation, Firm Growth, and Firm Transformation.

Chapter 3 is modified from Fu-Lai Tony Yu (2012) "Turning Trash Papers into Gold: Entrepreneurship and International Coordination of China's Paper Queen, Zhang Yin," *Journal of Chinese Entrepreneurship*, 4(1): 88–96.

Chapter 4 is modified from Fu-Lai Tony Yu (2011) "Entrepreneurial Alertness and Spontaneous Learning in the Market Process: The Case of Mama Moon in China," *Journal of Women's Entrepreneurship and Education*, 3–4: 29–44.

The content in Chapter 5 was presented at the 7th Annual Conference, Asian Studies Association Hong Kong held at Hong Kong Shue Yan University on 2–3 March 2012. The paper was published as Fu-Lai Tony Yu and Diana S. Kwan (2011) "Entrepreneurship as a Global Coordinator: The Li & Fung Group," *Journal for Global Business Advancement*, 4(4): 387–400. Special Issue on Global Business Advancement and Competitive Advantage.

A modified version of Chapter 6, entitled "A Subjectivist Approach to Advertising: The Success of Vitasoy" appears in *Asia-Pacific Journal of Management Research and Innovation*, 11(2/June): 153–160.

The content in Chapter 7 was presented at the 8th Annual Conference of Asian Studies Association Hong Kong held at the Hong Kong Institute of Education, March 8–9, 2013. The paper was later published in Fu-Lai Tony Yu and Diana S. Kwan (2013) "Family Business Succession in Hong Kong: The Case of Yung Kee," *Frontiers in Business Research in China*, 7(3): 433–460.

Chapter 8 is about the supermarket war in Hong Kong. Its content was presented at the 9th Annual Conference organized by the Asian Studies Association of Hong Kong (ASAHK), held at the University of Hong Kong on 14–15 March 2014.

An earlier version of Chapter 9 was presented at the 7th International Conference on "Branding & Marketing in a Global Marketplace – An Emerging Markets Perspective" organized by the Asian Centre for Branding & Marketing (ACBM), the Hong Kong Polytechnic University, on 18 November 2013. It was also presented at the International Workshop on the Cultural Foundations of Entrepreneurship in China, Department of Sociology, the University of Hong Kong, 2 November 2013. The revised version appears in Fu-Lai Tony Yu and Diana S. Kwan (2015) "Co-Evolution of Culture and Technology: The Business Success of Lee Kum Kee," *Global Business Review*, 16(1/February): 182–195.

A revised version of Chapter 10 appears in Fu-Lai Tony Yu and Diana S. Kwan "African Entrepreneurs and International Coordination in Petty Businesses: the Case of Low-end Mobile Phones Sourcing in Hong Kong," forthcoming in *Journal of African Business*.

Part I
The theoretical framework

1 Entrepreneurship in the history of the Austrian school of economics

It is generally known that entrepreneurship has no role in contemporary neo-classical economics. The entrepreneur disappears completely in the mainstream economic analysis where quantitative method and optimization technique are adopted. The market process in the neoclassical paradigm is simply a mechanic movement from disequilibrium to equilibrium through information searching. Learning in neoclassical economics is a static process involving known options (Boland 1982: 161–163). Though contemporary mainstream economists ignore entrepreneurship, the subject has been alive and well in the Austrian school of economics. This chapter discusses both Austrian and quasi-Austrian[1] economists who shed significant light on the theories of entrepreneurship.

Richard Cantillon (1680–1734): the entrepreneur as a bearer of uncertainty

The *Essai sur la Nature du Commerce en Général* [Essay on the Nature of Trade in General] in 1775 takes Richard Cantillon to the high place in the history of economics. In particular, William S. Jevons, one of the founders of Marginal Revolution, refers to the *Essai* to as the "first treatise on economics" (Thornton 1999: 13). Joseph Schumpeter describes the *Essai* as "the first systematic penetration of the field of economics" (Thornton 1999: 13–14). Murray Rothbard, a noted Austrian economist, crowns Cantillon the "founding father of modern economics" (Thornton 1999: 14). The Austrian school of economics was founded by Carl Menger 150 years later, with the publication of *Grundsätze* [Principles of Economics] in 1871. There is definitely no chronological link between Cantillon and Menger. However, Hébert (1985) demonstrates that "the Austrian tradition in economic analysis – [begun] in the last century by Menger and maintained in our own by von Mises, Hayek, Kirzner, and others – has quite a lot in common with the economics of Richard Cantillon." Jörg Guido Hülsmann (2002) even refers to Cantillon as a proto-Austrian.

One of Cantillon's remarkable contributions to economics is that he was the first economist to stress and analyze the entrepreneur (Rothbard 1995), use the term "entrepreneur," and distinguish it from other factors of production.

Cantillon begins economic analysis by classifying people in the economy into three classes:

1. Princes and the proprietors of lands
2. Wage earners
3. Entrepreneurs, who conduct "all the exchange and circulation of the state" and keep the economic system in adjustment.

The real-world market is inherently uncertain, and it is the function of the entrepreneur or "undertaker" to bear that uncertainty by investing, paying expenses, and then hoping to reap a profit. For Cantillon (1755/1931: 501), bearing uncertainty is the essence of entrepreneurial activity:

> These entrepreneurs can never know the volume of consumption in their city, nor even how long their customers will buy of them, seeing that their rivals will try in every way to get away their business: all this causes so much uncertainty among all these entrepreneurs that we see failures among them every day.

Profit, for Cantillon, is a reward for successful forecasting and uncertainty bearing in the process of production. Rothbard (1995) concludes that Cantillon's view of entrepreneurship "anticipates Mises and the modern Austrians in another respect: his entrepreneur performs not a disruptive (as in Schumpeter) but an *equilibrating* function – that is, by successfully forecasting and investing resources in the future, the entrepreneur helps adjust and balance supply and demand in the various markets" (italics original).

Unfortunately, Cantillon's pioneering insight into the uncertainty of the market process was totally neglected until independently resurrected by Frank Knight, Ludwig von Mises and Friedrich A. Hayek in the 20th century.

(Rothbard 1995)

Carl Menger (1840–1921): uncertainty, knowledge problems, and entrepreneurial functions

Carl Menger, the founder of the Austrian school of economics, was probably the first economist to acknowledge the significance of time and ignorance in economic analysis. Menger (1871/2007: 120–121) argues that

> the value of goods is therefore nothing arbitrary, but always the necessary consequence of *human knowledge* that the maintenance of life, of well-being, or of some ever so insignificant part of them, depends upon control of a good or a quantity of goods. Regarding this knowledge, however, men can be in error about the value of goods just as they can be in error with respect to all other objects of human knowledge. . . . [*I*]*t is a judgment made by*

economizing individuals about the importance their command of the things has for the maintenance of their lives and well-being [italics added].

Hence, for the first time in economics, we understand human action in terms of time, uncertainty, error, knowledge, and judgment. Such elements constitute what we now call Mengerian economics.

Menger (1871/1994: 159–160) analyzes the production process by classifying producer goods (goods of higher order) and consumer goods (goods of lower order):

> The process of transforming goods of higher order into goods of lower or first order, provided it is economic in other respects, must also always be *planned and conducted, with some economic purpose in view, by an economizing individual*. This individual must carry through the economic computations . . . and he must actually bring the goods of higher order, including technical labor services, together . . . for the purpose of production [italics added].

For Menger (1871/1994 : 160), the entrepreneur "makes not only the underlying economic calculations but also the actual decisions to assign goods of higher order to particular productive purposes." Due to uncertainty, entrepreneurs play four major roles in the economy, namely (a) obtaining information about the economic situation; (b) economic calculation – all the various computations that must be made if a production process is to be efficient (provided that it is economic in other respects); (c) the act of will by which goods of higher order (or goods in general – under conditions of developed commerce, where any economic good can be exchanged for any other) are assigned to a particular production process; and finally (d) supervision of the execution of the production plan so that it may be carried through as economically as possible.

Ludwig von Mises (1881–1973): uncertainty, economic calculation, and the market process

Eugen von Bohm-Bawerk and Friedrich von Wieser, the disciples of Carl Menger, made significant contributions to the theories of capital and subjective costs respectively. However, neither of them extends the Mengerian method of subjectivism. It was left to Ludwig von Mises, who single-handedly restored economics as a study of human action, which is known as praxeology and further extends the subjectivist method in economics. Mises directly imports Max Weber's method into his seminal work *Human Action: A Treatise on Economics* (1949). He explains the theory of human action with respect to time and uncertainty. The aim of human action according to Mises (1949/1966: 100)

> is always to render future conditions more satisfactory than they would be without the interference of action. The uneasiness that impels a man to act is caused by a dissatisfaction with expected future conditions as they would

probably develop if nothing were done to alter them. In any case action can influence only the future, never the present that with every infinitesimal fraction of a second sinks down into the past. Man becomes conscious of time when he plans to convert a less satisfactory present state into a more satisfactory future state.

While Bohm-Bawerk constructs a theory of capital based on Menger's classification of goods, Mises introduces the entrepreneur who conducts economic calculation for the capital deployed in the production process. In *Human Action*, Mises (1949/1966: 301) claims, "the marvelous economic improvements of the last two hundred years were an achievement of the capitalists who provided the capital goods required and of the elite of technologists and entrepreneurs." Furthermore, Mises (1949/1966: 297) argues:

> The vehicle of economic progress is the accumulation of additional capital goods by means of saving and improvement in technological methods of production, the execution of which is almost always conditioned by the availability of such new capital. The agents of progress are the promoting entrepreneurs intent upon profiting by means of adjusting the conduct of affairs to the best possible satisfaction of the consumers. . . . An excess of the total amount of profits over that of losses is a proof of the fact that there is economic progress and an improvement in the standard of living of all strata of the population. The greater this excess is, the greater is the increment in general prosperity.

Entrepreneurs are guided by profit and loss, which are ultimately related to consumers' tastes and preferences. As Mises (1949/1966: 299) argues:

> The entrepreneurial function, the striving of entrepreneurs after profits, is the driving power in the market economy. Profit and loss are the devices by means of which the consumers exercise their supremacy on the market. The behavior of the consumers makes profits and losses appear and thereby shift ownership of the means of production from the hands of the less efficient into those of the more efficient. It makes a man the more influential in the direction of business activities the better he succeeds in serving the consumers. In the absence of profit and loss, the entrepreneurs would not know what the most urgent needs of the consumers are. If some entrepreneurs were to guess it, they would lack the means to adjust production accordingly. Profit-seeking business is subject to the sovereignty of the consumers, while nonprofit institutions are sovereign unto themselves and not responsible to the public. Production for profit is necessarily production for use, as profits can only be earned by providing the consumers with those things they most urgently want to use.

Business success or profit is then a result of entrepreneurs' correct judgment or correct interpretation of the market. On the other hand, business failure or loss is the result of entrepreneurs' misinterpretation of the market signals. As Mises (1949/1966: 291) convincingly argues:

> [L]ike every acting man, the entrepreneur is always a speculator. He deals with the uncertainty of the future. His success or failure depends on the correctness of his anticipation of uncertain events. If he fails in his understanding of things to come, he is doomed. The only source from which an entrepreneur's profits stem is his ability to anticipate better than other people the future demand of the consumers. If everybody is correct in anticipation of the future state of the market of a certain commodity, its price and the prices of the complementary factors of production concerned would already today be adjusted to this future state. Neither profit nor loss can emerge for those embarking upon this line of business.[2]

Hence, Mises (1949/1966: 293) concludes, "the ultimate source from which entrepreneurial profit and loss are derived is the uncertainty of the future constellation of demand and supply." Hence, profit and loss serve as the signals for entrepreneurs to interpret and reinterpret market phenomena and allow the ideas of market participants to coordinate.

Frank Knight (1885–1972): uncertainty, entrepreneurial judgment, and profit

Frank Knight is generally regarded as one of the founding fathers of the Chicago school of economics (Emmett 2001). Ironically, the second generation of the Chicago school[3] never follows the Knightian spirits. Largely under Milton Friedman's influences, most contemporary Chicago economists maintain that economics should adopt the methodology of natural science, a view that Knight himself utterly rejects. Yu (2002: 1–23) argues that Knight is more like an Austrian than a Chicagoan. He is one of the leading American economists pertaining to subjectivism. His contributions of, notably, economic methodology, the theories of human agency, profit, entrepreneurship, and economic organization have left much to be appreciated by neoclassical mainstream economists in general and contemporary Austrians in particular.

In Knight's view, uncertainty bearing is an inseparable function of the entrepreneur (Knight 1921: 278, 281, 289). Future situations depend upon a large number of factors, for which entrepreneurs seldom conduct mathematical studies (Knight 1921: 210–211). Instead, they use instinct. Agreeing with Alfred Marshall that business managers are guided by "trained instinct" rather than knowledge, Knight (1921: 211) argues that entrepreneurs use judgment, common sense, or intuition when facing uncertainty. For Knight, entrepreneurs "infer" largely from their experience of the past as a whole, somewhat in the same way that we deal with intrinsically simple (unanalyzable) problems like estimating distances, weights, or other physical magnitudes when measuring instruments are not at hand.

Knight (1921: 210) argues that entrepreneurs bet on their judgments. The ordinary decisions of life are made on the basis of "estimate" of a crude and superficial character. Entrepreneurs try to determine what kinds of people to hire, what orders to give, which non-human factors to be utilized, and how their employees will be used. Entrepreneurs also predict future demand conditions, which they recognize, depending upon the actions of competitors. Having made their determinations and predictions, entrepreneurs proceed to make judgments concerning the profitability of alternative actions. When they ultimately decide to hire factors and produce a product for eventual sale, they are in effect betting that their judgments about the value of the factors they employ are more accurate than the judgments of others who are unwilling to bid as high as they. In this way, factors come to be controlled and allocated by those who have the most faith and trust in their judgments (Knight 1921: 268).

Who will be engaged in the entrepreneurial function? Knight (1921: 244) argues that different views on uncertainty by individuals give rise to a class of people who specialize in risk bearing. Knight (1921: 241–242) puts forward five variable elements[4] in individual attributes and capabilities that contribute to the specialization of entrepreneurial judgment: (1) people differ in their capacity by perception and inference to form correct judgments as to the future course of events in the environment, (2) difference in agents' capacities to judge means and discern and plan the steps and adjustments necessary to meet the anticipated future situation, (3) variation in the power to execute the plans and adjustments believed to be requisite and desirable, (4) diversity in conduct in situations involving uncertainty due to differences in the amount of confidence which individuals feel in their judgments, and (5) difference in conative attitude to a situation upon which judgment is passed with a given degree of confidence. In simple terms, some people are risk averse while others are risk takers.

Estimates or judgments are liable to error (Knight 1921: 203, 230). Hence, profit arises from error, or imperfect foresight, on the part of the responsible entrepreneur (Knight 1956: 24). The success of business enterprises in general is largely dependent upon the estimating powers of entrepreneurs in assigning people to their respective positions and for fixing the remunerations which they are to receive for filling positions (Knight 1921: 229). The level of profit is neither stipulated in any agreement nor fixed in an exchange but is contingent upon the success of an enterprise or undertaking.

Knight's notion of entrepreneurship is very much in line with the one elaborated by Mises (High 1982: 165). Hebert and Link (1988: 130) rightly conclude that "there appear to be no significant differences at all between Mises and Knight on the matter. Mises, of course, brought some traditional Austrian concerns to the discussion, but on practically every fundamental point dealing with the subject of entrepreneurship he comes across as a Knightian."

Joseph Schumpeter (1883–1950): technological breakthrough and a process of creative destruction

Though Joseph Schumpeter was born in Austria and studied under Eugen Bohm-Bawerk, he never followed Austrian methodology. Schumpeter regarded

Léon Walras as the greatest economist who ever lived. He hailed Walrasian economics and "became enamored of equilibrium in mathematical models, a big epistemological no-no in the Austrian method."[5] Therefore, Schumpeter's works cannot be regarded as orthodox Austrian economics (Paniagua 2012). At most, we regard him as a quasi-Austrian. Despite this, Schumpeter makes a significant contribution to the theories of entrepreneurship which incorporate the notion of human experience.

Schumpeter's concept of entrepreneurship introduces a new dimension into economics. According to Schumpeter (1934/1961: 81–86), entrepreneurs exert a disturbing force on an economy, which is termed "creative destruction." The entrepreneur was described by Schumpeter as the economic agent who performs the service of innovating, introducing changes that radically change the framework of the economic system. Entrepreneurs are defined as people who innovate, and innovating is the act of combining productive factors in some new ways. They include the introduction of a new good or quality of a good, the introduction of a new method of production, the opening of a new market, the utilization of some new source of supply for raw material or intermediate good, and the carrying out of the new organization of any industry (Schumpeter 1934/1961).

Schumpeter (1947: 150) further argues that entrepreneurship encompasses three essential characteristics:

> Firstly it can always be understood ex post; but it can practically never be understood ex ante; that is to say, it cannot be predicted by applying the ordinary rules of inference from the pre-existing facts. . . .[6] Secondly, it shapes the whole course of subsequent events and their long run outcome . . . it changes social and economic situations for good, it creates situations from which there is no bridge to those situations that might have emerged in its absence. . . . Thirdly, the frequency of its occurrence has something to do with the quality of the personnel available in the society, with the relative quality of personnel and with individual decisions, actions and patterns of behaviours [footnote added].

Furthermore, Schumpeter recognizes that entrepreneurial innovation is a difficult job because it lies outside the routine framework, and the environment resists in many ways. Therefore, the entrepreneurial function does not essentially consist in either inventing or creating the conditions which the enterprise exploits. It consists in "getting [new] things done" (Schumpeter 1934/1961: 93).

Friedrich A. Hayek (1899–1992): competition as a discovery process

Hayek (1952) contributes significantly to the theory of sensory order. In particular, his notion of classification of incoming events by the mind has much to be commented. He also understands well how the price system and market work. Hayek makes a famous statement that economic problems are knowledge problems, "arise always and only in consequence of change" (Hayek 1949: 82). Hayek (1949) emphasizes one kind of knowledge which is particularly relevant for coordination problems. This is "the knowledge of the particular circumstances of time and place." Hayek (1949: 77) explains the significance of dispersed knowledge in economic progress as follows:

> The peculiar character of the problem of a rational economic order is determined precisely by the fact that the knowledge of the circumstances of which we must make use never exists in concentrated or integrated form but solely as the dispersed bits of incomplete and frequently contradictory knowledge which all the separate individuals possess. The economic problem of society is thus not merely a problem of how to allocate "given" resources – if "given" is taken to mean given to a single mind which deliberately solves the problem set by these "data." It is rather a problem of how to secure the best use of resources known to any of the members of society, for ends whose relative importance only these individuals know. Or, to put it briefly, it is a problem of the utilization of knowledge which is not given to anyone in its totality.

Given limited knowledge, competition forces market participants to make adjustment towards their own expectation. As Hayek (2002: 15) contends:

> It is precisely through the disappointment of expectations that a high degree of agreement of expectations is brought about. This fact . . . is of fundamental importance in understanding the functioning of the market order. But the market's accomplishments are not exhausted in bringing about a mutual adjustment of individual plans. It also provides that every product is produced by those who can produce it more cheaply (or at least as cheaply) as anyone who does not in fact produce it, and that goods are sold at prices that are lower than those at which anyone could offer the goods who does not offer them.

More importantly, "competition is important only because and insofar as its outcomes are unpredictable and on the whole different from those that anyone would have been able to consciously strive for; and that its salutary effects must manifest themselves by frustrating certain intentions and disappointing certain expectations" (Hayek 2002: 10). Thus, Hayek's concept of competition is essentially a process of formation of opinion, a process which involves a continuous change in data. Hayek incorporates learning, the trial-and-error process, and market selection in his notion of spontaneous order. Moreover, he captures the essential element of competition, namely "surprise and unexpected" (O'Driscoll and Rizzo 1985: 102).

Despite his seminal contribution to the theory of market process, Hayek "did not focus explicitly upon the role of entrepreneurship in explaining the market process. Rather, he emphasizes the role of knowledge and mutual learning. He examines how, in the course of the market process, market participants come to obtain more accurate knowledge of each other's plans" (Harper 2003: 20). Klein

(2007) also argues that Hayek "did not develop a theory of the entrepreneur per se." In Klein's view (2007),

> Hayek does use the term "entrepreneur" in his writings on socialist calculation and capital theory. But he seems to mean simply "businessman," and does not distinguish sharply among entrepreneurs, managers, capitalists, and other business professionals.

Horwitz (2007) holds a somewhat different view: Hayek does recognize the discovery function that the entrepreneur plays in the market. This is evidenced by Hayek's work (1949: 196) in which the words "discovery" and "entrepreneur" appear:

> [T]he method which under given conditions is the cheapest is a thing which has to be discovered, and to be discovered anew, sometimes almost from day to day, by the entrepreneur, and that, in spite of the strong inducement, it is by no means regularly the established entrepreneur, the man in charge of the existing plant, who will discover what is the best method.

Horwitz (2007) concludes that Hayek anticipates Israel Kirzner's theory of the entrepreneurship, though Hayek did not put elements of entrepreneurship all together in the way Kirzner did. Klein (2007) states that the entrepreneurship literature on the whole regards "Hayek as an important theorist of knowledge and the competitive process . . . but not a contributor to the theory of entrepreneurship per se." He calls for constructing a theory of entrepreneurial learning that is more explicitly in Hayekian perspective (see the last section of this chapter).

Israel M. Kirzner (1930–): entrepreneurial alertness and arbitrageurship

Israel M. Kirzner was the most significant Austrian scholar contributing to the theory of entrepreneurship in economics during the 20th century (Gunning 1997).[7] Horwitz (2007) argues that "Kirzner's entrepreneur, who is in most ways Mises's entrepreneur, is the answer to that Hayekian question. . . . [Kirzner] brought Mises's entrepreneur into Hayek's epistemic conception of the market process. It is the entrepreneur who drives the social learning that characterizes the discovery process of the market."

Kirzner, as a follower of Mises, builds his concept of entrepreneurship entirely upon the foundation of Mises' action theory. He repeatedly stresses Mises' thesis that "each human actor is always, in significant respects, an entrepreneur" (Kirzner 1982: 139). It is important to note the link between action theory and entrepreneurship, more specifically, action and alertness. Kirzner (1973: 33) notes:

> Human action, in the sense developed by Mises, involves the course of action taken by the human being to remove uneasiness and to make himself better

off. Being broader than the notion of economising, the concept of human action does not restrict analysis of the decision to the allocation problem posed by the juxtaposition of scarce means and multiple ends . . . but also the very perception of the ends-means framework within which allocation and economising are to take place. . . . Mises' homo agens . . . is endowed not only with the propensity to pursue goals efficiently, once ends and means are clearly identified, but also with the drive and alertness needed to identify which ends to strive for and which means are available.

Hence, we can trace an important element of Kirzner's concept of entrepreneurship, namely alertness, from Mises. In the market, the opportunity that human agents are alert to is monetary profit. Kirzner (1973: 39) argues that "the entire role of entrepreneurs lie[s] in their alertness to hitherto unnoticed opportunities." In the market, entrepreneurs proceed by their alertness to discover and exploit situations in which they are able to sell for high prices that which they can buy for low prices. Alertness implies that the actor possesses a superior perception of economic opportunity. It is like an "antenna that permits recognition of gaps in the market that give little outward sign" (Gilad et al. 1988: 483).

For Kirzner, alertness to profit opportunity implies arbitrage activities. Indeed, Kirzner does not distinguish arbitrageurship from entrepreneurship (White 1976: 4). Regarding the arbitrage theory of profit, Kirzner (1973) argues that the existence of disequilibrium situations in the market implies profit opportunity. The entrepreneur endeavors to exploit profit opportunity, eliminate errors, and move the economy toward equilibrium. Such an argument has raised a number of criticisms from both within and outside the Austrian camps. Specifically, White (1976) comments that Kirzner fails to recognize the highly important part played by entrepreneurial imagination. Defending his position, Kirzner subsequently differentiates two kinds of markets, namely single period and multi-period markets (Kirzner 1982). For the multi-period market, with the passage of time and uncertainty, Kirzner accepts the elements of creativeness and imagination into his model. Hence, "incentive for the market entrepreneurship along the intertemporal dimension is provided not by arbitrage profits generated by imperfectly coordinated present markets but more generally, by the speculative profits generated by the as yet imperfectly coordinated market situations in the sequence of time" (Kirzner 1982: 154). In a multi-period situation, the entrepreneur "must introduce . . . his own creative actions, in fact construct the future as he wishes it to be" (Kirzner 1982: 63). Accordingly, his position comes closer to Schumpeter's vision. However, in a personal correspondence to the author (13 January 1994), Kirzner remarked that he preferred to consider Kirznerian entrepreneurship as a subset of entrepreneurship, confining it to those activities which take advantage of existing scattered knowledge.

If entrepreneurial alertness is so important in economic growth, then what are the causes of it? Kirzner argues that entrepreneurial vision may not arrive deliberately or rationally, but neither is it arrived at purely by chance. It is the "purposefulness of human action that tends to ensure, in some degree, that opportunities come to be noticed" (Kirzner 1979: 170). Spontaneous learning or alertness to profit opportunity is a subconscious process. It can be encouraged by the possibility of gain. He says: "[i]f we know anything at all about the process of spontaneous discovery of information, it is that this process is somehow altogether more rapid when the relevant information will be of benefit to the potential discoverer" (Kirzner 1979: 149). Gunning (2004) elaborates:

> Subconscious learning can be encouraged by institutional arrangements. Institutional arrangements determine the gains that are available to different individuals when they subconsciously learn. Because subconscious learning in some individuals is superior to that in others, it is important that those who are superior receive higher gains.

Kirzner (1979: 150) argues that institutional arrangements are private property rights, free enterprise, and the use of money in economic calculation. That is, the free market system provides an environment for subconscious learning to occur. This setting allows market participants to translate unnoticed opportunities into the forms that tend to excite the alertness of those most likely to notice (Gunning 2004).

Kirzner (1985: 162) concludes that entrepreneurship is the engine of the capitalist system. As he notes, entrepreneurship consists of

> the social integration of the innumerable scraps of existing information that are present in scattered form throughout society. . . . Yet the same entrepreneurial spirit that stimulated the discovery of the value of information now existing throughout the market also tends to stimulate the discovery or creation of entirely new information concerning ways to anticipate or to satisfy consumer preferences. The entrepreneurial process at this second level is what drives the capitalist system toward higher and higher standards of achievement.

Ludwig M. Lachmann (1906–1990): the entrepreneur as a systematic capital structure builder under uncertainty

Ludwig Maurits Lachmann was a student and colleague of Friedrich Hayek at the London School of Economics in the 1930s. In the market process, the entrepreneur needs to combine capital resources in a meaningful way or profitable manner. Lachmann (1956: 13) refers to this as the true function of the entrepreneur. As he puts it:

> The entrepreneur's function as regards capital is not exhausted by the hire of services. Here his function is to *specify* and make decisions on the concrete form the capital resources shall have. He specifies and modifies the shape and layout of his plant, which is something he cannot do to his typists, desirable though that may seem to him.
>
> (Lachmann 1956: 16; italics original)

The term "capital resources" implies time dimension and uncertainty in production. On the one hand, entrepreneurs predict consumer wants. They know that wants can never be correctly predicted. On the other hand, they hire capital resources, including managers, labor, equipment, and so on to produce goods and services. The prices of capital resources direct the whole mechanism of production. Betting on their judgments, entrepreneurs bear uncertainty in the form of profits or losses in future (Mises 1949/1966: 256).

In Lachmann's view (1956: 8), capital goods must process the capabilities to produce what consumers are prepared to pay for. Plans which are inconsistent with either the consumer's or producer's plans will be revised. By trial and error, capital goods will be oriented towards this direction. Furthermore, capital uses must fit each other in order to produce capabilities. A piece of capital equipment may have to be discarded because it does not fit into any combination to yield capabilities that generate profit. Eventually, an acceptable network of plans will emerge with certain patterns of capital use. In this regard, the firm, as a realization of an entrepreneurial plan, consists of a meaningful combination of capital resources.

If a production plan fails, this implies the capital structure of the firm lacks capabilities to yield profit. Accordingly, entrepreneurs will revise their production plans, and the capital structure of the firm either needs to be restructured or dissolved. The capital gains and losses of a firm are effective tests of entrepreneurial plans (Lachmann 1977: 203).[8] Similarly, if the entrepreneur perceives an expansion opportunity for the firm, then the previous production plan needs to be revised accordingly. The capital structure of the firm needs to be reshuffled so that the capabilities of these capital resources match the firm's expansion goal.

As economic change indicates that there is a need for the firm to expand, the entrepreneur will soon find that the original capital combination is inappropriate to yield capabilities to serve the new demand. Whether the firm possesses "the ability to integrate, build, and reconfigure internal and external competences to address rapidly changing environments" is related to the dynamic capabilities of the firm (Teece et al. 1997: 509–533). As the firm expands, new strategic capital resources with capabilities need to be integrated into the company. Old strategic capital resources have to be transformed or reconfigured. For instance, alliance and acquisition enable firms to bring new strategic capital resources into the firm from external sources.

Encountering new demand, entrepreneurs adapt and learn. New technology associated with superior capital combinations in the production process will eventually be learned and adopted by the firm. In the world of rapid change, capital combinations in the firm will be reshuffled and reformed. Given heterogeneous and complementary natures of capital resources,[9] on some occasions, the cost of restructuring the existing capital structure of a firm is so high that the entrepreneur may be better off simply starting another new plant in another location with a new combination of capital in order to meet new market demand.

In summary, production plans in the form of capital structure will be executed according to entrepreneurial wishes. Hence, the entrepreneur can be regarded as a systematic capital structure builder under uncertainty.

Towards a Hayekian perspective of entrepreneurial process: interpretation, classification, and discovery

As mentioned, Hayek contributes significantly to the theories of sensory order, market competition, and the discovery process. However, he does not have a theory of entrepreneurship. It is possible to formulate a theory of entrepreneurial process based on Hayek's thinking. In the Hayekian formulation (Hayek 1952, 1962), perceiving other people's action is a complicated undertaking, involving the capacity to identify, imitate and internalize patterns, and transfer action or perception across domains of space and time. Hayek (1952) argues that sensory experiences in the mind process are not unitary, but entail a collection of impulses. It is like a folder in a computer filled with an assortment of files. Sensory experiences compose many impulses corresponding to various aspects of the observed event. Furthermore, these impulses do not just originate from one, but from many neighboring receptors in the sensory system, and they occur in conjunction with other impulses associated with activities such as touching, looking, or listening. This package of impulses then goes through memory archives (or folders in the computer metaphor) and creates links between archives. Simply put, the mind is building up a record of past stimuli or, more accurately, of associations or connections between stimuli with which to compare new incoming stimuli. As Hayek (1952: 142) notes:

> [W]hat we perceive can never be unique properties of individual objects but always only properties which the objects have in common with other objects. Perception is thus always an interpretation, the placing of something into one or several classes of objects.

As there are a multiplicity of impulses associated with each sensory experience, impulses from different sensory experiences may employ one or more of the same neural pathways. In other words, an overlapping of memory will occur. This overlapping leads to simultaneous classification (Hayek 1952: 180–181). This means that sensory experiences are at the same time related to all sorts of other sensory experiences via shared neural pathways. These shared pathways have the effect of grouping common sensory experiences together. It also implies that at any given moment a sensory experience will be a member of more than one class of events, related through memory to many other sensory experiences (Dempsey 1996: 139–150).

Entrepreneurial interpretation and the perception process

Hayek's perception process can be applied to the entrepreneurial process. Before imitation and therefore actions take place, entrepreneurs have to identify certain actions which may have never been observed before. However, it is unlikely that business phenomena are completely novel; rather, they are likely to resemble something that has been previously experienced (Hayek 1952; see also Fleetwood

1995: 111). In other words, the entrepreneur performs "an act of classification" (Hayek 1952). The mind of the entrepreneur is able to classify sensory elements and recognize patterns as "one of the same kind" even though it has never been experienced before. If the event and a series of stimuli are repeated, a pattern begins to register in the mind. Each time the same event and subsequent stimuli are experienced, the same interpretation is triggered. This means that the impulse travels via the same route, forming the same linkage and establishing the same following. The result is that these events are classified as the same (Fleetwood 1995: 115). It is worth iterating that perception is founded upon the experience of an entrepreneur. All that is perceived is immediately confronted with classes of already recorded data. Every perception of a new stimulus, or class of stimuli, will be influenced by previously implemented classifications. A new phenomenon will always be perceived in association with other events with which it has something in common (Hayek 1952: 142–143).[10]

Entrepreneurs are not passive receptors of information. They learn selectively and engage in the ordering and selection of information pertinent to their particular situation and objectives. Knowledge and history shape entrepreneurs' interpretations of their environments, hence their discoveries and institutions. Gifford's concept of limited entrepreneurial attention (1992: 276–278) postulates that facing complexity in everyday life and the possibility of the projection of many imagined worlds, entrepreneurs tend to expose themselves to ideas that are in accordance with their interests, needs, or existing attitudes. They consciously or unconsciously avoid messages that are in conflict with their predispositions. Rogers (1983: 166) calls this "selective exposure." As Hayek (1952: 139) puts it, attention "is thus always directed, or confined to a particular class of events for which we are on the look-out and which, in consequence, we perceive with greater distinctness when one of them occurs."[11]

Entrepreneurship and the discovery process

Entrepreneurs do not only adapt themselves to the external world but also adjust the environment to their needs through deliberate and conscious choices. Besides being diffusers and users of knowledge, entrepreneurs are also the source of knowledge. In other words, they are the builders and users of knowledge, creators of economic possesses, and above all the engines of change (Hayek 1952; see also Rizzello 1999, 2000). In this regard, economic change is connected with the fact that entrepreneurs constantly create the reasons for their own existence, trying to have influence as much as possible and thus to determine the future states of the world in a direction that favors their own development as much as possible (Rizzello 2000: 127–150). This is the foundation of entrepreneurial discoveries.

Learning, trial and error, and discovery

Entrepreneurs learn and discover by trial and error, a measure adopted by most organisms. Karl Popper (1972: 242) argues that all organisms are constantly engaging in problem solving, which "always proceeds by the method of trial and error; new reactions, new forms, new organs, new modes of behavior, new hypothesis, are tentatively put forward and controlled by error-elimination." Agreeing with Popper, Hayek argues that discovery is an evolutionary process of cumulative growth of problem-solving knowledge. In Hayek's view (2002), the market is an ongoing, open-ended process of trial and error-elimination, a process in which constantly a number of potential alternative solutions of various kinds of problems are tried out and selected through the choices of market participants. It is a process in which new tentative problem solutions are continuously explored and in which the problems themselves are subject to change, as solutions to old problems tend to create new problems. The learning or discovery process involves the history of the entrepreneur's own experience of success and failure. Entrepreneurs interpret or classify incoming events according to their own experience. Whenever expectations resulting from the existing interpretation are disappointed, or when beliefs so far held are disproved by new experience, then reinterpretation or reclassification occurs. The whole process of entrepreneurial learning, of the growth of knowledge, is then seen as consisting of such reinterpretation or reclassification, as a process in which our "frame of reference" is corrected, adjusted, or refined (Vanberg 1993: 97).

In the following chapters, we shall use the Austrian theories of entrepreneurship to illustrate successful Chinese entrepreneurship in mainland China and Hong Kong.[12]

Notes

1 By "quasi-Austrian economists," we refer to those economists whose methodologies are not from the Austrian school of economics in the strictest sense. However, their views are very close to or at least consistent with the Austrian school of economics. In this chapter, we refer to Richard Cantillon, Frank Knight, and Joseph Schumpeter.

2 Elsewhere, Mises (1962: 120) argues that it is the entrepreneurial decision that gives rise to profit or loss. "What makes profit emerge is the fact that the entrepreneur who judges the future prices of the products more correctly than other people do buys some or all the factors of production at prices which, seen from the point of view of the future state of the market, are too low. . . . On the other hand, the entrepreneur who misjudges the future prices of the products allows for the factors of production prices which, seen from the point of view of the future state of the market, are too high" (Mises 1962: 109).

3 It is known that the Chicago school consists of the 'old' and the 'new'. Frank Knight is generally regarded as the spokesperson of the old Chicago school, while Milton Friedman is the representative of the new Chicago school (Hirsch and Hirsch 1993: 59).

4 Knight (1921: 242) argues that since the amount of uncertainty effective in a conduct situation is the degree of subjective confidence felt in the completed act as correct adaptation to the future, five items can be reduced to two, namely the subjective or felt uncertainty and his conative feeling toward it.

5 See http://archive.freecapitalists.org/forums/p/2371/31774.aspx; retrieved 11 April 2014.

6 DeBono (1992: 15) argues that every valuable creative idea must always be logical in hindsight.

7 Israel M. Kirzner was awarded the International Award for Entrepreneurship and Small Business Research in 2006. For a recent review of Kirzner's contributions, see Douhan et al. (2007).

8 As a Misesian follower, Rothbard (1962/1993: 494) argues that "the entrepreneur is an adjuster of the discrepancies of the market toward greater satisfaction of the desires of the consumers. When he innovates he is *also* an adjuster, since he is adjusting the discrepancies of the market as they present themselves in the potential of a new method or product. In other words, if the ruling rate of (natural) interest return is 5 percent, and a business man estimates that he could earn 10 percent by instituting a new process or product, then he has, as in other cases, discovered a discrepancy in the market and sets about correcting it. By launching and producing more of the new process, he is pursuing the entrepreneurial function of adjustment to consumer desires, i.e., what he estimates consumer desires will be. If he succeeds in his estimate and reaps a profit, then he and others will continue in this line of activity until the income discrepancy is eliminated and there is no 'pure' profit or loss in this area."

9 Lachmann's original insight that capital resources are essentially heterogeneous and complementary has been recognized in modern theories of the firm. For example, see Foss et al. (2012) and Foss and Garzarelli (2007).

10 Lane et al. (1996: 53), in Hayekian perspective, argue that when confronting a new situation requiring action, a mental system "categorises the situation according to patterns motivated by previously experienced situations. The categories are associated with particular actions: the association depends upon the valuations of the effects of the actions taken in past situations that were characterised similarly to the present situation. The categorization–action system then generates an action on the basis of this association."

11 In a cognitive study, March and Simon (1958) highlight entrepreneurial attention by classifying actions which maintain current program and actions which devise and evaluate new programs. Along this line of thinking, Gifford (1992: 276–278) proposes a concept of limited entrepreneurial attention. He postulates that the entrepreneur will allocate his/her attention between current operations and prospective new projects, depending on the relative profit between two projects. This implies that there is an opportunity cost to the growth of the firm. Gifford's concept allows the number of targets of attention to be endogenous.

12 This chapter lays the theoretical framework for the case studies in Part II. Hence, some materials in this chapter will be used and cited again in the following chapters.

References

Boland, Lawrence A. (1982) *The Foundations of Economic Method*, London: George Allen & Unwin.

Cantillon, Richard (1755/1931) *Essai sur la Nature du Commerce en Général* [Essay on the Nature of Trade in General], ed. and trans. by Henry Higgs, London: Macmillan & Co.

deBono, Edward (1992) *Serious Creativity*, New York: Harper Business.

Dempsey, G. T. (1996) "Hayek's Evolutionary Epistemology, Artificial Intelligence, and the Question of Free Will," *Evolution and Cognition*, 2: 139–150.

Douhan, Robin; Eliasson, Gunnar; and Henrekson, Magnus (2007) "Israel M. Kirzner: An Outstanding Austrian Contributor to the Economics of Entrepreneurship," *Small Business Economics*, 29(1/June): 213–223.

Emmett, Ross B. (2001) *The Chicago Tradition in Economics, 1892–1945*, London: Routledge, 8 vols.

Fleetwood, Steve (1995) *Hayek's Political Economy: The Socio-economics of Order*, London: Routledge.

Foss, N. and Garzarelli, Giampaolo (2007) "Institutions as Knowledge: Ludwig Lachmann's Institutional Economics," *Cambridge Journal of Economics*, 31: 789–804.

Foss, N.; Bylund, Per; and Klein, Peter G. (2012) "Entrepreneurship and the Economics of the Firm," in Daniel Hjorth (ed.) *Handbook on Organisational Entrepreneurship*, Cheltenham, UK: Edward Elgar, pp. 49–63.

Gifford, S. (1992) "Allocation of Entrepreneurial Attention," *Journal of Economic Behaviour and Organisation*, 19: 265–283.

Gilad, B.; Kaish, S.; and Ronen, J. (1988) "The Entrepreneurial Way with Information," in Shlomo Maital (ed.) *Applied Behavioral Economics*, Vol. II, Somerset: Wheatsheaf, pp. 481–503.

Gunning, Patrick (1997) "The Theory of Entrepreneurship in Austrian Economics," in W. Keizer et al. (eds.) *Austrians in Debate*, London: Routledge.

Gunning, Patrick (2004) "Israel Kirzner's Entrepreneurship," www.constitution.org/pd/gunning/subjecti/workpape/kirz_ent.pdf; retrieved 27 April 2015.

Harper, David A. (2003) *Foundations of Entrepreneurship and Economic Development*, London: Routledge.

Hayek, F. A. (1949) *Individualism and Economic Order*, London: Routledge and Kegan Paul.

Hayek, F. A. (1952) *The Sensory Order*, Chicago: University of Chicago Press.

Hayek, F. A. (1962) "Rules, Perception and Intelligibility," in *Proceedings of the British Academy*, XLVIII, 321–344, reprinted in F. A. Hayek (1967) *Studies in Philospophy, Politics and Economics*, New York: Clarion Book, pp. 43–65.

Hayek, F. A. (2002) "Competition as Discovery Process," *Quarterly Journal of Austrian Economics*, 5(3): 9–23.

Hébert, Robert F. (1985) "Was Richard Cantillon an Austrian Economist?" *Journal of Libertarian Studies*, 7(2/Fall): 269–279.

Hebert, Robert F. and Link, Albert N. (1988) *The Entrepreneur: Mainstream Views & Radical Critiques*, 2nd ed., New York: Praeger.

High, Jack (1982) "Alertness and Judgement: Comment on Kirzner," in Israel M. Kirzner (ed.) *Method, Process and Austrian Economics: Essays in Honour of Ludwig von Mises*, Lexington, MA: D. C. Heath, pp. 161–168.

Hirsch, Eva and Hirsch, Abraham (1993) "The Heterodox Methodology of Two Chicago Economists," in Warren J. Samuels (ed.) *The Chicago School of Political Economy*, New Brunswick, NJ: Transaction Publishers, pp. 59–78.

Horwitz, Steve (2007, November 8) "Klein on Hayek and Entrepreneurship," *Coordination Problem* blog, http://austrianeconomists.typepad.com/weblog/2007/11/klein-on-hayek-.html; retrieved 14 April 2014.

Hülsmann, Jörg Guido (2002) "More on Cantillon as a Proto-Austrian," *Journal des Economistes et des Etudes Humaines*, 11(4): 693–703.

Kirzner, I. M. (1973) *Competition and Entrepreneurship*, Chicago: University of Chicago Press.

Kirzner, I. M. (1979) *Perception, Opportunity and Profit*, Chicago: University of Chicago Press.

Kirzner, I. M. (1982) "Uncertainty, Discovery and Human Action: A Study of the Entrepreneurial Profile in the Misesian System," in I. M. Kirzner (ed.) *Method, Process and Austrian Economics*, Lexington, MA: Lexington Books, pp. 139–160.

Kirzner, I. M. (1985) Discovery and the Capitalist Process, Chicago: University of Chicago Press.

Klein, Peter (2007, November 7) "Hayek and Entrepreneurship," *Organizations and Markets*, http://organizationsandmarkets.com/2007/11/07/hayek-and-entrepreneurship/; retrieved 7 April 2014.

Knight, Frank H. (1921) *Risk, Uncertainty, and Profit*, New York: Houghton Mifflin.

Knight, Frank H. (1956) *On the History and Method of Economics*, Chicago: University of Chicago Press.

Lachmann, L. M. (1956) *Capital and Its Structure*, Kansas City, MO: Sheed Andrews and McMeel.

Lachmann, L. M. (1977) *Capital, Expectations and the Market Process*, Kansas City, MO: Sheed Andrews and McMeel.

Lane, D.; Malerba, M.; Maxfield, R.; and Orsenigo, L. (1996) "Choice and Action," *Journal of Evolutionary Economics*, 6: 43–76.

March, J. G. and Simon, H. A. (1958) *Organisation*, New York: Wiley.

Menger, Carl (1871/2007) *Principles of Economics*, Auburn, AL: Mises Institute.

Mises, L. v. (1949/1966) *Human Action: A Treatise on Economics*, 3rd ed., Chicago: Contemporary Books.

Mises, L. v. (1962) "Profit and Loss," in *Planning for Freedom*, South Holland, IL: Libertarian Press, pp. 112–150.

O'Driscoll, G. P. Jr. and Rizzo, M. (1985) *The Economics of Time and Ignorance*, Oxford: Blackwell.

Paniagua, Pablo (2012, May 28) "Joseph Alois Schumpeter, Entrepreneurship, Innovation and Disequilibrium," http://libertarian-economics.blogspot.hk/ 2012/05/joseph-alois-schumpeter.html; retrieved 11 April 2014.

Popper, K. (1972) *Objective Knowledge: An Evolutionary Approach*, Oxford: Oxford University Press.

Rothbard, Murray N. (1962/1993) *Man, Economy and State*, Auburn, AL: Ludwig von Mises Institute.

Rothbard, Murray N. (1995) "The Founding Father of Modern Economics: Richard Cantillon," in *Economic Thought before Adam Smith: An Austrian Perspective on the History of Economic Thought*, Vol. I, Auburn, AL: Ludwig von Mises Institute, pp. 345–361.

Rizzello, S. (1999) *The Economics of the Mind*, Aldershot: Edward Elgar.

Rizzello, S. (2000) "Economic Change, Subjective Perception, and Institutional Evolution," *Metroeconomica*, 51(2): 127–150.

Rogers, E. M. (1983) *Diffusion of Innovations*, 3rd ed., New York: The Free Press.

Schumpeter, J. A. (1934/1961) *The Theory of Economic Development*, New York: Oxford University Press.

Schumpeter, J. A. (1947) "The Creative Response in Economic History," in R. Clemence (ed.) (1951) *Essays of J. A. Schumpeter*, Cambridge, MA: Addison-Wesley, pp. 216–226.

Teece, David; Pisano, Gary; and Shuen, Amy (1997) "Dynamic Capabilities and Strategic Management," *Strategic Management Journal*, 18(7/August): 509–533.

Thornton, Mark (1999) "Richard Cantillon and the Origin of Austrian Economic Theory," in R. G. Holcombe (ed.) *The Fifteen Greatest Austrian Economists*, Auburn, AL: Ludwig von Mises Institute, pp. 13–28.

Vanberg, J. V. (1993) "Rational Choice, Rule-Following and Institutions: An Evolutionary Perspectives," in Uskali Maki, Bo Gustafsson, and Christian Knudsen (eds.), *Rationality, Institutions and Economic Methodology*. London: Routledge, pp. 171–200.

White, L. H. (1976) "Entrepreneurship, Imagination and the Question of Equilibrium," reprinted in S. Littlechild (ed.) (1990) *Austrian Economics*, Vol. III, Aldershot: Edward Elgar, pp. 87–104.

Yu, Fu-Lai Tony (2002) "Economics of Frank H. Knight: An Austrian Interpretation," *The Forum for Social Economics*, 31(2/Spring): 1–23.

Part II

Chinese entrepreneurship in theory and practice

2 Entrepreneurship, capital structure, and enterprise reform

Zhang Ruimin and the Haier Group

Introduction

This chapter will construct a theory of the growth of the firm by combining the insights of Austrian economics with entrepreneurial leadership and capabilities theories. In particular, it will utilize the contributions of Ludwig M. Lachmann[1] and scholars in entrepreneurship, leadership, and dynamic capabilities to examine how firms grow and expand in the global market. The new perspective will be used to explain how a Chinese manufacturing firm in household consumer products grows. In what follows, an entrepreneurial theory of the growth of the firm will be devised. Background of the Haier group will then be given. The empirical analysis of the Haier group will be covered, followed by a concluding remark in the last section.

Towards an entrepreneurial theory of the growth of the firm

The theory of the growth of the firm developed here is based upon three blocks: (1) entrepreneurial leadership, (2) Lachmann's theory of capital structure, and (3) theories of dynamic capabilities in evolutionary economics. This chapter adopts a "first person perspective" (Addleson 1995) or "businessman's common sense" (Skousen 1990: 134) approach in understanding the growth of the firm and focuses on coordination of production activities under uncertainty.

Entrepreneurial leadership

Entrepreneurship and leadership are traditionally treated as two separate concepts. However, researchers in the past decades have attempted to integrate these two concepts into one. One of the early works in this direction is by Lippitt (1987), who defines the entrepreneurial leader as a person who is able to innovate, take risks, focus on the task, assume personal responsibility, and initiate economic orientation. He argues that the entrepreneurial leader is more than an administrator or a manager. He or she orchestrates the enterprise with energy, self-confidence, persistence, and learning capabilities. Tarabishy et al. (2003) believe that entrepreneurial leaders help develop and sustain organizational culture, including adaptation to change, dealing with external forces, goal achievement, coordination, shared values, and beliefs. The entrepreneurial aspect of leadership is the ability to recognize opportunities in a dynamic market. In addition, entrepreneurial leaders excel in leading firms that compete on the edge. They possess the ability to learn, handle sudden change, and understand their resources and capabilities. Other notable scholars (Surie and Ashley 2008; Kuratko 2007; Gupta et al. 2004) define entrepreneurial leadership as the process of creating an entrepreneurial vision and inspiring the team to enact the vision in rapidly changing uncertain environments. Entrepreneurial leadership, in these literatures, has three main components, namely innovativeness, proactiveness, and risk-taking (see also Bagheri et al. 2009: 178–179). In this chapter, one additional component, namely organizing and conducting, is added.

1. **Innovativeness.** It is defined as the ability to think creatively and develop novel and useful ideas in resource utilization and problem solving (Mattare 2008; Okudan and Rzasa 2006; Gupta et al. 2004). Fernald and Solomon (1996) argue that entrepreneurial leadership provides a vision to the development of a new product, service, or organization.
2. **Proactiveness.** Entrepreneurial leadership is a proactive response to environmental opportunities (Surie and Ashley 2008). The leader exploits opportunities and accepts the responsibility of failure (Kuratko et al. 2007). He or she also anticipates the need for change and makes improvement (Okudan and Rzasa 2006).
3. **Risk-taking.** Risk-taking is an important quality in entrepreneurial leadership (Okudan and Rzasa 2006). Facing uncertainty, the entrepreneurial leader is willing to bear uncertainty and take responsibility for future development (Chen 2007). Risk-taking is a common characteristic of entrepreneurial leaders in the initial stages of the entrepreneurship process (Robinson et al. 2006).
4. **Organizing and conducting.** Having an entrepreneurial vision is not enough. A major function of the entrepreneur is to "get the things done" (Schumpeter 1934/1961). In practice, the entrepreneurial leader needs to combine resources to produce outputs to yield profit. Jean B. Say (1842) argues that the role of the entrepreneur is "organizing." The entrepreneur puts resources together for production and shifts economic resources from a lower to a higher area of productivity for greater yield. Entrepreneurial leaders are able to mobilize resources for firms to grow (Gupta and MacMillan 2002).

The entrepreneurial leader as an organizer of production activities under uncertainty: a systematic capital structure builder

In the market process, the entrepreneurial leader needs to combine capital resources in a meaningful way or profitable manner. Lachmann (1956: 13) refers to this as the true function of the entrepreneur. As he puts it:

> The entrepreneur's function as regards capital is not exhausted by the hire of services. Here his function is to *specify* and make decisions on the concrete

form the capital resources shall have. He specifies and modifies the shape and layout of his plant, which is something he cannot do to his typists, desirable though that may seem to him.

(Lachmann 1956: 16; italics original)

The term "capital resources" implies a time dimension and uncertainty in production. On the one hand, entrepreneurs predict consumer wants. They know that wants can never be correctly predicted. On the other hand, they hire capital resources, including managers, labor, equipment, and so on to produce goods and services. The prices of capital resources direct the whole mechanism of production. Betting on their judgments, entrepreneurs bear uncertainty in the form of profits or losses in future (Mises 1949/1966: 256). In Mises' own words (1949/1966: 290), "the entrepreneur is always a speculator. He deals with the uncertainty conditions of the future. His success or failure depends on the correctness of his anticipation of uncertain events . . . the only source from which an entrepreneur's profits stem is his ability to anticipate better than other people the future demand of the consumers."

In summary, production plans in the form of capital structure will be executed according to entrepreneurial wishes. Hence, the entrepreneur can be regarded as a systematic capital structure builder under uncertainty. The firm, in the Lachmann-ian perspective, can be defined as a collection of capital resources.[2]

The formation of a firm's capabilities through a meaningful combination of capital resources

A firm's capabilities are manifested in its capital structure. Hence, the most important issue in the capitalistic theory of the firm is to examine how capital resources are combined in production. In other words, what are the determinants of the firm's capital structure? – in particular, why capital resources are used in the way they are; why in a given situation some alternatives are rejected while others are selected; and what factors govern the choice or rejection of alternative uses when unexpected change compels plan revision.

In Lachmann's view (1956: 8), capital goods must possess the capabilities to produce what consumers will be prepared to pay for. Plans which are inconsistent with either the consumer's or producer's plans will be revised. By trial and error, capital goods will be oriented towards this direction. Furthermore, capital uses must fit each other in order to produce capabilities. A piece of capital equipment may have to be discarded because it does not fit into any combination to yield capabilities that generate profit. Eventually, an acceptable network of plans will emerge with certain patterns of capital use. In this regard, the firm, as a realization of an entrepreneurial plan, consists of a meaningful combination of capital resources.

According to the Resources-Based View, capabilities of the firm depend primarily on a bundle of capital resources at the firm's disposal (Wernerfelt 1984, 1995; Rumelt 1984; Penrose 1959/1995). The capital structure of the firm forms its organizational routines for gathering and processing information, linking customers' plans, and coordinating factories and component suppliers. Furthermore, competitive advantage of the firm requires the integration of internal capital structure linked with external technologies in the form of alliances, joint ventures, mergers and acquisitions, etc. Hence, the firm's capital structure determines the performance and the direction of the growth of the firm too.

Growth of the firm: capital structure reshuffling and capabilities enhancement

As mentioned, if a production plan fails, this implies that the capital structure of the firm lacks capabilities to yield profit. Accordingly, entrepreneurs will revise their production plans, and the capital structure of the firm either needs to be restructured or dissolved. The capital gains and losses of a firm are effective tests of entrepreneurial plans (Lachmann 1977: 203).[3] Similarly, if the entrepreneur perceives an expansion opportunity for the firm, then the previous production plan needs to be revised accordingly. The capital structure of the firm needs to be reshuffled so that the capabilities of these capital resources match the firm's expansion goal.

Penrose (1959/1995: 31) argues that the decision on the part of a firm to investigate the prospective profitability of expansion is an enterprising decision, in the sense that

> whenever expansion is neither pressing nor particularly obvious, a firm has the choice of continuing on its existing course or of expending effort and committing resources to the investigation of whether there are further opportunities of *which it is not yet aware*. This is a decision which depends on the "enterprise" of the firm . . . and it is here that the "spirit of enterprise," or a general entrepreneurial bias in favour of "growth" has perhaps its greatest significance [italics added].

As economic change indicates that there is a need for the firm to expand, the entrepreneur will soon find that his or her original capital combination is inappropriate to yield capabilities to serve the new demand. Whether the firm possesses "the ability to integrate, build, and reconfigure internal and external competences to address rapidly changing environments" is related to the dynamic capabilities of the firm (Teece et al. 1997). As the firm expands, new strategic capital resources with capabilities need to be integrated into the company. Old strategic capital resources have to be transformed or reconfigured. For instance, alliance and acquisition enable firms to bring new strategic capital resources into the firm from external sources.

Encountering new demand, entrepreneurs adapt and learn. New technology associated with superior capital combinations in the production process will eventually be learned and adopted by the firm. In the world of rapid change, capital combinations in the firm will be reshuffled and reformed. Given heterogeneous and complementary natures of capital resources,[4] on some occasions the cost of restructuring the existing capital structure of a firm is so high that the entrepreneur may be better off simply by starting another new plant in another location with a new combination of capital in order to meet new market demand.

A firm's capabilities enhancement through imitation and international cooperation

Rapidly changing market conditions challenge the entrepreneur's ability to reconfigure the firm's capital structure and accomplish necessary internal and external transformation (Amit and Schoemaker 1993). To keep up with the change, the entrepreneur assesses the environment, revaluates markets, and quickly accomplishes reconfiguration and transformation ahead of the competition. In doing so, the entrepreneur knows that he or she needs to upgrade his or her firm's capabilities. Capabilities of the firm can be upgraded by reshuffling the capital structure through product imitation or international cooperation with technologically advanced firms in the forms of joint ventures, strategic alliances, or mergers or acquisitions.

Capabilities enhancement via learning and imitation

In the initial stage of a firm's formation, due to low level of absorptive capacity[5] and poor technological capabilities, entrepreneurs conduct replication or pure copying. To conduct imitation, the firm needs skilled technicians or engineers. Bringing new engineers or skilled workers means a change in the capital structure. Of course, new manpower needs to be fit into the existing capital structure. The entrepreneur perceives that extra skilled workers can fit into the firm's existing production pattern and help conduct imitation to earn profit. Furthermore, to produce a mature product by imitation, the firm may need to buy a secondhand assembly line. Again new capital equipment has been fit into the overall capital structure – for example, the newly hired engineer knows how to operate the assembly line. By hiring new manpower and an assembly line, the firm's capabilities to produce an imitated product to penetrate the world's market is raised.

Capabilities enhancement via strategic alliance

Another method to enhance a firm's capabilities is to form an alliance with a foreign technologically advanced firm. By signing an agreement with the foreign firm from the advanced economy, the latecomer firm can learn technology from its partner. Although this form of strategy has less influence on a latecomer firm's capital structure, the latecomer firm still needs to modify its capital structure in order to accommodate new skills and technology. For example, the foreign firm may advise the latecomer firm to have stricter quality control on product in order to gain a higher quality standard, then the latecomer firm may need to discard old routines. This in turn requires the latecomer firm to discard old equipment or add new technologies to detach the flaws. Hence, the capital structure of the latecomer firm needs to be modified, though the change may be slight.

Capital structure enlargement via mergers or acquisitions

Alliance is a loose form of agreement without capital commitment. Through merger or acquisition, firms can enhance capabilities by tapping into the technology of foreign firms. Mathews (2006: 5–27) argues that initially latecomer firms from emerging economies such as China's deliberately link up with global players and draw into collaborative networks with them, with rapid catching up as a goal (linkage). These firms then exploit the resources and capabilities available from the acquired firm. In other words, it is a technology leverage from links with advanced firms (leverage). Eventually, repeated application of linkage and leverage leads to learning to perform operations more effectively, resulting in capabilities enhancement (learning).[6] For example, Geely Holding Group from Zhejiang province in China bought the Swedish luxury car brand Volvo from US giant carmaker Ford for $1.8 billion on 28 March 2011. The acquisition will offer Geely, a producer with a lower-end image, access to a high-end brand and technology which needs to compete with much bigger rivals globally (*China Daily* 2010). Capabilities enhancement by merger or acquisition implies that two independent firms with different capital structures combine into one. As a result, some capital assets will be made obsolete and discarded. The acquisition also means that there is a saving by deleting some duplicate capital assets. Furthermore, if two capital structures merge into one, some capital assets fit in and some do not. Those not fitting in well will be deleted. By combining two capital structures into a new structure, resources are saved and capabilities are enhanced. A new mode of production is then able to compete globally and bring in profit. The theoretical framework on the growth of the firm is summarized in Figure 2.1.

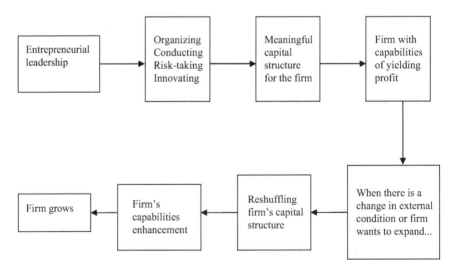

Figure 2.1 The growth of the firm

Background of the Haier Group

The Haier Group is a consumer electronics and home appliances company head-quartered in Qingdao city, Shandong province, China. Its products include air conditioners, mobile phones, computers, microwave ovens, washing machines, refrigerators, and televisions. Haier was formerly a refrigeration factory under the name of Qingdao Refrigerator Co., founded in the 1920s. In 1949, the firm was nationalized by the Communist government. The company under state enterprise performed poorly and the factory was close to bankruptcy. In desperation, the Qingdao government appointed Mr. Zhang Ruimin as the managing director of the factory in 1984. Under Zhang's management reform, Qingdao Refrigerator had returned to profitability, and sales growth averaged 83 percent per year by 1986. Having diversified its product line covering other consumer products, the company adopted a new name, Haier, in 1991. By the end of the 1990s, Haier had become a well-known brand in China, with products ranging from mobile phones to computers. It also captured a dominant market share in its core white goods division. Having success in the domestic market, Haier moved onto the international stage with the goal of building a global brand name. The company opened a production facility in Indonesia in 1996, and the Philippines and Malaysia in 1997. Haier moved into the United States market in 1999, making it in direct confrontation with established American giants such as General Electric (GE), Whirlpool, Frigidaire, and Maytag. As of 2008, Haier surpassed rival Whirlpool as the world's top refrigerator producer in terms of sales. Haier continued its expansion into other international markets. Haier entered Pakistan in 2002 and Jordan in 2003. In Africa, Haier has plants in five countries: Tunisia, Nigeria, Egypt, Algeria, and South Africa. The company also purchased a factory in Italy so as to enter the European market. In 2010, the Haier brand had the world's largest market share in white goods, with 6.1 percent. It has become the world's largest manufacturer of domestic appliances and the fifth largest manufacturer of consumer goods in the world (www.haier.com; Liu and Li 2002: 699–706; Sun 2002: 266–282; Yi and Ye 2003).

The capital structure and capabilities of Qingdao Co. under the radical communist regime

In the 1920s, a refrigerator factory was built in Qingdao to supply the Chinese market.[7] After the establishment of the People's Republic of China in 1949, Haier was then taken over by the central government and turned into a state-owned enterprise. The plant was a manually operated, old workshop run by the Communist cadre, Yang Mianmian, who studied at Shandong Institute of Technology. Through self-learning and a site visit to the Beijing Snowflake refrigerator factory and with the help of a consultant from Shanghai, technicians and workers of Qingdao Co. learned and acquired knowledge and skills to make refrigerators. The manufacturing methods they acquired were native and naive. Nevertheless, these were the early forms of the firm's capital structure and capabilities. Under the socialist regime, the market was strictly enclosed and protected. All production was controlled by the government. Competition was shielded from the outside world. Qingdao's production enjoyed full protection from the government. All Yang needed to do was to follow the instruction of the central planning committee and produce according to the central orders. We can imagine that the capital structure of the factory at that time did not need to be changed. The person in charge of the plant did not need to learn new methods and compete. According to our theory, the entrepreneur will reshuffle the capital structure if the production plan fails due to the change in environment. The faster the change in environment, the quicker the change in the capital structure of the firm is needed so that capabilities of the firm can be enhanced to face new competition. In the case of Qingdao Co., the capital structure of the firm remained unchanged without challenge. In other words, the production and innovation capabilities of Qingdao Co. remained at low levels. Qingdao's production and management lacked efficiency before state enterprise reforms in 1984.

Enter the entrepreneurial leader and the rebirth of the Haier Co.

Under communist central planning, the Qingdao Refrigeration Co. suffered from worn-out infrastructure, poor management, and lack of quality control. Production rarely reached 80 refrigerators a month. By the 1980s, the company had incurred a debt of over ¥1.4 million[8] and was close to bankruptcy. Following Deng's economic reform in 1984, Zhang Ruimin[9] was appointed the managing director of the factory by the Qingdao government. Therefore, Qingdao Co. was not created by Zhang. However, Zhang's entrepreneurial leadership and vision have brought life back into the firm. Hence, the rebirth of Haier can be said to be attributed to Zhang. It is not hard to envisage that Zhang encountered many obstacles in the enterprise reform. As Schumpeter (1934/1961) argues, the entrepreneur is able to overcome social resistance.[10] As we shall illustrate, Zhang was able to transform a rotten factory into a modern multinational giant. Before Zhang joined the firm, the factory could produce only 80 refrigerators per month (see above). The manufacturing equipment was inferior and the refrigerators were produced with poor quality control. More devastatingly, Qingdao's poor-quality refrigerators selling at a price of ¥800 at that time had no demand in the market. Zhang realized that the capital structure of his firm yielded inadequate production skills, low technological standards, and poor quality control that would threaten the firm's survival. After Deng embarked on his "Four Modernizations" policy in 1983, state enterprises were allowed to initiate "responsibility systems" so that businesses were allowed to perform in a capitalist way. Zhang then undertook a radical reform in the capital structure of the firm, with the view of raising the firm's capabilities in order to compete. Receiving growing complaints about the faulty fridges from his customers in 1985, Zhang had 76 faulty refrigerators lined up on the factory floor and ordered his employees to destroy them with hammers. Zhang preached to his workers, "Destroy them! If we sell these refrigerators, we'll continue making mistakes and the company will go bankrupt," showing Zhang's determination in restructuring the company. Embarking on a radical reform in the company, Zhang introduced a strict employee performance evaluation process, called the OEC system.[11] Targets (both quantity and quality) were given to each employee at the start of his or her work. Employees had to meet these targets if they wanted to receive their full salary. Bonuses and promotions were given to employees who exceeded their daily targets. Those who fell short of the target would have their pay stopped or were demoted to probationary status. One key feature of the OEC system was that workers could find out immediately the relationship between their performances and their financial remuneration at the end of the day. When combined with other methods, such as making errant workers stand on red footprints painted on the factory floor to publicly confess their failures, Zhang's new reform provides a major incentive for workers to perform well every day (Hawes and Chew 2011: 67–83).

Capabilities enhancement via strategic alliances and joint ventures

Zhang realized that "every multinational set up in China. Margins are low here. If we don't go outside, we can't survive" (*The Economist*, 18 March 2004[12]; see also Bonaglia et al. 2007: 5). Zhang wanted to raise his product quality to international standards. To achieve this goal, Haier formed joint ventures and strategic alliances with foreign partners.

In order to survive in the industry, Zhang focused on producing high-quality products. One way was to acquire foreign technologies through direct purchases from, or forming strategic alliances with, leading global firms. In 1984, Haier acquired new technology in manufacturing refrigerators from abroad. After a careful assessment of 32 potential cooperative partners, Haier established an alliance with the Liebherr Company of Germany. Liebherr had 70 years of experience in producing high-quality refrigerators. Its refrigerators were generally regarded as the leading ones in the world. Cooperating with Liebherr, Haier was able to import Liebherr's four-star refrigerator production technology and equipment to China. Compared with Liebherr's refrigerators with four-star technology, the capital structure of Haier could perform the very old-fashioned two-star technologies with a freezing capability of −12°C. The freezing capability of a four-star refrigerator was −18°C. By acquiring four-star refrigerator technology, Haier became the only company in China that was able to offer this modern refrigerator. In other words, technology capabilities of Haier were greatly raised. After establishing an R&D department, Haier sent more than 40 top engineers and managers to Liebherr to master technological skills required for developing advanced refrigerators. In 1985, a year after it licensed Liebherr's technology, Haier was able to introduce its first four-star refrigerator in the Chinese market. This product instantly established Haier as the leading refrigerator producer in China (Duysters et al. 2009: 329–330). This implies that the capabilities of the capital structure of Haier were upgraded, with new skilled workers replacing outdated unskilled workers. The installation of Liebherr's equipment and technology was accompanied by a new and rigorous commitment to quality. Combined with Zhang's disciplined management techniques, which broke from the tradition of the iron rice bowl in Chinese state-owned enterprises, the company began to turn around. By 1986, Qingdao Refrigerator had returned to profitability and sales growth averaged 83 percent per year. As a result, sales increased from ¥3.5 million in 1984 to ¥40.5 billion by 2000, a tremendous growth.

Expanding capital structure by mergers and acquisitions

By the late 1980s, Haier was able to establish itself as a leading national brand in the refrigerator market in China. Since then, Haier has continued to expand and diversify into freezers and air conditioners by acquiring companies with good choices of products, facilities, equipment, and distribution channels but with poor management.[13] In other words, these companies possessed good capital equipment but with a capital structure that was incapable of yielding profit in the competitive market. In 1991, Haier took over the Qingdao Air Conditioner Factory and the Qingdao Freezer Factory, both of them experiencing falling sales and financial trouble. After acquisition, Haier imposed its capital structure and capabilities on the new firm. Specifically, Haier transmitted its own management practices to the acquired company. The Haier brand name was given to the products of the acquired company only after they had met Haier quality standards. By the early 1990s, the company had three profit centers: refrigerators, air conditioners, and freezers. It took Haier about 3 years to successfully establish itself in these two new industries. By 1994, Haier's sales had grown to ¥2.56 billion and its profits to ¥200 million. Subsequently, Haier also successfully developed washers, microwave ovens, and water heaters. In August 1997, Haier made its entry into the black household appliances sector; until then, Haier's products were primarily white household appliances (Duysters et al. 2009: 330–331).

Reengineering the capital structure to face market competition

Facing the challenges of e-commerce and China's access to the World Trade Organization, Zhang modified the firm's capital structure in order to compete in the world market. Haier implemented the market-chain-based business process reengineering system in late 1998. It is a management-restructuring program focusing on improved information dissemination for contract performance, logistics, capital investment, after-sales services, inventory, and operation cost reduction.

Such restructuring is backed by an efficient market-chain system and an order-process performance. According to Zhang Ruimin, "a market chain is a series of business process activities to make products to satisfy customers' needs. A market chain links every employee's work with the market, which can be external or internal. Hence, each Haier employee's next downstream activity or process is a market, and every employee faces a market with a direct link to a customer.

This allows the firm to convert external market competition into a type of internal competition. With the worker's reward tied to market performance, there is an incentive for each employee to provide the best performance to meet his or her customers' needs" (Lin 2009: 42).

Restructuring its production and management systems has enabled the company to diversify internal and external resources. Additionally, its worldwide logistics, distribution, and manufacturing facilities ensure customer satisfaction through their efficient operations (Lin 2009: 43–44).

Testing the firm's capital structure in the tough American market

After acting as an Original Equipment Manufacturer (OEM) for foreign companies, Haier attempted to establish its own branded products in overseas markets in 1999. In entering foreign markets, many enterprises from mainland China will first export to developing economies such as Southeast Asia's, where there is no strong competitor. However, Haier did otherwise. Taking an unconventional path, Haier penetrated markets in the United States, where there were the largest global competitors with top quality products. There are two major reasons for Haier taking this route.

First, Haier saw entering developed markets as a way to challenge its product. In the developed countries such as the United States, the requirements of both customers and retailers were very tough and not easy to meet. Zhang believed that if Haier could succeed in markets in advanced nations, then Haier could easily conquer other, emerging markets. If Haier could compete in the US markets with brands such as GE, Matsushita, and Philips, then it could surely take the markets in the developing countries without much effort.

Second, if Haier could successfully launch branded products in the United States market, then its products would be easily accepted by the customers in the emerging markets because it had already gained a reputation in an advanced nation (Palepu et al. 2006: 10–12).

However, entering markets in the United States is a challenging job. Haier had performed well in domestic markets. However, going global is another story. In particular, Zhang needed to prove that Haier could succeed in advanced economies such as the United States and Europe as well. Zhang again exercised his entrepreneurial leadership and successfully competed in the US market through two key strategies.

Identifying market opportunities in the United States

As mentioned, the United States market is flooded with top competitors such as GE, Matsushita, Philips, etc. If Haier wanted to share the pie, it needed a strategy. Haier could not afford head-to-head confrontation with these brand rivals. Instead, it would enter a market that was not adequately served. According to Kirzner (1973), the role of entrepreneurs lies in their alertness to hitherto unnoticed opportunities. When Haier entered the United States markets, they discovered that there was a gap in supplying good refrigerators for students and for offices. Haier sought this golden opportunity and offered mini-fridges that doubled as computer desks, aimed at college students living in dorms. Having a very successful product like compact refrigerators or wine cellars in the United States, Haier was able to get the attention of the major retail chains like Walmart and Best Buy. Having developed a relationship with them, Haier was in a stronger position to get the major chains to consider other appliances such as standard refrigerators, apartment refrigerators, air conditioners, washing machines. In 2005, *Euromonitor* reported that Haier had a 26 percent share for compact refrigerators, over 50 percent of the wine cellar market and 17 percent of air conditioner sales in the United States (Palepu et al. 2006: 10–12).

Capital structure has its cultural dimension too

With its specific capital structure originally designated for Chinese consumers, Haier did possess the capabilities to yield profit in China. However, the United States and China are two markets with entirely different cultures. If Haier wanted to produce for the United States customers, its capital structure might have to be revised in order to obtain new capabilities in the new market. In other words, some capital resources might need to be deleted or replaced. One of the major capabilities of capital assets lies in human capital. Therefore, human resources might need to be replaced.

When entering the United States market, Haier hired local people in the United States to overcome cultural barriers. This implied that the cultural content of the capital structure had to be changed too. Hiring staff in the United States, Haier could expand very quickly because local people knew the local market very well. In this way, staff at Haier were a group of people with local thinking to satisfy the needs of customers in the United States (Palepu et al. 2006: 10–12). With a team of foreign personnel, Haier then placed its own people in key positions overseas in order to get better market intelligence. As a result, in the United States, it is the Americans who built up Haier America. Similarly, in Europe, it was the Europeans who built up Haier Europe. To conclude, the capital structure and capabilities of the firm are never fixed in the market process. They need to be modified, revised, and changed according to the time and place and the company's goal.

Conclusion

Under Zhang's entrepreneurial leadership, Haier had its capital structure restructuring continuously. Each modification has led to an upgrade of the firm's capabilities so that Haier has been able to compete in the world market. As a result, Haier has successfully transformed from a state enterprise of heavy debt into a modern multinational giant. In 2008, Haier ranked number 1 on "Overall Leadership of Mainland China Corporations" for the fifth consecutive year by *The Wall Street Journal Asia*. In 2008, R&F and Beijing Famous-Brand Evaluation Co.

announced that Haier topped the list for seven consecutive years as the "China Most Valuable Brand," with a brand value of US$11.7 billion. In 2009, the China National Household Electric Appliances Service Association ranked Haier number 1 in the Year Customer Satisfaction Survey. In 2009, Haier was the only Chinese household appliances enterprise to win *Businessweek*'s Top 10 Chinese and Foreign Enterprises in China "Green Economy Award" (Lin 2009: 47).

On Haier's success, Duysters et al. (2009: 343) comment that the greatest driving force in the emergence of the business group has been "its leadership whose vision and entrepreneurial dynamism made (the company) stand out domestically, if not globally. The top management . . . exhibited dynamic capabilities, keeping with the changes in the business environment."

Notes

1 Although the works of Ludwig Lachmann have drawn some attentions from scholars in the Austrian camp (e.g., see Foss and Garzarelli 2007; Foss et al. 2007, 2011), few works have applied Lachmann's contributions to the theories of the firm and corporate strategies in the real world.

2 Penrose (1959/1995) defines the firm as a collection of resources. In her book, she implicitly recognizes the "capital" nature of resources.

3 As a Misesian follower, Rothbard (1962/1993: 494) argues that "the entrepreneur is an adjuster of the discrepancies of the market toward greater satisfaction of the desires of the consumers. When he innovates he is *also* an adjuster, since he is adjusting the discrepancies of the market as they present themselves in the potential of a new method or product. In other words, if the ruling rate of (natural) interest return is 5 percent, and a business man estimates that he could earn 10 percent by instituting a new process or product, then he has, as in other cases, discovered a discrepancy in the market and sets about correcting it. By launching and producing more of the new process, he is pursuing the entrepreneurial function of adjustment to consumer desires, i.e., what he estimates consumer desires will be. If he succeeds in his estimate and reaps a profit, then he and others will continue in this line of activity until the income discrepancy is eliminated and there is no 'pure' profit or loss in this area."

4 Lachmann's original insight that capital resources are essentially heterogeneous and complementary has been recognized in modern theories of the firm. For example, see Foss et al. (2011), Foss and Garzarelli (2007), and Foss et al. (2007). However, the literature has not yet developed a Lachmannian model of the growth of the firm and corporate strategies.

5 Cohen and Levinthal (1990: 128) define absorptive capacity as "the ability of a firm to recognize the value of new, external information, assimilate it, and apply it to commercial ends."

6 Mathews (2006) refers to the linkage, leverage, and learning as the LLL framework for Chinese latecomer firms to catch up.

7 The name of its founder cannot be traced.

8 ¥ is Chinese currency yuan (CNY); US$1= ¥6.256 on 23 February 2015.

9 For further information on Zhang Ruimin, see Tang (2005) and Zhang (2011).

10 Schumpeter (1947) refers this phenomenon to as "creative response."

11 "O" stands for over the whole firm; "E" stands for every task, every day, and every employee; and "C" stands for control, i.e., every task is controlled.

12 *The Economist*, "Haier's Purpose," 18 March 2004, www.economist.com/node/2524 347; retrieved 30 December 2011.

13 Zhang Ruimin referred to these types of companies as "stunned fishes."

References

Addleson, Mark (1995) *Equilibrium versus Understanding: Towards the Restoration of Economics as Social Theory*, London: Routledge.

Amit, R. and Schoemaker, P.J.H. (1993) "Strategic Assets and Organizational Rent," *Strategic Management Journal*, 14(1): 33–46.

Bagheri, Afsaneh; Akmaliah, Zaidatol; and Pihie, Lope (2009) "An Exploratory Study of Entrepreneurial Leadership Development of University Students," *European Journal of Social Sciences*, 11(1): 177–190.

Bonaglia, F.; Goldstein, A.; and Mathews, J. A. (2007) "Accelerated Internationalization by Emerging Markets' Multinationals: The Case of the White Goods Sector," *Journal of World Business*, 42(4): 369–383.

Chen, Ming-Huei (2007) "Entrepreneurial Leadership and New Ventures: Creativity in Entrepreneurial Teams," *Creativity and Innovation Management*, 16(3): 239–249.

China Daily (2010) "Focus on Geely's Purchase of Volvo," www.chinadaily.Com.cn/bizchina/2010–03/29/content 9658301.htm; retrieved 29 March 2010.

Cohen, W. M. and Levinthal, D. A. (1990) "Absorptive Capacity: A New Perspective on Learning and Innovation," *Administrative Science Quarterly*, 35(supplement 1): 128–152.

Duysters, G.; Jacob, J.; Lemmens, C.; and Yu, J. T. (2009) "Internationalization and Technological Catching up of Emerging Multinationals: A Comparative Case Study of China's Haier Group," *Industrial and Corporate Change*, 18(2): 325–349.

Fernald, L. W. Jr. and Solomon, G. T. (1996) "Entrepreneurial Leadership: Oxymoron or New Paradigm?" *Journal of Management Systems*, 8: 2–16.

Foss, Kirsten; Foss, N.; Klein, P.; and Klein, S. (2007) "The Entrepreneurial Organization of Heterogeneous Capital," *Journal of Management Studies*, 44(7): 1165–1186.

Foss, Nicola J.; Klein, P. G.; and Bylund, P. L. (2011) "Entrepreneurship and the Economics of the Firm," SMG WP 6/2011, Department of Strategic Management and Globalization Copenhagen Business School.

Foss, Nicolai J. and Garzarelli, Giampaolo (2007) "Institutions as Knowledge Capital: Ludwig M. Lachmann's Interpretative Institutionalism," *Cambridge Journal of Economics*, 31(5/September): 789–804.

Gupta, V. and MacMillan, I. C. (2002) "Entrepreneurial Leadership: Developing a Cross-cultural Construct," *Proceedings from the Academy of Management Science*, Denver, Colorado.

Gupta, V., MacMillan, I. C. and Surie, G (2004) "Entrepreneurial Leadership: Developing and Measuring a Cross-cultural Construct," *Journal of Business Venturing*, 19(2/March): 241–260.

Hawes, Colin and Chew, Eng (2011) "The Cultural Transformation of Large Chinese Enterprises into Internationally Competitive Corporations: Case Studies of Haier and Huawei," *Journal of Chinese Economic and Business Studies*, 9(1/Feb): 67–83.

Kirzner, I. M. (1973) *Competition and Entrepreneurship*, Chicago: University of Chicago Press.

Kuratko, D. F. (2007) "Entrepreneurial Leadership in the 21st Century," *Journal of Leadership & Organizational Studies*, 13(4): 1–11.

Kuratko, D. F.; Hornsby, J. S.; and Goldsby, M. G. (2007) "The Relationship of Stakeholder Salience, Organizational Posture, and Entrepreneurial Intensity to Corporate Entrepreneurship," *Journal of Leadership and Organizational Studies*, 13(4): 56–72.

Lachmann, L. M. (1956) *Capital and Its Structure*, Kansas City, MO: Sheed Andrews and McMeel.

Lachmann, L. M. (1977) *Capital, Expectations and the Market Process*, Kansas City, MO: Sheed Andrew and McMeel.

Lin, Thomas W. (2009) "Haier Is Higher: A Chinese Company's Roadmap to Success via Its Reengineering System," *Strategic Finance*, 91(6/Dec): 41–49.

Lippitt, G. L. (1987) "Entrepreneurial Leadership: A Performing Art," *Journal of Creative Behavior*, 21(3): 264–270.

Liu, H. and Li, K. Q. (2002) "Strategic Implications of Emerging Chinese Multinationals: The Haier Case Study," *European Management Journal*, 20(6): 699–706.

Mathews, John (2006) "Dragon Multinationals: New Players in 21st Century Globalization," *Asia-Pacific Journal of Management*, 23(1/March): 5–27.

Mattare, M. (2008) "Teaching Entrepreneurship: The Case for an Entrepreneurial Leadership Course," USASBE Proceedings, pp. 78–93.

Mises, Ludwig von (1949/1966) *Human Action: A Treatise on Economics*, 3rd ed., Chicago: Contemporary Books.

Okudan, G. E. and Rzasa, S. E. (2006) "A Project-Based Approach to Entrepreneurial Leadership Education," *Technovation*, 26: 195–210.

Palepu, Krishna G.; Khanna, Tarun; and Vargas, Ingrid (2006) "Haier: Taking a Chinese Company Global," Case 9-706-401, 25 August, Harvard Business School.

Penrose, E. (1959/1995) *The Theory of the Growth of the Firm*, Oxford: Basil Blackwell.

Rothbard, Murray N. (1962/1993) *Man, Economy and State*, Auburn, AL: Ludwig von Mises Institute.

Robinson, D. A.; Goleby, M.; and Hosgood, N. (2006) "Entrepreneurship as a Values and Leadership Paradigm," paper presented to Fourth AGSE International Entrepreneurship Research Exchange, 7–9 February 2007 BGSB, QUT, Brisbane.

Rumelt, R. P. (1984) "Towards a Strategic Theory of the Firm," in R. Lamb (ed.) *Competitive Strategic Management*, Englewood Cliffs, NJ: Prentice-Hall, pp. 556–570.

Say, Jean Baptiste (1842) *A Treatise on Political Economy; or the Production, Distribution and Consumption of Wealth*. Translated from the 4th edition of the French. Kitchener, Ontario: Batoche Books.

Schumpeter, J. A. (1934/1961) *The Theory of Economic Development*, New York: Oxford University Press.

Schumpeter, J. A. (1947) "The Creative Response in Economic History," in R. Clemence (ed.) (1951) *Essays of J. A. Schumpeter*, Cambridge, MA: Addison-Wesley, pp. 216–226.

Skousen, M. (1990) *The Structure of Production*, New York: New York University Press.

Sun, J. (2002) *The Corporate Strategy of Haier*, Beijing: Enterprise Management Press, pp. 266–282.

Surie, G. and Ashley, A. (2008) "Integrating Pragmatism and Ethics in Entrepreneurial Leadership for Sustainable Value Creation," *Journal of Business Ethics*, 81: 235–246.

Tang, Ivy Yanxia (2005) "A Case Study of a Leader Zhang Ruimin," www.runsky.com/homepage/dl/spec/2004/usa4/guo/userobject1ai551524.html; retrieved 30 December 2011.

Tarabishy, Ayman; Fernald, Lloyd W. Jr.; and Solomon, George T. (2003) "Understanding Entrepreneurial Leadership in Today's Dynamic Markets," Proceedings of the United States Association for Small Business and Entrepreneurship (USASBE) Conference held at Hilton Head Island, South Carolina, 23–26 January 2003.

Teece, David; Pisano, Gary; and Shuen, Amy (1997) "Dynamic Capabilities and Strategic Management," *Strategic Management Journal*, 18(7/August): 509–533.

Wernerfelt, B. (1984) "A Resource-Based View of the Firm," *Strategic Management Journal*, 5(2): 171–180.

Wernerfelt, B. (1995) "The Resource-Based View of the Firm: Ten Years After," *Strategic Management Journal*, 16(3): 171–174.

Yi, Jeannie Jinsheng and Ye, Shawn Xian (2003) *The Haier Way: The Making of a Chinese Business Leader and a Global Brand*, Dumont, NJ: Homa & Sekey Books.

Zhang, Xinglong (2011) *Ruimin Zhang's Wisdom of Confucian Entrepreneurs*, Hangzhou: Zhejiang University Press.

3 Turning trash paper into gold

Zhang Yin and her paper recycling business

Introduction

Unlike Bill Gates, who is well known for the personal computer revolution in the United States, Zhang Yin,[1] a woman entrepreneur without any knowledge in high tech, has become one of the richest persons in China by recycling waste papers. While Bill Gates will leave his name in human history through his extraordinary technological breakthrough, Zhang Yin makes herself known in Chinese entrepreneurship through her alertness to opportunity. While Bill Gates represents the Schumpeterian theory of entrepreneurial innovation, Zhang Yin can be regarded as a celebrated illustration of the Kirznerian theory of entrepreneurial discovery.[2] This chapter will introduce an Austrian perspective of international entrepreneurship and coordination. This theory will be applied to understand the economic success of a paper tycoon, Zhang Yin and the Nine Dragons Paper Company. This chapter concludes by showing how the world is unintentionally linked together by the efforts of entrepreneurs who consciously seek profits for their own good. In what follows, a theory of entrepreneurship and international coordination based on Austrian economics will be presented. This will be followed by a brief introduction of Nine Dragons Paper and Zhang Yin, a woman entrepreneur in paper recycling. Her entrepreneurship and global coordination will be analyzed in the subsequent sections. A conclusion will be given in the last section.

Invisible hand, economic coordination, and the market

Adam Smith (1776: 208) portrays the market as "an obvious and simple system of natural liberty." In Smith's view, the market "encourages every man to apply himself to a particular occupation, and to cultivate and bring to perfection whatever talent or genius he may possess" (ibid: 14). As a result, "the most dissimilar geniuses are of use to one another; the different produces of their respective talents . . . being brought, as it were, into a common stock, where every man may purchase whatever part of the produce of other men's talents he has occasion for" (ibid: 7).

The market coordinates economic activities not from benevolence, but through self-interest. Smith (1776: 354) contends that the individual "intends only his own gain, and he is, in this, as in many other cases, led by an invisible hand to promote an end which was not part of his intention. Nor is it always the worse for the society that it was no part of it. By pursuing his own interest he frequently promotes that of the society more effectually than when he really intends to promote it."

Hayek's knowledge problems and market coordination[3]

Hayek adds insight into the functioning of the market in terms of knowledge problems. For Hayek, the market is a process in which the outcome is produced in a decentralized way. The acting agents' aims are coordinated with the actual outcome that the agents don't have any knowledge of. For Austrian economists, knowledge about means and ends is dispersed among each and every individual member of society. Under such circumstance, when planning his/her actions with the goal of furthering his/her own ends, each individual has to incorporate expectations of what the others might do in order to have a chance of success in his/her action plan. The economic problem is then a matter of how to coordinate the multitude of individual plans. It is with this knowledge problem in mind that Austrian economists consider the market to be the most effective way humans have stumbled upon through history to address the problem compared with alternatives like central planning. Prices in a market system perform two functions which help coordinate individual plans. The first function is best illustrated from an example Hayek used in his classic paper on dispersed knowledge (Hayek 1945). Imagine that a source of supply of tin is exhausted or suddenly men find a new way to use tin – the price of tin will increase as a result. There is no need for the users of tin to figure out the real reason for the rise of the tin price. All they need to do is to conserve their use of tin. The price of tin serves as a signal communicating to the users of tin that the material has become relatively less available without the need for them to know exactly why that is the case. The price thus also economizes the knowledge individuals need to formulate plans that would be consistent with those of the others.

In the example above, the price of tin is assumed to accurately reflect the relative scarcity of tin in every moment in time. Prices are presumed to adjust automatically subsequent to changes in demand and/or supply conditions. The above portrait of the market order is incomplete. Someone has to bring about the needed changes in the prices of goods for them to be an accurate reflection of the underlying demand and supply conditions. That role is fulfilled by entrepreneurs' alertness to profit opportunities (Kirzner 1973). Suppose apples are sold at different prices in two nearby markets. The price for an apple in market A is 10 dollars while the same apple sells for 5 dollars in market B. The price differential indicates that the underlying market conditions in two places are not accurately reflected in apple prices. Some apple lovers in market A are left without apples because they would pay 7 dollars for an apple at the maximum, a valuation higher than the marginal customer places on the same apple in market B. Prices will not change automatically but need to be changed. Who is going to do the job? The answer is the entrepreneur. The price differential in the example above entails a profit opportunity for someone who keeps alert to it. An entrepreneur can buy apples at 5 dollars in market B and resell them at higher prices in market A for a profit. The opportunity for such profitable arbitrage will be exhausted when the price differential is eliminated. By buying apples from market B and reselling them in market A, the entrepreneur would be able to pocket the price difference for apples. So long as current prices do not accurately reflect the underlying market conditions, systematic forces exist for them to align with those conditions as a by-product of entrepreneurial activities in pursuit of profits. The second function of price is therefore to provide an incentive for entrepreneurs to bring about the change needed for price to accurately reflect underlying the market condition. In Mises' words (1949: 328):

> The driving force of the market process is provided neither by the consumers nor by the owners of the means of production – land, capital goods, and labor – but by the promoting and speculating entrepreneurs. These are people intent upon profiting by taking advantage of differences in prices. Quicker of apprehension and farther-sighted than other men, they look around for sources of profit. They buy where and when they deem prices too low, and they sell where and when they deem prices too high. They approach the owners of the factors of production, and their competition sends the prices of these factors up to the limit corresponding to their anticipation of the future prices of the products. They approach the consumers, and their competition forces prices of consumers' goods down to the point at which the whole supply can be sold. Profit-seeking speculation is the driving force of the market as it is the driving force of production.

Economic calculation as a function of entrepreneurship

Carl Menger (1871/2007: 160), the founder of the Austrian school of economics, argues that one of the entrepreneurial activities is "economic calculation – all the various computations that must be made if a production process is to be efficient (provided that it is economic in other respects)." Mises (1949) adds that in the market process, entrepreneurs discover discrepancy between current factor prices and future product prices and exploit it for their own advantages. More importantly, every single step of entrepreneurial activities is subject to scrutiny by economic calculation. As Mises (1949: 210–211) notes:

> The task which acting man wants to achieve by economic calculation is to establish the outcome of acting by contrasting input and output. Economic calculation is either an estimate of the expected outcome of future action or the establishment of the outcome of past action. But the latter does not serve merely historical and didactic aims. Its practical meaning is to show how much one is free to consume without impairing the future capacity to produce. It is with regard to this problem that the fundamental notions of economic calculation – capital and income, profit and loss, spending and saving, cost and yield – are developed.

Moreover, "monetary calculation is the guiding star of action under the social system of division of labor. It is the compass of the man embarking upon production. He calculates in order to distinguish the remunerative lines of production from the unprofitable ones. . . . Monetary calculation is the main vehicle of planning and acting in the social setting of a society of free enterprise directed and controlled by the market and prices" (Mises 1949: 229–230). More importantly, resources can be efficiently allocated via entrepreneurs' economic calculation.

International entrepreneurship and global coordination

The Austrian theories of market can be applied to global economy too. Global markets coordinate economic activities worldwide. For instance, consumers in China may have little knowledge about production in the Unites States and yet people in China can buy and enjoy American products. Thus, the market "is a system which enables the dispersed knowledge and skill of millions of people to be coordinated for a common purpose. Men in Malaya who produce rubber, in Mexico who produce graphite, in the state of Washington who produce timber, and countless others, cooperate in the production of an ordinary rubber-topped lead pencil – to use Leonard Read's vivid image – though there is no world government to which they all submit, no common language in which they could converse, and no knowledge of the purpose for which they cooperate" (Friedman 1976: 16).

Economic coordination in global markets is conducted by international entrepreneurs. Oviatt and McDougall (2005: 7) define international entrepreneurship as "the discovery, enactment, evaluation and exploitation of opportunities *across national borders* to create future goods and services" (italics added). These entrepreneurs, with a world perspective, are on constant alert to the development of world politics. They travel extensively and deal effectively with foreigners. They initiate joint ventures and establish overseas branches. They are willing to understand different cultures of the world and are often the first group of businesspeople to penetrate unexplored foreign markets.

The most important role of international entrepreneurship is to coordinate global economic activities, i.e., matching plans of millions of individuals around the globe. For example, in the global economy, computer producers in Taiwan (say, Acer) today need to estimate what consumers (Walmart) in the United States want tomorrow. Likewise, American producers are also keen to know their rivals' plans so that they can formulate their selling or pricing strategies. Charging a wrong price or producing a wrong product (i.e., mismatches of plans) can be disastrous and leads to business failure.

Using Kirzner's insights (Kirzner 1973) again, this chapter argues that the role of international entrepreneurs lies in their alertness to hitherto unnoticed global opportunities. In the world market, the opportunity that entrepreneurial agents are alert to is monetary profit. They discover and exploit global opportunities according to their hunches. International entrepreneurs, with their superior ability of reading market data, exploit profit opportunities around the world. According to Martin (2007: 6), profit opportunities in the world market come in three ways. The first is the recognition of previous errors or mismatches of plans. The second is the introduction of new opportunities. The third is the uncertainty of the future. Furthermore, international entrepreneurs are able to integrate "innumerable scraps of existing information that are present in scattered form" throughout the world (Kirzner 1985: 162). The international coordination process is thus "the systematic plan changes generated by the flow of market information released by market participation – that is, by the testing of plans in the market" (Kirzner 1973: 10). Increased coordination means that entrepreneurs' plans are made more compatible (Martin 2007: 4).

More importantly, it is the spirit of international entrepreneurship that improves the well-being of the human race. In Kirzner's (1985: 162) words, "the entrepreneurial spirit that stimulates the discovery in the market of the value of information now existing throughout the market also tends to stimulate the discovery or creation of entirely new information concerning ways to anticipate or to satisfy consumer preferences. The entrepreneurial process at this second level is what drives the capitalist system toward higher and higher standards of achievement." Our Austrian theories of market, international entrepreneurship, and global coordination will be used to explain the economic success of Zhang Yan and her paper business empire, namely the Nine Dragons Paper Company.

Introducing Zhang Yan and the Nine Dragons Paper Company

Zhang was born in Guangdong, China in 1957. Her family originally comes from northern Heilongjiang province near the Russian border. She was the eldest of eight children of a military family. During the Cultural Revolution, her father was branded as "counter-revolutionary" and sent to prison. When the Cultural Revolution ended in 1976, her father was released from prison and "reeducated." Zhang Yin was able to study commerce and work as an accounting clerk (China Investment Consulting 2008; He 2009).

Moving to Shenzhen (southern China)

Deng Xiaoping embarked on the "Four Modernizations" and the Open Door Policy in 1979. China's officials learned how to catch up with economically advanced nations. Without any precedent, China cruised into a journey of experimentation by "groping the stones to cross the river." Special economic zones were established as "guinea pigs" for the "Four Modernizations policies." Shenzhen was designated as a special economic zone to attract foreign investment. Overnight, Shenzhen turned into a city of opportunity for those who left their villages to seek a fortune in the "newfound land." Zhang Yin was one of the first such movers. She started working for a foreign–Chinese joint venture paper trading company (Barboza 2007; He 2009). This working experience enabled her to gain knowledge in the paper industry. In particular, Zhang was inspired by a man in the paper business. He told Zhang that "waste paper is like a forest. Papers recycle themselves, generation after generation" (He 2009). Zhang kept in mind that paper recycling could be a profitable business. At that time, Hong Kong had already gained a reputation as an international metropolis. Zhang felt that Hong Kong would provide her with more opportunities if she wanted to do big business. At the age of 27, she decided to give up the job in Shenzhen and moved to Hong Kong for a new life. Zhang dared to dream and venture, a vital trait of an entrepreneur.

From Shenzhen to Hong Kong

In 1985, Zhang moved to Hong Kong and became an accountant in a Chinese trading company. Zhang never wanted to be an employee. She perceived that there was a market gap in the paper manufacturing business that was not adequately serviced.[4] She assessed the opportunity cost of starting up a paper factory in Hong Kong. She was fluent in Putonghua, China's national language, and Cantonese, the dialect of Guangdong (including Hong Kong). With her working experience and capabilities at that time, she was offered an annual salary of HK$500,000[5] in Hong Kong. Zhang therefore felt that if her paper business failed, she could find a job in Hong Kong or simply return to China. After balancing the pros and cons, Zhang decided to fill the market gap by setting up a paper factory in Hong Kong. Moving from Shenzhen to Hong Kong, Zhang in fact reshuffled her own labor from the market (Shenzhen) where her labor was undervalued to the one (Hong Kong) where her labor was valued much higher.[6] Her entrepreneurial migration allowed a more efficient use of labor resources.

Supplying better paper at a lower price in Hong Kong

During that period, many paper factories in Hong Kong filled water into paper pulp in order to increase profit margins. However, this dishonest act lowered the quality of the paper. Zhang wanted to ensure that the paper manufactured in her factory was of top quality and refused to do this kind of trick. By so doing, Zhang irritated other manufacturers in the industry, who alleged that she violated business practices. As a result, Zhang received a lot of threats and condemnation from her peers. However, Zhang refused to compromise. This gained Zhang goodwill and trust in the paper industry in Hong Kong. Her business was able to expand rapidly.

From Hong Kong to Los Angeles

After all, Hong Kong's paper market proved to be too small for the ambitious lady. Zhang moved to Los Angeles in 1990 and married for the second time, to a Taiwanese who was fluent in both Chinese and English. Life in the United States was not easy for the couple initially. At that time, China's economy grew rapidly and consumed a lot of paper. However, China was short of lumber and pulp after many forests in the country were ruined during the "Great Leap Forward" movement in 1958–62. Chinese manufacturers were desperate for scrap paper. Moreover,

China's own paper products were of poor quality, often made from grass, bamboo, or rice stalks. Most paper made in the United States and Europe were derived from wood pulp. China began to look for used paper overseas (Cheng 2007). Zhang saw the profit opportunity and was one of the first entrepreneurs to sell scrap paper to China. In 1990, Zhang and her husband established America Chung Nam (ACN) and made deals with American scrap yards. The couple drove around the city in a used minivan, asking garbage dumps to give them their scrap paper. Garbage dumps were more than happy to have her haul off the paper for a minimal payment. As a result, her overhead was very low (Cheng 2007). The company began shipping huge containers of papers back to China for profit. In 2002, the company shipped 3 million tons of paper out of the United States to China (*Global Entrepreneur* 2008).

International coordination via self-interest and economic calculation

What Zhang did was an international coordination. Such global connection was made possible through self-interest and economic calculation. This is the magic of the market. In Los Angeles, an aged pensioner and/or non-skilled laborer collected trash paper from supermarkets or garbage dumps and sold them to buyers of trash paper. In this way, they could earn US$80 a day (China Investment Consulting 2008). This non-taxed income, together with old-age pensions or unemployment insurance deterred this group of people from entering the formal labor market,[7] because they could obtain a better income by collecting trash paper.

Buyers of trash paper in the United States sold it to ACN collection centers for US$30–40 per ton (China Investment Consulting 2008). In the seven ACN collection centers, trash papers were pressed, packaged, and transported to the containers ready for shipping to China. Zhang was able to secure the lowest shipping rates because many vessels were almost empty on the way back to China after unloading their cargoes in the United States. In two weeks' time, trash paper was sold to paper manufacturing companies for recycling at the Shanghai port at a price of US$100 per ton. This procedure was repeated once a week for twenty years, made possible by Zhang's America Chung Nam. As raw materials for making paper rose, collecting and shipping trash paper could bring ACN an impressive profit margin of over 10 percent (China Investment Consulting 2008).

From Los Angeles back to Dongguan (southern China)

As the demand for paper and cardboard packaging in China grew rapidly, Zhang felt that instead of selling scrap paper to paper manufacturers in China, she would be better off by being directly involving in paper manufacturing. In other words, she conducted international vertical integration by linking (1) trash paper collection in the USA, (2) shipping trash paper to China's ports, and (3) producing paper in China.[8] In 1995, Zhang returned to her mother country, China, and opened her first paper factory (namely the Nine Dragons Company) in Dongguan, a major manufacturing hub in the Pearl River Delta region near Hong Kong (Barboza

2007). Nine Dragons became one of the fastest growing paper companies, and yet it could not keep up with the demand for container board, the material used to make boxes, because of the rapid growth in the Chinese economy and exports. The Nine Dragons Paper Company was able to raise nearly US$500 million when it was listed public in Hong Kong's stock market in March 2006. Shares of Nine Dragons quadrupled, giving the company a market value of more than US$5 billion. The Zhang family controlled 72 percent of the company, which made it one of the richest families in China (Barboza 2007). In June 2007, the company owned 13 giant papermaking machines, hired about 8,600 full-time employees, with US$1.4 billion in annual revenue and US$300 million in profits (Ko and Joshi 2008: 1). In 2008, Nine Dragons was the largest producer of container board products in China and one of the largest producers in the world in terms of production capacity. The company offered a comprehensive product range in three major categories of packaging paper products, namely linerboard, high performance corrugating medium, and coated duplex board (Ko and Joshi 2008: 3). In May 2008, the company acquired a controlling interest of 60 percent in a paper mill in Vietnam, thereby utilizing cheap labor and land there as well as penetrating the Southeast Asian markets, a significant milestone for the company (Ko and Joshi 2008: 3).

Investigating factors for Zhang's success

It remains to examine the factors that led to Zhang's success. This chapter identifies four major factors.

Ability to identify profit opportunities

As mentioned, Kirzner's role of the entrepreneur lies in his/her alertness to hitherto unnoticed opportunities (Kirzner 1973). Kirzner's view of entrepreneurship describes exactly what Zhang has done. To be sure, paper recycling is hardly a high-tech business. However, the entrepreneur survives by being able to identify and exploit the profit opportunity in the low-tech business. Zhang was able to identify profit opportunity in the paper recycling business by being the first to ship trash paper back to China. As Zhang claims, "forecasting the market ahead of our competitors . . . is what made us into the market leader" (*MoneyWeek* 2006). Zhang is always ahead of other traders in the competition. For example, while "most domestic producers were using machines with a production capacity of less than 50,000 tons, Zhang's first machine already had a capacity of 200,000 tons" (*MoneyWeek* 2006). In this regard, Hutton (2006) rightly concludes that "scrap paper is one of the few industries the party considers non-strategic and which it indulges – another smart choice for an ambitious woman."

Correct foresight

Knight (1921: 281) argues that "profit arises out of the inherent, absolute unpredictability of things, out of the sheer brute fact that the results of human activity cannot be anticipated. The receipt of profit is the result of superior judgment. The amount of income depends on his success in producing the anticipated excess, and . . . the correctness of his judgment." In line with Knight, Mises (1949: 290) argues that "the entrepreneur . . . deals with the uncertain conditions of the future. His success or failure depends on the correctness of his anticipation of uncertain events. If he fails in his understanding of things to come, he is doomed." The success of Zhang is her ability to read the market. Zhang correctly anticipated the changing market condition and acted upon it to exploit profit.

Venturesome and thinking globally

Zhang Yin is venturesome and not afraid of dreaming big. She belongs to what Mises describes as "promoting entrepreneurs," who are "especially eager to profit from adjusting production to the expected changes in conditions, those who have more initiative, [are] more venturesome, and [have] a quicker eye than the crowd, the pushing and promoting pioneers of economic improvement" (Mises 1949: 255). These entrepreneurs are restless. Zhang wanted to make the Nine Dragons Company number one in paper manufacturing and the world's largest paper corporation by 2009. She is regarded by market analysts as "visionary" (Ko and Joshi 2008: 10). "She doesn't mind putting a lot of money in at the beginning, to build the company" (Barboza 2007). Thinking globally, she started business in Hong Kong, moved to the United States, then returned to China. This global vision enables Zhang to link the world together, something that domestic entrepreneurs fail to do.

Overcoming cultural barriers

International exchange is a market structured by political, economic, and cultural contexts. The issue of culture and knowledge justifies the role of the middleman in global trade. In mainstream neoclassical price theory, the role of the middleman is to reduce the transaction costs (for example, see Casson 1982). However, a middleman is more than just a person who links both trading parties together. The middleman is also an entrepreneur who makes exchange possible under a set of cultural values and beliefs. Zhang describes her management style as a combination of Western and Chinese culture. She is able to ride both worlds to her company's benefit. Grasping the Western trend of environmental conservation, the Nine Dragons Company adopts the Chinese way of management in its operations. Being able to combine her Chinese origin with the American base, Zhang's company gains support from both sides of the globe and fills the trade gap efficiently. Zhang's international coordination efforts raise the well-being of both trading parties around the globe.

Hopping around the globe: the Hong Kong–USA–China Connection

Zhang Yin started her career in Shenzhen, moved to Hong Kong, ventured into the United States, and set up paper plants in Dongguan, China. For Zhang Yin, life is like hopping around the globe. Each of Zhang's entrepreneurial moves is driven by self-interest and scrutinized by careful economic calculation. As a result of her entrepreneurship and economic coordination, the world has been linked as "one" market. Zhang's entrepreneurship has paid off too. She is now richer than many women in the world, including the chief executive of eBay, Meg Whitman. Zhang's personal wealth was estimated at over US$1.5 billion in 2007 (Barboza 2007). From a humble recycling "trash to cash" business, she is now one of the richest self-made women in the world.

Notes

1 Zhang is the surname and Yin is the given name. She is also known as Cheung Yan in Hong Kong due to Cantonese pronunciation.
2 Two kinds of entrepreneurship are mentioned. Joseph Schumpeter (1934/1961) regards the entrepreneur as a person who innovates. Isaac M. Kirzner (1973) argues that the role of entrepreneurs lies in their alertness to opportunity hitherto not yet noticed. See also Yu (1997).
3 This part is adopted from Yu and Shiu (2011).
4 Leibenstein (1968) regards the entrepreneur as a gap filler.
5 US$1 = HK$7.8 (Hong Kong dollar has been pegged to the US dollar at this rate since 1983).
6 Jean Baptist Say argues that the entrepreneur "shifts economic resources out of an area of lower and into an area of higher productivity and greater yield" (cited in Drucker 1995:19). Thus, Say's entrepreneur is an organizer (Philipsen 1998; Hebert and Link 1988: 152).
7 In 1974, a waiter working in a Chinese restaurant earned US$700 per week, or US$70 a day (the author's personal observation in Philadelphia, USA).
8 Vertical integration is a controversial issue in the theory of the firm. In entrepreneurial perspective, Penrose (1959) argues that firm expansion is limited by the entrepreneur's vision. Williamsons (1981) uses the concepts of bounded rationality and transaction costs to explain vertical integration.

References

Barboza, David (2007) "China's Queen of Trash Finds Riches in Waste Paper," *International Herald Tribune*, January 15.

Casson, Mark (1982) *The Entrepreneur: An Economic Theory*, Oxford: Blackwell.

Cheng, Allen T. (2007) "Cardboard Queen Zhang Recycles to Become China's Richest Person," *Bloomberg News*, January, www.bloomberg.com/apps/news?pid=newsarchive&sid=aX2DENqYvouU&refer=news; retrieved 28 July 2010.

China Investment Consulting (2008) *Zhang Yin: China's First Female Rich*, Shenzhen, China.

Drucker, Peter F. (1995) *Innovation and Entrepreneurship*, London: Butterworth Heinemann.

Friedman, M. (1976) "Adam Smith's Relevance for 1976," Chicago: University of Chicago Graduate School of Business, Occasional Papers #50.

Global Entrepreneurs (2008) "Double Faces of Zhang Yin," http://magazine.sina.com/genius/200806/2008-06-02/104411949.shtml; retrieved 15 July 2011.

Hayek, F. A. (1945) "The Use of Knowledge in the Society," *American Economic Review*, 35: 519–530.

He, Chunmei (2009) *China's Top Female Rich, Zhang Yin: From Paper Recycling to Paper Queen*, Beijing: Zhong Yang Bian Yi Publishers.

Hebert, Robert and Link, Albert (1988) *The Entrepreneur: Mainstream Views and Radical Critiques*, 2nd ed., New York: Praeger.

Hutton, Will (2006) "Thanks to Mao, Zhang Yin's a Billionaire," *The Observer*, 15 October (Sunday); available at www.guardian.co.uk/commentisfree/2006/oct/15/comment. china; retrieved 13 July 2011.

Kirzner, I. M. (1973) *Competition and Entrepreneurship*, Chicago: University of Chicago Press.

Kirzner, I. M. (1985) *Discovery and the Capitalist Process*, Chicago: University of Chicago Press.

Knight, Frank (1921) *Risk, Profit and Uncertainty*, Boston: Houghton Mifflin Company.

Ko, Stephen and Joshi, Havovi (2008) "Cheung Yan: China's Paper Queen," The Asia Case Research Centre, The University of Hong Kong, HKU799, 3 November.

Leibenstein, H. (1968) "Entrepreneurship and Development," *American Economic Review*, 58: 72–83.

Martin, Adam (2007) "Mises, Kirzner and Knight on Uncertainty and Entrepreneurship: A Synthesis," working paper, http://adamgmartin.com/Site/Working%20Papers/B1F98 99F-6D08-43B9-A8A7-E2B6FA0644EC.html; retrieved 25 February 2008.

Menger, C. (1871/2007) *Principles of Economics*, Auburn, AL: Mises Institute.

Mises, Ludwig von (1949) *Human Action*, 3rd ed., Chicago: Contemporary Books.

MoneyWeek (2006) "Zhang Yin: The World's Richest Self-made Woman," 26 October, www. moneyweek.com/news-and-charts/zhang-yin-the-worlds-richest-self-made-woman; retrieved 14 July 2011.

Oviatt, Benjamin M. and McDougall, Patricia P. (2005) "Defining International Entrepreneurship and Modelling the Speed of Internationalization," *Entrepreneurship: Theory and Practice*, 29(5/September): 537–554.

Penrose, Edith T. (1959) *The Theory of the Growth of the Firm*, New York: John Wiley.

Philipsen, Kristian (1998) "Entrepreneurship as Organizing: A Literature Study of Entrepreneurship," paper presented at the DRUID Summer conference, 9–11 June, Bornholm, Denmark.

Schumpeter. J. A. (1934/1961) *The Theory of Economic Development*, New York: Oxford University Press.

Smith, Adam (1776) *An Inquiry into the Nature and Causes of the Wealth of Nations*, New York: Modern Library Classics.

Williamson, Oliver E. (1981) "The Economics of Organization: The Transaction Cost Approach," *American Journal of Sociology*, 87(3): 548–577.

Yu, Tony Fu-Lai (1997) *Entrepreneurship and Economic Development in Hong Kong*, London: Routledge.

Yu, Fu-Lai Tony and Shiu, Gary Moon Cheung (2011) "A New Look at the Austrian School of Economics: Review and Prospects," *International Journal of Pluralism and Economic Education*, 2(2/June): 145–161.

4 Entrepreneurial alertness and spontaneous learning in the market process

The case of Mama Moon in Guilin

Introduction

Apart from Joseph Schumpeter and Frank Knight, Israel M. Kirzner was the most significant scholar contributing to the theory of entrepreneurship in economics during the 20th century (Gunning 1997).[1] Kirzner argues that the role of entrepreneurs lies in their "alertness to hitherto unnoticed opportunities" (Kirzner 1973: 39). His view on entrepreneurial alertness triggers scholars in searching for the causes and nature of alertness. Although Kirzner argues that there are opportunities to be discovered by entrepreneurs, Baron and Markman (1999: 3) contend that entrepreneurs create opportunities more than discover them. Baron and Markman postulate that an existing opportunity, like raw material, can be molded into a business concept. The quality of an opportunity is largely a function of the person who discovers it. The more alertness human agents have, the more likely they are to identify hidden profit opportunities (see also Kandel 2003). Yu (2001) interprets Kirzner's concept of entrepreneurial alertness and discovery in a subjectivist perspective. He argues that the entrepreneurial discovery process is associated with the actor's interpretative framework, which is derived from everyday life experiences. Koppl (2002) uses Schutz's theory of relevance to explain the origin of alertness. Gunning (2004) interprets Kirzner's entrepreneurship in the strictly Misesian tradition. Very few empirical studies apply Kirzner's theory of entrepreneurial alertness and discovery in terms of Austrian subjectivism. Most empirical applications are in the field of psychology. For example, Kaish and Gilad (1991) conduct psychological testing on the theory of entrepreneurial alertness. Their results reveal that entrepreneurs raise alertness to possible business opportunities by different types of relevant information. Yu (1997) interprets Kirzner's view as pertaining to adaptive entrepreneurs and applies the concept to explain Hong Kong's economic success. This chapter will follow Kirzner's subjectivist view that entrepreneurial alertness is spontaneous or subconscious learning which cannot be obtained by deliberate search or conscious scientific investigation. Kirzner's insight will be applied to a successful business operated by a woman entrepreneur in Guilin, China. In what follows, we shall review Kirzner's theory of entrepreneurial alertness. The application of Kirzner's insight to a female entrepreneur, "Mama Moon" in Guilin (China) is then given. The conclusion will be presented in the last section.

Kirzner's theory of entrepreneurship revisited: alertness, subconscious learning, and arbitrageurship

The entrepreneurial process in Kirznerian perspective involves alertness to profit opportunities, spontaneous discovery, and profit arbitrageurship. Alertness to profit opportunity is a mind process involving subconsciousness. It is a hunch. Once the hunch is known, it becomes a resource to the entrepreneur. With the resource (knowledge), through deliberate learning, search, and experimentation, the entrepreneur attempts to exploit profit manifested in price discrepancy. Finally, profit arbitrage allows mistakes to be eliminated, economic activities to be coordinated, and the economy to move towards equilibrium.

Alertness to profit opportunity and spontaneous learning

For Kirzner (1973), the most important feature of entrepreneurs lies in their alertness to profit opportunities which hitherto have not yet been noticed by others. Put differently, an entrepreneur is a human agent who has the ability to be alert to opportunities. Kirzner (1985: 11) contends that the ability does not come from deliberate learning. Instead, it comes from subconscious learning or spontaneous discovery.[2]

From a cognitive perspective, subconscious learning refers to a collection of mental phenomena that manifest in a person's mind but that the person is unaware of at the time of their occurrence. These phenomena include unconscious feelings, skills, perceptions, thoughts, and habits, as well as automatic reactions, complexes, hidden phobias, and concealed desires.[3] Subconscious learning can be seen as a source of spontaneous thoughts (which appear without apparent cause), the stored memories which are neglected but nevertheless can be accessible to consciousness at some later time. One familiar example of the operation of subconscious learning is the phenomenon where one fails to immediately solve a problem and then suddenly has a flash of insight that provides a solution later. Hayek (1952) argues that sensory experience in the human mind entails a collection of stimuli in the past. It identifies, imitates, and classifies the impulses in conjunction with human senses. Sensory order puts a collection of impulses into different folders or archives and creates a linkage between folders (Hayek 1952: 121). When patterns are created, novel ideas or hunches will emerge.

Human agents lack self-consciousness concerning the hunch before the pattern of hunches is organized. In simple words, human agents do not know that they possess such a hunch or a vision of the future. They do not act by deliberately utilizing their hunch for profits. Instead, their actions reflect their hunch. As Kirzner (1985: 21–22) argues:

> [I]f an entrepreneur's discovery of a lucrative arbitrage opportunity galvanizes him into immediate action to capture the perceived gain, it will not do to describe the situation as one in which the entrepreneur has decided to use his alertness to capture this gain. He has not deployed his hunch for a specific purpose; *rather, his hunch has propelled him to make his entrepreneurial*

purchase and sale. The entrepreneur never sees his hunches as potential inputs about which he must decide whether they are to be used. To decide not to use a hunch means . . . that a businessman realizes that he has no hunch. . . . If one has become sufficiently alerted to the existence of an opportunity – that is, one has become sufficiently convinced regarding the facts of a situation – it becomes virtually impossible to imagine not taking advantage of the opportunity so discovered.

Entrepreneurship is thus not something to be deliberately introduced into a potential production process: it is, instead, something primordial to the very ideas of a potential production process awaiting possible implementation. Entrepreneurial alertness is not an ingredient to be deployed in decision making; it is rather something in which the decision itself is embedded and without which it would be unthinkable [italics original].

Let's illustrate this with an example. Assume that a used reference book, valued at $5 in a flea market, is sold in a campus secondhand bookstore for $35. There is a profit opportunity of $30 available in the market, but it remains unnoticed. Assume that Mary, a college student, comes across this price discrepancy. Due to some unexplained reason, she does not notice this opportunity at once. Kirzner (1979: 120–136) refers to this as an economic error. Nevertheless, the knowledge of this profit opportunity at $30 has been spontaneously absorbed in the student's mind but will slowly fade away over time. Assume that this student later discovers again that the same used book is sold at the price of $35 in a downtown second-hand bookshop. In other words, a profit opportunity of $30 still exists. Previous unnoticed information that comes cross the student's mind does not mean that information will remain unnoticed forever. Kirzner (1979: 146) argues that as time passes by, human agents may spontaneously increase the "awareness of information hitherto veiled in ignorance." In simple terms, it is a continual renewal of ignorance. The student's second experience in the downtown bookshop "intensifies" her hunch. This time, she comes to be alert to the profit opportunity. Though the student is not at once alert to the profit opportunity in her first encounter in the campus bookstore, spontaneous learning eventually triggers entrepreneurial vision. Human agents cannot be said to have planned their learning. Rather, it is subconsciousness that functions in the actor's mind. Subconscious learning is thus "synonymous with the transformation of a previously unrecognized 'entrepreneurial vision' (the subconscious hunch) into a recognized contributor to satisfaction. It is also synonymous with spontaneous learning" (Gunning 2004).

Kirzner (1979) emphasizes that hunch is never an ingredient for deliberate action. When the agent comes to be aware of the vision, that vision ceases to be entrepreneurial and becomes a resource and can be utilized through deliberate learning. As Kirzner (1979: 168–169, italics original) writes, the human agent's "*realization* that he possesses this definite information resource may itself be entrepreneurial. As soon as he 'knows' that he possesses an item of knowledge, *that* item ceases to correspond to entrepreneurial vision; instead, as with all resources, it is [the] belief that he has the resources at his disposal that may now constitute his entrepreneurial hunch."

Spontaneous learning and discovery of error

There are forces in the market process "that bring about changes in the buying, selling, producing, and consuming decisions" (Kirzner 1973: 70). These forces consist of learning from mistakes. To "explain how yesterday's market experiences can account for changes in plans that might generate alterations in prices, in outputs, or in the uses of inputs . . . it is necessary to introduce the insight that men . . . learn from their experiences in the market. It is necessary to postulate that out of the mistakes which led market participants to choose less-than-optimal courses of action yesterday, they can be expected to develop systematic changes in expectations concerning plans" (Kirzner 1973: 71). Hence, the scope of entrepreneurship is grounded in the possibility of discovering error. For Kirzner, error occurs not because of resource misallocation or inefficiency due to an information problem, as portrayed by neoclassical mainstream economists. Instead, error occurs when a person fails to be alert to an opportunity that he or she comes across. Kirzner provides us a subjectivist theory of knowledge and error. Suppose that an individual has mistakenly attached a low valuation to resources or placed an incorrectly low value on labor time. This implies room for improvement. If this person discovers that he/she can reallocate the time far more valuably by switching production activities, this implies entrepreneurial insight. Through entrepreneurial discovery, and hence resources reshuffled, the ends achievable with the same amount of labor time now have higher value than the ends that were previously achieved. The discovery of error brings about pure entrepreneurial profit.

Assume further that the individual learns from his/her previous subconscious hunch that a certain strategy enables him or her to gain in a market. The hunch becomes a useful piece of knowledge to be utilized. Later, when the same individual experiences a similar choice situation, knowledge, not hunch, will enable the person to make a correct choice. In hindsight, the individual can be said to have realized that he or she possesses a means of satisfying the wants which he/she was previously unaware of. By the time the person knows the hunch, the hunch transforms into a resource – knowledge (Gunning 2004). The utilization of this knowledge is then associated with conscious learning.

Furthermore, as a situation changes, yesterday's decision can become incorrect today. Entrepreneurs will constantly be alert to the changing condition in the market and renew their ends–means framework in order to seek pure entrepreneurial profit. Thus, the entrepreneurial process in the Kirznerian sense consists of alertness, subconscious learning, and continual adjustment.

Promoting entrepreneurial alertness

According to Kirzner (1985), there are two kinds of knowledge.

1. Technical knowledge. This comprises skills in utilizing given physical resources which can be obtained by deliberate search or research and development (R&D).
2. Knowledge of opportunities. This knowledge cannot be obtained by deliberate search. It requires entrepreneurial alertness.

For Kirzner (1985: 73–74), economic growth of a nation occurs in two ways:

1. Improvement in technical knowledge. Neoclassical growth theories emphasize this kind of knowledge, which can be conducted by R&D.
2. Increased awareness of the availability of opportunities. In this category, economic growth occurs not only because of the availability of new opportunities, but because of expanded awareness of unexploited opportunities. Hence, economic growth requires not only expanded productive possibilities, but also entrepreneurial alertness and discovery.

If entrepreneurial alertness is so important to economic growth, then what are the causes of this alertness? In literature, the problem-solving argument contends that most people will awaken when they encounter a sudden crisis or a rapidly changing external condition (Choi 1993). The theory of self-competition argues that people compete with their inner selves. It is defined as "inter-temporal competition between future and past selves stemming from the desire of the present self to test self-ability" (Khalil 1997). In simple terms, human agents have a desire and passion to fulfill a vision, to see things become true.

Kirzner argues that entrepreneurial vision may not arrive deliberately, rationally, but neither is it arrived at purely by chance. It is the "purposefulness of human action that tends to ensure, in some degree, that opportunities come to be noticed" (Kirzner 1979: 170). Spontaneous learning or alertness to profit opportunity is a subconscious process. It can be encouraged by the possibility of gain. He says: "[i]f we know anything at all about the process of spontaneous discovery of information, it is that this process is somehow altogether more rapid when the relevant information will be of benefit to the potential discoverer" (Kirzner 1979: 149). Gunning (2004) elaborates:

> Subconscious learning can be encouraged by institutional arrangements. Institutional arrangements determine the gains that are available to different individuals when they subconsciously learn. Because subconscious learning in some individuals is superior to that in others, it is important that those who are superior receive higher gains.

Kirzner (1979: 150) argues that institutional arrangements are private property rights, free enterprise, and the use of money in calculation. That is, the free market system provides an environment for subconscious learning to occur. This setting allows market participants to translate unnoticed opportunities into the forms that tend to excite the alertness of those most likely to notice (Gunning 2004).

In this chapter, Kirzner's concept of entrepreneurial alertness and its contribution to economic progress will be illustrated by the case of Mama Moon, who is a legendary tourist guide from a well-known tourist attraction in Yangshuo, Guilin (China).

Mama Moon in Guilin, China

Yangshuo, Guilin (China) is well known for its superb landscape. At the foot of Mountain Moon in Yangshuo, there is an old tourist guide called Xiuzhen Xu, who is now around 70 years old. Xu had an education equivalent to third grade and yet had the ability to communicate with tourists in eight foreign languages.[4] A tourist described her in his blog this way, "I didn't take notice of this old lady who couldn't appear more common – an outmoded brown gingham shirt shouldered by a bony body, face tanned and deeply wrinkled – a concrete example of women working in farm fields in South China. Nevertheless, amazement rose up from my heart when she spoke in fluent English to invite us to have lunch in her home."[5] Xu is described by many tourists as kind, friendly, warm, and fun, and her hospitality captured the hearts and friendship from people around the world. As a result, overseas tourists honor her as "Mama Moon,"[6] who is like a caring mother for people coming from everywhere.

Mama Moon came from a village nearby Yangshuo, Guilin. She married to a man who was eight years senior. Life in the rural area was harsh and income from the field was barely enough for her family. Human agents would like to improve their well-beings whenever possible. As Mises (1949/1966: 14) argues, "acting man is eager to substitute a more satisfactory state of affairs for a less satisfactory. His mind imagines conditions which suit him better, and his action aims at bringing about this desired state." Mama Moon was no exception.

In 1995, the Yangshuo City Government promoted Mountain Moon as an international tourist attraction. Since then, many overseas tourists poured in. This provided business opportunities for people living in the area. In order to make daily ends meet, Xu, like other villagers, went to the town to seek her fortune. Xu's action cannot be regarded as 'entrepreneurial'. As Kirzner (1973) contends, the role of an entrepreneur is to identify hitherto unnoticed opportunity. Seeking her fortune in a tourist town was too obvious for Xu and other villagers to ignore. Xu merely surfed on the wave of fortune-seeking in a new place. Without any education, skill, and business experience, the thing that a rural woman could do in a tourist town was very limited. Xu eventually managed to sell soft drinks to the tourists. Yet, her business was not good. Sometimes, she could not even sell out any bottle of soft drink. On the contrary, her fellow vendors could sell around 30 bottles a day. She sought the reasons and found out that her soft drinks were not cold because she did not have a fridge, while other vendors sold icy cold soft drinks. Secondly, she could not speak English. When foreigners complained that her soft drinks were not cold, she did not understand. She then asked her son-in-law to teach her simple English conversation in order to upgrade her competitive edge. This is deliberate learning in Kirzner's view. Xu purposively pursued a means to achieve an end in order to survive in the market.

Mama Moon's alertness to opportunities and her first spontaneous learning

One day, as Mama Moon felt bored while waiting for customers, there were two Italian tourists who did not know the way to reach a stalactite cave (a famous cave in Yangshuo). They approached Mama Moon for help. Showing her hospitality, Mama Moon used simple English words and hand gestures to show them the way as they walked on. As they became familiar with each other, Mama Moon even voluntarily served as a tourist guide for them. At the end of the day, the Italians asked Mama Moon how much they should pay her. Mama Moon said not to worry. However, they paid 50 yuan to her out of gratitude. After she got the money, she discovered that being a tourist guide was a good way to earn a living. This hunch occurred in Mama Moon's mind. She was alert to a profit opportunity. She discovered that her labor had previously been spent on a low-value production activity. This was an error. Being a tourist guide for three hours, she could earn 50 yuan, while selling soft drinks for three days could not even get that reward. Alert to the price discrepancy of her labor, Mama Moon decided to act as a tourist guide. This change represented a kind of arbitrage activity in the sense that she made better use of her labor, which had previously been valued wrongly. She knew that she needed to improve her English if she wanted to be a tourist guide for foreigners. She then deliberately learned English. The discovery of a new opportunity (being a tourist guide) was a hunch, while seeking English skills was deliberate learning. It was very hard for an old woman to learn English. At the beginning, Mama Moon pronounced English words by using Chinese characters and memorized some English words via rote learning. After studying hard for several years and having frequent conversations with foreign tourists, Mama Moon could speak eight basic foreign languages. Apart from learning foreign languages, Mama Moon also established good friendships with foreigners. This helped her business in future.

Keen competition in the market

Kindness, honesty, and friendliness earned Xu a good brand name in Yangshuo's sightseeing business. As a matter of fact, many local tourist guides earned commissions from discounts given by hotels and souvenirs shops. While other tourist guides only aimed at earning commissions from tourists, Xu stood on the tourists' side and bargained with local shops or vendors for the tourists. Hence, local people accused Mama Moon of violating the rules of the game in the market. They united to condemn Mama Moon and tried to push her out of business. For instance, whenever tourists made an inquiry about her, the local people would reply that she was dead or retired. Public Choice School argues that the demand for government regulation is a common method to eliminate competitors. The local tourist and hospitality industry lobbied the city government to issue tourist guide licenses. Mama Moon needed to apply for a tourist guide license. This made life difficult for an old lady such as Xu, for she did not have any formal education.[7] The city government at first refused to issue her a license, for they hardly believed that Xu could speak any foreign language. Eventually, after a series of appeals, the city government was convinced that she was capable of being a tourist guide. They issued her a license by special permission and allowed her to continue to operate as a tourist guide.

Entering the catering business

Xu was happy to charge 60 yuan per person as her tourist guide fee. At the peak of the season, she could earn around 200 yuan a day, which was quite an income for a farm lady at that time. Xu had never considered entering the catering business. She did not know that another opportunity was waiting to be discovered by her. One day, five Americans finished touring at Mount Moon and were walking down the hill with Mama Moon. One man asked Xu where she lived. She pointed to the farmhouse down the hill. The Americans found that her little farmhouse was surrounded by a green field and creek. The scenery was as charming as a Monet painting. Xu then invited them to visit her house. However, five Americans hesitated because they were starving after a full-day trip. They asked Xu where they could find something to eat before going to see her house. Xu replied that they could eat in her farmhouse. However, she reminded them that she could only provide some raw farm foods, nothing to compare to the fare at restaurants downtown. The Americans replied that they did not mind trying anyway. Xu then prepared a typical farm meal, with vegetables and meats freshly obtained from the home farmyard, including pumpkin, eggplant, beans, pork, and eggs. Five Americans enjoyed a very gorgeous farm meal with rice wine and beautiful scenery. At the end of the day, each of them put US$15 on the table as a kind of remuneration to Xu. This was a good payoff for Mama Moon. Suddenly, a hunch popped up in her mind: "Hey, I can also enter into the restaurant business and earn more income by utilizing the manpower of my family members." She put her hunch to trial and found that the idea worked. In this way, Xu entered the catering industry and promoted "Mama Moon's farm meal." Her restaurant business blossomed because foreigners enjoyed fresh and uncontaminated vegetables and meats, and beautiful scenery.[8]

Offering the full package: from tourist guide to catering to accommodations

It has to be noted that those tourists approaching Mama Moon were mostly backpackers. They could only afford cheap food and budget accommodations. Rich foreigners usually traveled by organized tours and stayed in relatively expensive hotels. Furthermore, backpackers in general preferred to stay in guest houses or farmhouses, so that they could experience the local lifestyle. Fancy hotels and facilities were not of importance to them. Villagers such as Mama Moon were able to fill in this market gap by providing budget food and accommodations. Mama Moon's farmhouse was a large two-storey building with plenty of open space and rooms. With her experience in providing farm meals, Mama Moon then thought of providing budget accommodations to the tourists on the upper floor of her farmhouse. Her foresight was again proven to be correct. All visitors' rooms on the upper floor were quickly occupied by young backpackers. She called her guest house "Mama Moon Inn." In this way, Mama Moon transformed from a farm lady to an entrepreneur in the tourist, catering, and accommodations businesses.

Explaining China's recent economic miracle: entrepreneurship in unfettered capitalism

Mama Moon is not an isolated case in China. After Deng's Open Door Policy in 1979, thousands of entrepreneurs in China have moved to the city to "look" for an opportunity just like Mama Moon did. Many of them have started small enterprises which then turned into gigantic multinational firms via their entrepreneurship. Among them are Wenbing Lu (Little Sheep Hotpot), Jack Ma (Alibaba. com), Qinghou Zong (Wahaha Beverage), Shufu Li (Geely Automobile Holdings), and Cheng Fei Zhang (Nine Dragons Paper).[9] These entrepreneurs have used their alertness capabilities and exploited profit opportunities to their advantage. As a result of their efforts, China has achieved high income growth in the last decade. Again, the crucial issue is what factors stimulated alertness to profit opportunity for Mama Moon and many other entrepreneurs in mainland China, which was once a radical communist society. Kirzner (1980) argues that human agents tend to notice that which it is in their interest to notice.[10] In other words, it is the self-interest motive that enhances the entrepreneur to be alert. It follows that, for Kirzner, in order to switch on the alertness of potential discoverers, gain must be offered to them. Accordingly, the free market system is conducive to entrepreneurial alertness, for it permits agents to reap gains from their discoveries (Kirzner 1979: 148–151).

China has a huge pool of human resources. During the Cultural Revolution (1966–76), China pursued radical socialism, in which all resources were communally owned and shared. Private ownership of property was prohibited. During ten years of extreme communism, private entrepreneurs vanished, though political entrepreneurs participated enthusiastically in unproductive rent-seeking activities. As a result, China became one of the poorest nations in the world. Correcting extreme communism, Deng's government pursued the Open Door Policy and the Four Modernizations. One of the most important institutional reforms has been to allow rural farmers to keep part of their rewards through the incentive device of the "rural responsibility system." Later, "capitalism in Chinese socialist style" extended to industrial and service sectors. As a result of the institutional reform, talented entrepreneurs have continued to spring up in mainland China. They identify and exploit profit opportunities and indirectly boost national economic growth. In other words, economic growth in China occurs because of expanded awareness of unexploited opportunities by these entrepreneurs. It can be said that profit-seeking in mainland China nowadays is relatively unfettered. The change from radical communism to unfettered capitalism is an important institutional change. It enhances entrepreneurial alertness hidden in every human agent's mind. Kirzner (1979: 149) rightly concludes:

> It would be a mistake to imagine. . . that spontaneous discovery is a wholly unexplainable process. . . . [I]t is clear that opportunities for social improvement will tend to be exploited most fruitfully if institutional arrangements

can be patterned so as to translate such opportunities into opportunities that will be encountered by those whose entrepreneurial alertness is the most acute, the most sensitive, the most accurate. . . . Entrepreneurial alertness, that is, is sensitive not so much to information per se as to information that can be deployed to one's advantage.

Economic reform in China has provided an environment for entrepreneurs to achieve self-gain by simulating their subconscious learning, hence contributing to China's economic growth.

Conclusion

There are many factors that explain China's economic growth in the last decade. This chapter has focused on one factor, namely entrepreneurial alertness, to explain China's recent economic growth. Mama Moon, a woman entrepreneur in the tourism, catering, and hotel industries in Guilin, is a celebrated illustration of Kirzner's theory of entrepreneurial alertness and arbitrageurship. It is believed that many interesting cases similar to Mama Moon's in mainland China can be found and are worthwhile to be reported. Further research on entrepreneurship in Kirzner's perspective is called for.

Notes

1 Israel M. Kirzner was awarded the International Award for Entrepreneurship and Small Business Research in 2006. For a recent review of Kirzner's contributions, see Douhan et al. (2007).
2 Kirzner (1979: 144–145) classifies knowledge into two types, namely knowledge that can be obtained from deliberate search and knowledge that cannot be obtained by deliberate search. The former can be obtained by deliberate acquisition or search. The ignorance of knowledge that might be known through deliberate search or learning can be justified by a high cost of search. In other words, knowing more of this knowledge means to sacrifice something else. Knowledge that cannot be obtained from deliberate search can only be absorbed spontaneously. The ignorance of such knowledge cannot be explained by a high cost of search. It is the result of "sheer failure to notice" something that has been there. Kirzner refers to it as a "lack of entrepreneurial alertness" (Kirzner 1979: 145).
3 http://en.wikipedia.org/wiki/Unconscious_mind; retrieved 24 June 2010.
4 She was able to communicate with tourists in English, French, German, Danish, Korean, Italian, Swedish, and Israeli. However, she could not read or write these languages.
5 http://blog.sina.com.cn/s/blog_5c4ea4610100bhk0.html; retrieved 2 July 2010.
6 It is reported that the name was given to her by an Australian girl, who left complimentary words in Xu's notebook: "How I want to call you Mama. You are a kind of 'Mama Moon' living at the foot of 'Moon Hill'" (*People's Daily* newspaper, 10 August 2000). In this chapter, Mama Moon and Xiuzhen Xu are used interchangeably.
7 www.Shanghaiexpat.com/MDForum-viewtopic-t-44337.phtml; retrieved 5 July 2010.
8 www.yoo66.com/zx/article.jsp?id=865; retrieved 2 July 2010.
9 See *Forbes* "400 Richest Chinese List 2009" (www.forbes.com/lists/2009/74/china-billionaires-09The-400-Richest-Chinese_Rank_2.html; retrieved 5 July 2010).
10 In cognitive literature, this is called selective entrepreneurial attention (Gifford 1992).

References

Baron, R. A. and Markman, G. D. (1999) "Cognitive Mechanisms: Potential Differences between Entrepreneurs and Non-entrepreneurs," in W. D. Bygrave et al. (eds.) *Frontiers of Entrepreneurial Research*, Babson Park, MA: Babson College.

Choi, Y. B. (1993) *Paradigms and Conventions: Uncertainty, Decision Making and Entrepreneurship*, Ann Arbor: University of Michigan Press.

Douhan, Robin; Eliasson, Gunnar; and Henrekson, Magnus (2007) "Israel M. Kirzner: An Outstanding Austrian Contributor to the Economics of Entrepreneurship," *Small Business Economics*, 29(1/2): 213–223.

Gifford, S. (1992) "Allocation of Entrepreneurial Attention," *Journal of Economic Behaviour and Organisation*, 19(3): 265–283.

Gunning, J. Patrick (1997) "The Theory of Entrepreneurship in Austrian Economics," in W. Keizer, B. Tieben, and R. Van Zijp (eds.) *Austrians in Debate*, London: Routledge, pp. 172–191.

Gunning, Patrick (2004) "Israel Kirzner's Entrepreneurship," working paper, www.constitution.org/pd/gunning/subjecti/workpape/kirz_ent.pdf; retrieved 28 June 2010.

Hayek, F. A. (1952) *The Sensory Order*, Chicago: University of Chicago Press.

Kaish, S. and Gilad, B. (1991) "Characteristics of Opportunities Search of Entrepreneurs versus Executives: Sources, Interest, and General Alertness," *Journal of Business Venturing*, 6: 45–61.

Kandel, Anatoly F. (2003) "A Critique of Kirzner's Concept of Sheer Ignorance," http://ssrn.com/abstract=388040 or doi:10.2139/ssrn.388040; retrieved 6 July 2010.

Khalil, E. (1997) "Buridan's Ass, Risk, Uncertainty, and Self-competition: A Theory of Entrepreneurship," *Kyklos*, 50(fasc. 2): 147–163.

Kirzner, I. M. (1973) *Competition and Entrepreneurship*, Chicago: University of Chicago Press.

Kirzner, I. M. (1979) *Perception, Opportunity, and Profit*, Chicago: University of Chicago Press.

Kirzner, I. M. (1980) "The Primacy of Entrepreneurial Discovery," in I. M. Kirzner (ed.) *Discovery and the Capitalist Process*, Chicago: University of Chicago Press, pp. 15–39.

Kirzner, I. M. (1985) *Discovery and the Capitalist Process*, Chicago: University of Chicago Press.

Koppl, Roger (2002) "What Is Alertness?" *Journal des Economistes et des Etudes Humaines*, 12(1): 3–13.

Mises, Ludwig von (1949/1966) *Human Action: A Treatise on Economics*, 3rd ed., Chicago: Contemporary Books.

Yu, Tony Fu-Lai (1997) *Entrepreneurship and Economic Development in Hong Kong*, London: Routledge.

Yu, Tony Fu-Lai (2001) "Entrepreneurial Alertness and Discovery," *Review of Austrian Economics*, 14(1): 47–63.

5 Global division of labor and international coordination

The Li & Fung Group

Introduction

> [Li & Fung] focuses on designing the best possible processes across a global net-
> work for delivering the right product to the right place at the right time at the right
> price.
>
> (Fung et al. 2008: 20)

Li & Fung is an exemplary multinational enterprise based in Hong Kong after
1949. The company deals with a wide range of products, including apparel, household goods, furnishings, toys, and health and beauty products. Today, it coordinates the manufacture of goods through a network of 70 offices in more than
40 countries. In 2009, Li & Fung was ranked at 27 in the World's Best Companies
by *Businessweek*, at 26 in "Asia's Fabulous 50" by *Forbes Asia*, and at 690 in
"World's Biggest Public Companies" by *Forbes* in 2014.[1]

In what business is the Li & Fung business group involved? Is it an exporter,
a merchandiser, manufacturer, retailer, customer, or supplier? Interestingly, the
answer can be any of them. In other words, Li & Fung performs all these functions. However, when viewed in the Austrian perspective of market process, Li &
Fung is properly regarded as an international entrepreneur. It earns profits via
global coordination. This chapter attempts to use Austrian theories of entrepreneurship in economics to explain the operations and practice of Li & Fung's business. Specifically, this chapter integrates the contributions of Ludwig von Mises,
I. M. Kirzner, and F. A. Hayek to entrepreneurship and market process to obtain
a theory of global coordination. This theory is then applied to reinterpret Li &
Fung's dynamic success.

Literature review

Being as successful an international empire as Li & Fung is, studies on the group
are not lacking. Material on the Li & Fung group can be found in interviews of
Victor and William Fung, the third generation of the business empire (for example, see Slater 1999, Holstein 2002, Fung 2007, and CNN 2009). In an interview
conducted by Magretta (1998), Victor Fung shares the concepts and strategies of

borderless manufacturing and supply chain management. Fung's brothers eluci-dated the management of the supply chain business (Fung 1997; Fung et al. 2008; Wind et al. 2009). Hutcheon (1992) and Feng (2007) wrote the biography of Li & Fung. In particular, Feng (2007) portrays the transition from a traditional Chi-nese family business to a multinational enterprise in terms of business strategy, entrepreneurship, and cultural values in the last century. Li & Fung collaborates with trading parties and adapts to each of them through coordination, learning, and innovation (Wind et al. 2009: 300–301). Hagel and Brown (2005) further define Li & Fung with the role of network orchestrator which enhances flexibility and connects the best capabilities in the world. Chang and Phi (2007) analyze the acquisition of the Integrated Distribution Services Group Limited (the IDS Group). Case studies of Li & Fung conducted by Harvard Business School include Loveman and O'Connell (1995), Long and Seet (1996), Yoshino and George (1998), Hagel (2002), McFarlane and Young (2002).[2] Despite extensive studies of biography, economic analysis, and supply chain management, an entrepreneurial explanation of Li & Fung's operation is still missing. This chapter fills this gap. More specifically, an Austrian theory of global coordination is called for. This chapter starts with an Austrian theory of international entrepreneurship and global coordination, followed by the case study of Li & Fung. The background of Li & Fung is given in the next section. Li & Fung's global coordination in Austrian economic perspectives will then be presented. The final section is the conclusion.

An Austrian theory of international entrepreneurship and global coordination

The most important role of international entrepreneurship is to coordinate global economic activities. Austrian economics argues that in the market, no individual is homogeneous.[3] Each market participant has his/her own experience and stock of knowledge, and hence each thinks and foresees the future differently. As a result, plans in the market often mismatch. Hayek (1945) refers to the compatibility of plans as a coordination problem. For example, computer producers in Taiwan (say, ASUS) today need to estimate what consumers (JC Penney) in the United States want tomorrow. Likewise, American producers are also keen to know their rivals' plans so that they can formulate their selling or pricing strategies. Charg-ing a wrong price or producing a wrong product (i.e., mismatches of plans) can be disastrous and lead to business failure.

In an Austrian economic perspective, entrepreneurs attempt to coordinate eco-nomic activities for profits. In Mises' words (1949: 328):

> The driving force of the market process is provided neither by the consum-ers nor by the owners of the means of production – land, capital goods, and labor – but by the promoting and speculating entrepreneurs. These are people intent upon profiting by taking advantage of differences in prices. Quicker of apprehension and farther-sighted than other men, they look around for sources of profit. They buy where and when they deem prices too low, and

they sell where and when they deem prices too high. They approach the owners of the factors of production, and their competition sends the prices of these factors up to the limit corresponding to their anticipation of the future prices of the products. They approach the consumers, and their competition forces prices of consumers' goods down to the point at which the whole supply can be sold. Profit-seeking speculation is the driving force of the market as it is the driving force of production.

I. M. Kirzner adds further insight into Hayek's and Mises' arguments. Using Kirzner's groundbreaking insights in 1973 (Kirzner 1973), we argue that the role of international entrepreneurs lies in their abilities to identify global profit opportunities. They discover and exploit global opportunities according to their hunches. International entrepreneurs, with their superior ability of reading market data, exploit profit opportunities around the world. According to Martin (2007: 6), profit opportunities in the world market come in three ways. The first is the recognition of previous errors or mismatches of plans. The second is the introduction of new opportunities. The third is the uncertainty of the future.

International entrepreneurs are able to integrate "innumerable scraps of existing information that are present in scattered form" throughout the world (Kirzner 1985: 162). The international coordination process is thus "the systematic plan changes generated by the flow of market information released by market participation – that is, by the testing of plans in the market" (Kirzner 1973: 10). Increased coordination means that entrepreneurs' plans are made more compatible (Martin 2007: 4).

Knowledge transmission in the global market

If economics is a coordination problem (Hayek 1945), then it is of utmost importance to analyze how knowledge is created and transmitted during the process of international exchange. Assuming two individuals Mr. A and Ms. B living in England and Hong Kong respectively, they each possess their own stock of knowledge and subjectively interpret incoming events each day. Mr. A wishes to attain end X, and Ms. B to end Y. Each person will do economic calculation and make judgment on his or her project with respect to the external environments. Assume that Mr. A would like to achieve his end but he does not have the means at his disposal. Furthermore, he does not know where and how to obtain such means. On the other hand, Ms. B owns an abundant resource/means which she has no use for at the moment, though the resource is suitable for Mr. A to attain his end. The economic problem is that both Mr. A and Ms. B do not know each other. Obviously, in this case, international trade cannot be carried out for lack of this mutual knowledge required for trade. According to the subjectivist theory of knowledge (Kirzner 1979: 137–153), the opportunity simply does not exist for these two parties.[4]

Even if merchants of two nations accidentally discover that both have the intention to trade, international transaction may not be carried out because both parties' thinking and actions are socially embedded. Traders' minds are governed by a set of habits, traditions, institutions, norms, customs, and legal rules which make them follow without being asked. This knowledge is taken for granted and socially constructed. Each trading party, with different cultures and values, will accordingly interpret the social world differently. Specifically, it takes lots of efforts to find out if a trading partner is trustworthy. This can be illustrated by the first-time trade between the English and the Chinese during the late Ch'ing dynasty. Their trade encounter unfortunately ended with a conflict, the Opium War. The cultural content of the Sino-British conflict can be seen by the fact that the British referred to this war as a "trade war." For the British, the purpose of the war was to demand free trade with China and eliminate unfair treatment laid down by the Ch'ing government officials. However, the Chinese referred to the conflict as an "Opium War" because of the enormous amount of opium shipped to China, leading to moral degradation and loss of foreign exchange (silver).[5] Hence, knowing your trading parties, making entrepreneurial moves, and learning and testing foreign markets by trial and error are the main elements in international trade. However, such important elements are missing in the neoclassical paradigm.

The issues of culture and knowledge justify the role of the middleman in international trade. To be sure, the role of middleman is well documented in the mainstream price and transaction costs theories (for example, see Casson 1982; Reekie 1984). However, in human agency perspective, a middleman is more than just a person who links both parties together. The middleman, in our case, is also an entrepreneur as well as a knowledge creator. He or she transmits knowledge and performs entrepreneurial discovery, and hence raises the well-being of both trading parties.

In the above example, assume that Mr. A and Ms. B do things routinely each day, and a Person C practices as a middleman.[6] Person C discovers that there is an opportunity in the international market. He contacts Ms. B in Hong Kong and offers to buy the resource which Ms. B has an abundance of and sells it to Mr. A in England. As a consequence of Person C's entrepreneurial action, all three parties gain. This is essentially the case of Kirznerian entrepreneurship (Kirzner 1973) which conducts arbitrageurship.[7] The neoclassical economic analysis argues that trade would continue until the marginal rate of substitutions between two goods for all parties are equal. Their analysis would end at the optimal equilibrium. Unfortunately, such technical analysis, though elegantly presented, loses the insight of how human agents behave and how knowledge is created and transmitted. According to de Soto (1995: 234–237), there are at least three significant implications due to the result of entrepreneurial arbitrageurship.

Firstly, by performing as a middleman, the entrepreneur Person C creates new information which did not exist before. An entrepreneurial act implies a creation of information which takes place in the agent's mind. In our case, information is created by Person C. Moreover, as soon as Person C enters into the international transaction with Mr. A and Ms. B, new information is also created in the minds of Mr. A and Ms. B. As a result of Person C's action, Mr. A in England becomes aware that the resource that he lacks is available in another part of the world.

Hence, Mr. A would take a new action that he did not consider before. On the other hand, Ms. B in Hong Kong becomes aware that the abundant resource she possesses can now be sold overseas at a good price too. Therefore, Ms. B also takes a new action previously not taken before. In short, Person C's entrepreneurial action gives rise to a chain of new knowledge in the world market.

Secondly, entrepreneurial creation of knowledge implies a simultaneous transmission of knowledge in the global market. Knowledge transmission means that people learn from others and create new knowledge in their minds as a result of learning. In our example, new ideas have been created in the minds of Mr. A and Ms. B at the same time as a result of Person C's entrepreneurial action: (1) Mr. A now may proceed to pursue his desired goal, which could not be attained due to the lack of a specific kind of resource owned by Ms. B. (2) Ms. B now realizes that her resource is useful and valuable, and therefore should not be wasted. It can be conceived that in general, through the price signal, such knowledge (received by both Mr. A and Ms. B) will be spread to the entire global community in the market process.

Thirdly, through learning, trading parties revise their plans, formulate new expectations (Lachmann 1956), and make economic judgments (Knight 1921) of the new situation. Hence, economizing resources or, more precisely, coordination of actors' expectations or plans will be possible. In our case, as a result of Person C's entrepreneurial action, both Mr. A and Ms. B will revise their plans in accordance with the new messages they perceive. In particular, Mr. A, now having the resource at his disposal, can attain his end and undertake action that he did not take previously. On the other hand, Ms. B does not waste her resource any more, but keeps and conserves it in order to sell it in the international market. Therefore, all trading parties in the market will learn, revise plans, and modify actions accordingly; thereby economic coordination is made possible. More importantly, the parties each adjust to the world market in the best possible way without knowing that they are actually learning. As Schutz and Luckmann (1989: 8) note, "one learns both to 'adjust' one's own conduct appropriately to the goal of action and also to improve one's interpretation of the conduct of others." This interactive market process, a simple and effective way of coordinating economic activities and improving human welfare, is precisely Adam Smith's concept of the invisible hand. In what follows, we shall adopt our Austrian theory of international coordination to understand the success of Li & Fung in global markets.

Background of the Li & Fung Group

Li & Fung was first established in Guangzhou, China by Mr. Fung Pak-Liu and Mr. Li To-Ming in 1906. As a former teacher of English, Fung spoke fluent English and was competent to be an intermediary between Chinese manufacturers and Western buyers. At the beginning, Li & Fung exported porcelain and silk from mainland China before diversifying into bamboo and rattan ware, jade, ivory handicrafts, and fireworks. In 1937, Fung Hong-Chu, Fung Pak-Liu's second son, moved the company to Hong Kong, where there was a deep harbor and a stable political situation.[8] When Fung Pak-Liu passed away in 1943, Li To-Ming retired and sold all his shares to the Fung family. Fung Hong-Chu then took over the business.[9] After 1949, a large influx of immigrants came from mainland China to Hong Kong. They worked in labor-intensive manufacturing industries such as toys, garments, electronics, and plastic flowers. Li & Fung sought the opportunities and shipped these products from Hong Kong around the world.

During the early 1970s, the US-educated third generation of the Fung family, Victor and William Fung, joined Li & Fung. They transformed the company from a traditional Chinese family business into a modern enterprise. They restructured two core businesses, namely export trading and retail. Li & Fung expanded the business and established regional offices in Taiwan, Singapore, and Korea. In 1979, when Deng Xiaoping's Open Door Policy was implemented in mainland China, manufacturing factories in Hong Kong were relocated to the mainland. The headquarters of Li & Fung in Hong Kong focused on design, sales, logistics, and banking. From 1995 onward, the company has transformed from a regional sourcing company into an international coordinator. It acquired Inchcape Buying Services (Dodwell), Swire & Maclaine Ltd., Camberley Enterprises Ltd., and Colby Group Holdings Ltd. Sales grew sevenfold between 1998 and 2008 and totaled US$14.3 billion in 2008 (CNN 2009). In 2009, it had 13,400 staff, of which 3,045 were based in Hong Kong and 10,357 around the world (Li & Fung Limited 2009). It generated a net income of HK$3.37 billion[10] with a network of nearly 11,000 suppliers served by over 80 offices in 40 countries (Li & Fung Limited 2009). It is one of the biggest apparel providers of such brands as Abercrombie & Fitch (A&F) and Tommy Hilfiger. It is also successful in the business of consumer goods like housewares, toys, and sports equipment. Despite the achievement in export trading, Li & Fung does not own any raw material, factory, or machine. Instead, it disperses manufacturing processes and finds a best-in-class supplier for each stage of production. Li & Fung coordinates economic activities around the world to meet the expectations in a changing market.

Li & Fung as an international coordinator

Li & Fung not only adapts to but also enacts the changing market situation. Victor Fung agrees with his father that "change is inevitable and that change is often for the good because the old way is not necessarily the best" (Fung 1997: 225). However, change brings uncertainty and opportunity. Li & Fung people are constantly alert to profit opportunities in the global market and are "able to pre-empt the market" (quoted in Slater 1999: 13). For William Fung, it is absolutely essential for the company to "anticipate change, strive for constant improvement and be prepared to reinvent the company, to start from zero base if necessary, and above all, institutionalize the change" (Fung 2003). Li & Fung exhibits its capabilities on global coordination. As an international coordinator, Li & Fung is capable of "drawing out the talent and creativity of the network, coordinating all the individual elements, and ensuring the success of the overall process" (Fung et al. 2008: 37). While it understands partners' visions, strategies, organizations, and needs, it does "actually *anticipate* customer needs and the needs of their end consumers" (ibid: 121, italics original). It creates a market and enables business parties to meet the demands in the market.

Dynamic global networking

Li & Fung believes that "companies don't compete against other companies. Networks compete against networks" (Fung et al. 2008: 16). Global networking enhances "the capability to connect to competencies – the capability for network orchestration – and the capability for learning might become as important as any firm-specific capabilities" (ibid: 208). Li & Fung exhibits capabilities in international coordination by (a) understanding capabilities of the market participants, (b) building mutual trust, (c) ensuring quality and on-time delivery, (d) constructing a global information network, and (e) internal organization and incentive system (Cheng 2001).

Li & Fung "dissects" manufacturing beyond national borders. The company itself does not hire any worker or own raw material, a factory, or machinery. Yet, it matches best-in-world capabilities and offers a one-stop shop or assortment package for customers around the world (quoted in Magretta 1998: 104). When a client thinks about a new product, Li & Fung customizes and assembles the components all over the world. The "suppliers supply the raw materials, the manufacturers manufacture the goods, and we [Li & Fung] handle all the logistics. No one in our supply chain is asked to do more than what he is capable of doing" (Long and Seet 1996). Li & Fung matches manufacturers and suppliers to meet customer's requirements on design, production, quality assurance, and delivery schedule. Its role is to "orchestrate the production, come up with samples and feed them [suppliers] information. All that is going way, way beyond that original matching function" (quoted in Slater 1999: 11). That is to say, Li & Fung integrates scattered knowledge and synchronizes "the best possible processes across a global network for delivering the right product to the right place at the right time" (Fung et al. 2008: 20).

Li & Fung as a knowledge broker

Li & Fung can be regarded as a global knowledge broker that transmits, assimilates, and creates knowledge around the world. It acts as a knowledge hub to share knowledge and collaborate with other market participants. Each specialized division in the company is an independent small business headed by an expert in a specific product. Li & Fung provides administrative support, infrastructure, facilities, finance, and human resources. These experts are empowered to act entrepreneurially but free from administrative duties to maximize their capabilities. They have "immediate access to the knowledge and resources of the larger parent organization, while maintaining their individual identities . . . to build creatively and rebuild flexibly, to respond to customers better and improve the operation of the business" (Fung et al. 2008: 96). In this way, these entrepreneurs, "Little

John Wayne," develop capabilities and maintain flexibility and innovation. They "take their wagon trains out into new business areas in search of opportunities, and they stand independently. They build and orchestrate networks. They are able to respond quickly to changes on the ground. On these frontiers, they live or die by their own abilities" (ibid: 83). They catch up with the latest market trend and pursue profit opportunities with other entrepreneurs around the world. Li & Fung coordinates flexible and diverse capabilities to quickly respond to the expectations of the market.

On the other hand, Li & Fung coordinates capabilities around the globe by "filling in the mosaic" (Yoshino and George 1998). It makes partial acquisition and receives priority attention from the partner, while the partner is not dependent on Li & Fung for business. For instance, the acquisition of Inchcape Buying Services (Dodwell) in the Asia-Pacific region in 1995 transformed Li & Fung from a regional trader to a multinational virtually overnight.[11] To promote "acting locally and thinking globally," Li & Fung encourages working teams to bring in local culture and diversify with an international perspective. It develops a knowledge-based environment. In collaborating with entrepreneurs around the world, Li & Fung believes that "local solutions are often distinctly tailored to the needs of a specific region" (Fung et al. 2008: 200). In the acquisition of Inchcape, Li & Fung empowers Inchcape to keep "very high retention rates of managers after acquisitions and creates opportunities to learn from the best practices of the acquired firm, . . . gives some freedom to local offices, . . . [and] allows overseas offices to develop their own management model that fits local circumstances" (ibid: 90).

To enhance the effectiveness of global coordination, Li & Fung promotes mutual understanding, trust, and tolerance, in contrast to traditional top-down Chinese family businesses. The company facilitates monthly English-speaking meetings and a twice-yearly international conference. It encourages the staff to express ideas and share information with fellow partners all over the world. In this way, Li & Fung integrates Chinese values and Western culture so that

> a totally new Chinese management model is in the making; such a model not only embraces traditional values like industry, thriftiness, and social harmony, but also borrows from the West qualities such as flexibility and innovation in doing things, as well as the readiness to assimilate foreign elements.
>
> (quoted in Feng 2007: 95)

Li & Fung provides the incentives of experimentation and diversity. It understands and compares the performance of business parties. Each business party is designated roles, job specifications, and performance benchmarks. Good performers are rewarded by bonuses, but poor performers are designated other assignments. A policy committee is established to ensure quality assurance. In the committee, a group of product managers meet once every five to six weeks. They share information and carry out the policies regarding business ethics, monitoring, compliance, and corporate social responsibility. Rigorous factory inspection and continuous training programs are carried out to develop entrepreneurial knowledge and capabilities (Loveman and O'Connell 1995). A three-year strategic plan enables the company and its partners to "anticipate changes and adjust or initiate reforms ahead of the others" (Feng 2007: 237) and "find gaps in the business and come up with new areas to develop" (*Telegraph* 2008). Li & Fung encourages business parties to adopt a new way of thinking and to discover profit opportunities in the market.

Online capabilities on knowledge coordination emerge in the modern digital world. Information technology, digital communication, and the Internet facilitate a fast and reliable way of knowledge coordination. Li & Fung develops an online communication network of product development and order fulfillment among trading parties. Electronic data exchange accommodates direct communication with the customers. Admittedly, while information technology increases the effectiveness and efficiency of decision making, human experience and knowledge are still complex and indispensable. Li & Fung recognizes the importance of human experience and knowledge.

> [T]echnology is not the technology itself, but how important human judgment and experience continues to be. . . . Advanced management science tools are important in addressing the complex challenges of managing global networks, but the decisions are so complex that they cannot be entirely entrusted to machines. Skilled experts, supported by information systems, make decisions about where to manufacture and how to design each chain.
>
> (Fung et al. 2008)

Li & Fung integrates information technology, human experience, and knowledge. It maintains a "close and deep" relationship with partners and customers (Li & Fung Research Center 2003: 154). It coordinates customer-oriented knowledge and enhances online capabilities on "boosting efficiency, improving coordination . . . creatively rethinking" (Fung et al. 2008: 148). In a sophisticated telecommunication network, entrepreneurs are able to understand market trend, anticipate demand and capture more value after a product leaves the factory. For example, in retail business, Li & Fung shares sales and consumer data with manufacturers, distributors, and retailers to prevent stockouts and excess inventory, ensure quality, and so forth (Quelch and Bartlett 2006: 61). Along with modern technology, Li & Fung's global coordination emphasizes understanding and collaboration, assimilates best-in-class knowledge, and shares new insights with partners around the globe.

Case study: Gymboree and Li & Fung[12]

Gymboree, a US-based children's wear retailer, plans to stock in 10,000 fleece-lined puffer jackets for next winter. The company initially contacts manufacturers in the United States because of close proximity, high quality, and efficiency. However, manufacturing costs are very high. Gymboree then considers sourcing from suppliers overseas. Although manufacturers in Pakistan produce good and cheap jackets, terrorism is Gymboree's main concern. In many regions in East Asia, the costs of manufacturing garments are low due to abundant cheap raw materials and labor forces. Hong Kong was once a famous place for garment manufacturing. Knowing that Li & Fung is one of the biggest apparel providers for other American brands, such as Tommy Hilfiger, and is as well an Asian-based agent with an extensive network of suppliers and manufacturers around the globe, Gymboree approaches Li & Fung and says, "Our company usually makes orders four or five times every year, including more than 2,000 styles per season. For this winter, this fleece-lined puffer jacket is what we are thinking about – such-and-such layout, fabric, lining, and quantities. Each jacket will be sold at US$40. Can you come up with a production program?" Li & Fung takes the deal and forms a working team for Gymboree. The team is responsible to source the best manufacturing capabilities around the globe in the cheapest way for Gymboree. As a result, all parties gain, including Gymboree, Li & Fung, suppliers, and manufacturers from developing economies. We take the fleece-lined puffer jacket as an example.

For each fleece-lined puffer jacket sold at US$40, Li & Fung notices that there is a profit opportunity of a "soft $4" which is achieved by the difference in manufacturing costs and the retail price (Fung et al. 2008: 146). Li & Fung estimates that the cost of cloth accounts for 35–45 percent of the retail price, and of accessories 5–7 percent (Li & Fung Research Center 2003). Li & Fung uses the cheapest and best quality resources all over the world. For example, it uses shell from a Korean producer, 100% polyester thermal fleece from China, reserves a factory in Taiwan for weaving and dying, and orders front zippers from YKK in Shenzhen, China (see Figure 1). Finally, Li & Fung calculates that if the costs of designing,

Borderless Manufacturing

Figure 5.1 Borderless manufacturing

Source: Li & Fung Research Center 2003: 121

sourcing, manufacturing, and logistics are kept at below US$10, it will make a profit. Since clothing techniques, such as insulating, waterproofing, zipping-in, are complex, Li & Fung frequently discusses with Gymboree and factories around the world. The extensive global network significantly shortens production time. Five weeks before delivery, Li & Fung receives the specification of the product from Gymboree and informs the factory in Taiwan of the style and color of the garments. For capabilities of an abundant labor force and cost-efficient production, China is the best place to do "cut, make, and trim," the final stage to producing jackets. To meet the tight deadline, all materials are shipped and assembled in three factories in Guangdong and Zhejiang, China. Li & Fung designates each manufacturer to assemble jackets at between 30 and 80 percent of its own total productivity. In this way, Li & Fung controls sourcing and manufacturing costs, increases the efficiency of manufacturing, and ensures cost-effectiveness and high profit margins for Gymboree.

In each listed factory, Li & Fung assigns a team of technicians and quality-control officers to monitor the manufacturing process and ensure products to meet minimum testing requirements. Defective products are flagged and will not be sold. The first batch of puffer jackets are made and checked by Li & Fung. They are then sent to Gymboree for approval. Li & Fung disperses manufacturing process at the right place at the right time. Each puffer jacket looks exactly the same as if it were produced in the same factory. Despite being labeled as "Made in China," each jacket "*moves the world*" (Fung et al. 2008: 184, italics original). It is "made by Hong Kong." Li & Fung also provides replenishment services to eliminate market mismatch, such as buying the wrong products and overstocking obsolete products (Li & Fung Research Center 2003: 123). Jackets are then attached with price tags before being packed in standard-sized containments and transported to over 600 retail stores and 140 outlet stores in North America right before the new season starts (www.gymboree.com).

Gymboree is astonished by the high-quality, efficient, and cost-effective global coordination given by Li & Fung. Gymboree regards Li & Fung as its "eyes and ears."[13] Li & Fung keeps up with the latest information on raw materials, technology, and fashion trends by regular on-the-job training and overseas visits to fashion capitals such as London and Paris. It helps Gymboree to forecast fashion trends in the coming year. With Li & Fung's international entrepreneurship, suppliers, manufacturers, and customers around the globe are linked and coordinated. For the next few years, Gymboree continues to collaborate with Li & Fung to expand its businesses in markets for shoes, hair accessories, umbrellas, and children's non-garment items. Mike Mayo, a senior vice president of Gymboree, says, "We are able to send all our products over to one agency. They go into Li & Fung's computer system and then are sent out to all of their locations throughout the world, whether they are in Indonesia, Bangkok, New Delhi, or Seoul. The different factories compete and get their costs as sharp as they can for a particular area" (Fung et al. 2008: 117). Li & Fung coordinates each stage of the production process conducted by suppliers, manufacturers, and Gymboree. In short, Li & Fung removes hassles in sourcing, manufacturing, and distribution and henceforth reduces information costs for all trading parties involved.

Conclusion

This chapter has developed an Austrian theory of international coordination which can be applied to understand the business dynamics of Li & Fung. In the global market, mismatches of plans and mutual distrust are common. International entrepreneurs coordinate global economic activities. These international entrepreneurs are not only middlemen but also knowledge creators. They transmit, create knowledge, and perform entrepreneurial discovery around the globe, and hence improve the well-being of humankind.

Li & Fung is one of the biggest providers of consumer goods in the world. It does not hire any worker or own any raw material, machinery, or factory for manufacturing household products. However, by adopting and linking up the most efficient and cheapest manufacturing process in different parts of the world, Li & Fung is able to gain pure entrepreneurial profit. As a result of dynamic entrepreneurship such as Li & Fung's, Hong Kong has evolved into a knowledge hub which integrates knowledge scattered in every corner of the world.

Notes

1 For the details of achievements made by Li & Fung, see www.lifung.com/eng/newsroom/lifung_news/news100205.pdf; retrieved 27 July 2010.
2 Both Victor and William Fung graduated with MBAs from Harvard Business School. Victor Fung taught in the school after completing PhD in economics at Harvard University. Since Fung's brothers returned to Hong Kong in the early 1970s, they have maintained close relationship with Harvard Business School.
3 Mainstream neoclassical economics assumes that market participants, firms, and products in the market are homogeneous.
4 The subjectivist approach does not stress knowledge itself, but rather what people know about knowledge. This approach focuses on the kind of knowledge about which people know nothing at all. It follows that "things about which men are completely ignorant are things that simply do not exist" (Kirzner 1979: 138; see also Yu 2001: 47–63).
5 For a further discussion of the Sino-British conflict, see Yu and Kwan (2003: 76–78).
6 Adopted from de Soto (1995: 228–253). Using simple stick figures as an illustration, de Soto is able to demonstrate the essence of Austrian entrepreneurial process.
7 White (1976: 4) argues that Kirzner does not distinguish arbitrageurship from entrepreneurship.
8 During the second Sino-Japanese war between 1937 and 1945, Hong Kong was comparatively accessible, immune from the Japanese invasion, and stable in its political situation.
9 Although the Li family was absent in Li & Fung, the name of Li & Fung has been kept until now. In Chinese, the characters of Li & Fung mean profit and abundance, respectively.
10 Currently, US$1 = HK$7.8.
11 Inchcape was a traditional British trading *hong* (company) led by Western managers. It has a large pool of customers in Europe and established sourcing offices in Europe, South Asia, the Mediterranean, and Latin America.
12 Adapted from Magretta (1998) and Fung et al. (2008).
13 Laura Willensky, the vice president of merchandising and design for Gymboree, says, "They [Li & Fung] are our eyes and ears" (*Time* 2007).

References

Casson, Mark (1982) *The Entrepreneur: An Economic Theory*, Oxford: Blackwell.

Chang, Ben and Phi, Joseph (2007) "The IDS Story: Reinventing Distribution through Value-Chain Logistics," in Hau L. Lee and Chung-Yee Lee (eds.) *Building Supply Chain Excellence in Emerging Economies*, New York: Springer, pp. 367–390.

Cheng, Leonard K (2001) "Li & Fung Ltd.: An Agent of Global Production," in Leonard K. Cheng and Henry Kierzkowski (eds.) *Global Production and Trade in East Asia*, Boston: Kluwer Academic, pp. 317–324.

CNN (2009, December 9) *The Unstoppable Fung Brothers*, http://money.cnn.com/2009/12/07/news/international/li_fung.fortune/; retrieved 21 July 2010.

de Soto, J. H. (1995) "Entrepreneurship and the Economic Analysis of Socialism," in Meijer Gerrit (ed.) *New Perspectives on Austrian Economics*, London: Routledge, pp. 228–253.

Feng, Bang-yan (2007) *100 Years of Li & Fung: Rise from Family Business to Multinational*, Singapore: Thomson Learning.

Fung, Victor K. (1997) "Evolution in the Management of Family Enterprises in Asia," in Gunwu Wang and Siu-lun Wong (eds.) *Dynamic Hong Kong: Business and Culture*, Hong Kong: University of Hong Kong Press, pp. 216–229.

Fung, Victor K. (2007) "How to Compete in a Borderless World: Eliminating Borders with Global Networks," *Knowledge Leadership*, Winter: 28–31.

Fung, Victor K.; Fung, William K.; and Wind, Yoram J. (2008) *Competing in a Flat World: Building Enterprises for a Borderless World*, Upper Saddle River, NJ: Wharton School Publishing.

Fung, William K. (2003) *Talking to CEOs' Show: Anticipate Change and Reinvent Yourselves Is Key to Survival*, www.cuhk.edu.hk/ipro/pressrelease/030417e.htm; retrieved 22 July 2010.

Hagel, John (2002) "Leveraged Growth: Expanding Sales without Sacrificing Profits," *Harvard Business Review*, October: 69–77.

Hagel, John and Brown, John Seely (2005) *The Only Sustainable Edge: Why Business Strategy Depends on Productive Friction and Dynamic Specialization*, Boston: Harvard Business School Press.

Hayek, F. A. (1945) "The Use of Knowledge in the Society," *American Economic Review*, 35: 519–530.

Holstein, William J. (2002) "Middleman Becomes Master," *CEO Magazine*, 182(October): 53–56.

Hutcheon, Robin (1992) *A Burst of Crackers: The Li & Fung Story*, Hong Kong: Li & Fung Ltd.

Kirzner, I. M. (1973) *Competition and Entrepreneurship*, Chicago: University of Chicago Press.

Kirzner, I. M. (1979) *Perception, Opportunity, and Profit*, Chicago: University of Chicago Press.

Kirzner, I. M. (1985) *Discovery and the Capitalist Process*, Chicago: University of Chicago press.

Knight, Frank H. (1921) *Risk, Uncertainty, and Profit*, Boston and New York: Houghton Mifflin.

Lachmann, L. M. (1956) *Capital and Its Structure*, Kansas City, MO: Sheed Andrews and McMeel.

Li & Fung Limited (2009) *Annual Report 2009*, www.irasia.com/listco/hk/lifung/annual/ar55263-e00494.pdf; retrieved 23 July 2010.

Li & Fung Research Center (2003) *Supply Chain Management – the Practical Experience of the Li & Fung Group*, Hong Kong: Joint Publishing (H.K.) Ltd. (Text in Chinese)

Long, Diane and Seet, Richard (1996) "Li & Fung (A)," *Harvard Business Case Studies*, 9-396-107, 15 April.

Loveman, Gary W. and O'Connell, Jamie (1995) "Li & Fung (Trading) Ltd.," *Harvard Business School Case*, 9-396-075.

Magretta, Joan (1998) "Fast, Global, and Entrepreneurial: Supply Chain Management, Hong Kong Style: An Interview with Victor Fung," *Harvard Business Review*, September-October: 102–114.

Martin, Adam (2007) "Mises, Kirzner and Knight on Uncertainty and Entrepreneurship: A Synthesis," working paper, http://mises.org/journals/scholar/martin.pdf; retrieved 26 September 2011.

McFarlane, Franklin W. and Young, Fred (2002) "Li & Fung (A): Internet Issues," *Harvard Business School Case*, 9-301-009.

Mises, Ludwig von (1949) *Human Action*, 3rd ed., Chicago: Contemporary Books.

Quelch, John A. and Bartlett, Christopher A. (2006) *Global Marketing Management: A Casebook*, Mason, OH: Thomson/South-Western.

Reekie, W. Duncan (1984) *Markets, Entrepreneurs, and Liberty: An Austrian View of Capitalism*, Brighton, Sussex: Wheatsheaf Books.

Schutz, A. and Luckmann, T. (1989) *The Structures of the Life World*, Vol. II, Evanston, IL: Northwestern University Press.

Slater, Joanna (1999, July 22) "Masters of the Trade," *Far Eastern Economic Review*, pp. 10–13.

Telegraph (2008, June 1) *Li & Fung – the Made in China Giant You Have Never Heard Of*, www.telegraph.co.uk/finance/newsbysector/retailandconsumer/2790870/Li-and-Fung-the-Made-in-China-giant-you-have-never-heard-of.html; retrieved 3 August 2010.

Time (2007, November 15) *Exports: Trading Up*, www.time.com/time/magazine/article/0,9171,1115648,00.html; retrieved 3 August 2010.

White, L. H. (1976) "Entrepreneurship, Imagination and the Question of Equilibrium," in S. Littlechild (ed.) *Austrian Economics*, Vol. III, 1990, Aldershot: Edward Elgar, pp. 87–104.

Wind, Yoram; Fung, Victor; and Fung, William (2009) "Network Orchestration: Creating and Managing Global Supply Chains without Owning Them," in Paul R. Kleindorfer and Yoram J. Wind (eds.) *The Network Challenge: Strategy, Profit, and Risk in an Interlinked World*, Upper Saddle River, NJ: Wharton School Publishing, pp. 209–315.

Yoshino, Michael Y. and George, Anthony (1998) "Li & Fung (A): Beyond 'Filling in the Mosaic'– 1995–98," *Harvard Business School Case* 9-398-092.

Yu, Tony Fu-Lai (2001) "Entrepreneurial Alertness and Discovery," *Review of Austrian Economics*, 14(1): 47–63.

Yu, Tony Fu-Lai and Kwan, Diana S. (2003) "Learning, Catching Up and the International Economic Order: The Trilateral Relationship between China, Britain and Hong Kong in the Entrepreneurial Perspective," in Tony Fu-Lai Yu (ed.) *East Asian Business Systems in Evolutionary Perspective: Entrepreneurship and Coordination*, New York: Nova Science Publishers, pp. 67–88.

6 A subjectivist approach to advertising

The success of Vitasoy

Weaknesses in contemporary neoclassical economics of advertising

In the mainstream neoclassical economic paradigm, products are portrayed as homogeneous. New institutional economists argue, however, that products are not homogeneous. They contend that product attributes need to be identified and valued by the trading parties concerned before a transaction can be carried out (Cheung 1983; Barzel 1989). Unfortunately, as in the neoclassical paradigm, New Institutional Economics adopts an "economics of information" approach, in which information is a commodity whose acquisition renders both cost and benefit. As with the neoclassical school, information is held to be a homogeneous good which is identical to everyone. It follows that every individual makes the same assessment of a piece of information and, accordingly, the same decision. This perspective disregards the actors' prior experiences, stocks of knowledge, and cultural and/or social backgrounds. In particular, the neoclassical economic approach attempts to find out the right (optimal) amount of information that should be produced and delivered by the advertising industry in response to consumers' desires. It follows that information can be bought and sold and even packaged. Neoclassical economists then conclude that extensive advertising in order to persuade potential customers during the competition is redundant and wasteful.[1] This argument ignores the subjective evaluation of a commodity (information) by consumers and therefore fails to explain the persuasive role of advertising.

Lancaster (1966) modifies the standard neoclassical theory of consumer behavior and develops a "new theory of consumer demand." He stipulates that what consumers are seeking to acquire is not only the goods themselves but the characteristics of the goods. Adapting Lancaster's attribute analysis, Robertson and Yu (2001) show how the interaction between supply and demand can be represented from the Austrian market process perspective. Yet a subjectivist theory of advertising has to be formulated. This chapter fills in this gap. In what follows, a subjective perspective of advertising and promotion strategies will be given. This theory will be applied to understand the successful advertising strategy of Vitasoy, a famous soybean drink in Hong Kong. Finally, a conclusion will be given.

A subjectivist approach to advertising

In contrast to mainstream neoclassical economics, the Austrian school of economics[2] interprets human behavior and social phenomena from the actor's point of view (O'Driscoll and Rizzo 1985) and argues that if a consumer or producer does not know of the existence of a commodity, the good simply does not exist to this person (Kirzner 1979: 137–153). Given human ignorance,[3] it is impossible for a person to search for something that he or she does not know about, let alone to estimate the cost and benefit associated with the search of a piece of information. Hence, according to the subjectivist view of knowledge, the demand of a commodity does not exist unless consumers are aware of the existence of a commodity. Suppose that a new product is manufactured and sold in the market, but consumers are ignorant of the consumption opportunity. Thus, there is room for the firm to inform its potential consumers that such a new product exists.[4] In terms of alertness to the opportunities, Kirzner (1973: 1979) rightly argues that the role of the firm lies not only in perceiving that there is an opportunity to serve consumers but also in making the consumers perceive that opportunity. When consumers are not even aware that this knowledge is available, the firm must then inform them (Kirzner 1973: 148). The crucially important role of the firm is to bring available opportunities to the notice of consumers (Kirzner 1973: 155). In short, producers are not only engaged in providing commodities for consumers to purchase, but are also concerned with making consumers know the existence of these purchase opportunities.

The persuasive role of advertising

The most significant feature of advertising in the modern society is its persuasive power. Knight (1923/1936: 51–52) contends that "one cannot condemn advertising and salesmanship out of hand, unless one is prepared to repudiate most of education, and of civilization in general; for most of the desires which distinguish man from the brutes are artificially created." Until consumers know about the new product/idea, they cannot begin to form an attitude toward it. In developing an attitude toward the innovation, individuals may mentally apply the new idea to their present or anticipated future situations before deciding whether or not to try it. In Rogers' words (1983: 170), "the ability to think hypothetically and counter-factually and to project into the future is an important mental capacity at the persuasion stage where forward planning is involved." The function of advertising is not only to present consumers with a particular buying opportunity, but also to present it to them in a way that they cannot fail to "notice" its availability. In other words, the supplier must get consumers to notice and absorb that information. In this regard, it is therefore not surprising to find that a piece of information that might be provided in a small advertisement in a newspaper is instead posted on giant billboards or repeatedly broadcast TV commercials (Kirzner 1973). More importantly, through persuasive promotion, consumers' tastes are altered. Advertising can change the knowledge consumers believe and possess concerning the factual state of the world. Very often, consumers' perceptions of the external world are "locked in" by their experiences, and people therefore show no interest in the new consumption opportunities, even though they may know of their existence. Advertising helps consumers unlock their preoccupied knowledge and perceptions. It is a process of unlearning. Furthermore, many products can be furnished with new images through the use of some well-known figures in the society, such as a celebrity in the entertainment industry. To consumers, the product that has been promoted by the use of a celebrity is different from the product that has not been promoted. The former becomes another product with a new value. Advertising, when explained in the subjectivist view, is therefore not a waste. Thus, it is correct to claim that "all effective communication is persuasive. . . . [B]oth information and recommendations must be presented persuasively if they are to have any effect on purchasing decisions" (Rogers 1983: 170).[5]

How can the persuasive power of advertising be possible? A phenomenological explanation

In this section, we use phenomenology, another form of subjectivism, to explain the persuasive power of advertising. We argue that the prerequisite for the advertising agent to persuade consumers to accept a product appearing on TV[6] is to make consumers understand the product. If a product or an idea promoted on TV cannot be understood, we cannot expect it to be accepted.[7] However, the term "understanding" is more than just an explanation as we usually think of it in science. It refers to what Weber terms "Verstehen" or "subjective understanding." This concept involves the sharing of the same definition of a situation, and can be made possible because of intersubjective relationships among human agents. In the following, we elucidate subjective understanding on two types of commodity, namely novel and familiar.

Promotion of a new product

If a product is entirely novel in the market, then the advertising campaign needs to introduce the physical nature of the product. It includes the introduction of the unique attributes of the product, boasts of its usefulness, etc. When consumers watch TV advertising, they will try to make some sense out of the promotion content. Making sense of the promotion content means subjective understanding. In other words, the actor attempts to interpret the story based on his or her stock of knowledge, which is accumulated from everyday life experience. The stock of knowledge is gained during a process of socialization. At the beginning, a child interprets experiences from family members. The primary social world implies familial identity. Children accept their parents without question. They take what their parents have told them and have learned from their parents. As children grow up and go to school, they learn and interact with schoolmates and teachers. They gradually experience and accept the outside world. Hence, "secondary socialization" occurs (Berger and Berger 1976). After finishing school, adults enter the workforce. Working people socialize with their colleagues. In general, as people grow up in the same environment, they socialize and share a common pool of knowledge (Schutz 1962: 7).

How can subjective understanding in advertising be possible in the commercial world? The answer is that the act of interpretation or sensemaking is essentially intersubjective, since all human agents find their experiences necessarily associated with other persons. Everyday lives build on the category of the "others" (Weigert 1981: 55). Individuals find themselves related to the surrounding world in order to create a meaningful life and share it with the others. Advertising agents are taken by the consumers to be "other I's" just as the advertising agents experience the consumers as "another you." In this way, "we" can make sense. Subjective understanding or interpretation, as Weigert (1981: 74) puts it, "is a process of perceiving the other and his or her interaction within symbolic frameworks so that we can make some sense out of what the other is doing. . . . *If we cannot make any sense out of the other's interaction, it may be that there is no sense in it, or worse, it may be that there is no sense in me*" (italics added).

Accordingly, when consumers find that the TV commercial for a novel product makes sense to them or, more precisely, is consistent with their stock of experience and hence expectation, then the product will be accepted and the chance of buying it will increase.

Promotion of an old product by arousing collective memories: sharing of the same biography

Many products promoted on TV are not new but are familiar to households, such as Coca-Cola, Vegemite, Heinz Ketchup, Bell's Whisky, Ovaltine, etc. For household brands, physical attributes are well known. In what way can TV commercials persuade consumers to repeatedly buy these items? Conventional wisdom in marketing argues in terms of brand loyalty. Perceived value, brand trust, customer satisfaction, and repeat purchasing behavior and commitment are said to be the key factors of brand loyalty (Taylor et al. 2004). This chapter relates brand loyalty with collective memories or sharing of consumers' biographies in phenomenology.

Many advertising campaigns for age-old products intend to capture brand loyalty by arousing consumers' collective memories. As mentioned above, making sense of an event each time implies that we are experiencing. As we experience, our stock of knowledge grows. Hence, the stock of knowledge has a biography (Berger and Berger 1976). This stock of knowledge is used as a framework or scheme of reference to interpret or understand an external event. If the incoming event is old and familiar, it is consistent with our experience or interpretive framework. Thus, understanding is possible.

We have learned and experienced a commodity since childhood. As we buy and consume the product each time, the experience becomes a part of our stock of knowledge. As a result, the product accompanies us as we grow up and is accepted without challenge. We simply take it as it was. Such experience may even turn into affection. Simply put, bias may overtake reasoning. We love our childhood product simply as it was.

Given such condition, to promote an old product, all the advertising agent needs to do is to rekindle our childhood memories by constructing some old familiar stories we once experienced together. In doing so, the advertising agent (on behalf of the product) and consumers are sharing common experience with each other. This type of subjective understanding involves consumers' relearning, which we call "biography sharing." The consumers are sharing the same everyday life experience with the people featured in the TV commercial directed by the advertising agent.

To summarize, when the story appearing in the advertising campaign is in line with our biography, this will arouse our memories. Hence, collective memory is a "sharing of biography" in the community. We shall argue that the advertising strategy of Vitasoy, a well-known soymilk in Hong Kong, has adopted the sharing of biography approach and successfully captures the hearts of Hong Kong people.

Background of Vitasoy

Soybean drink has a long history in China. Though it is widely consumed at breakfast in the Chinese community, it emerged as a commercial drink in Hong Kong in 1940 when Dr. Kwee Seong Lo (1910–1995) promoted it by the name of Vitasoy. As early as 9 March 1940, Vitasoy was delivered door to door in Hong Kong as a milk alternative. At that time, diseases of malnutrition, such as pellagra and beriberi, were widespread in Hong Kong. Lo tried to produce a nutritious, high-protein soybean milk drink at an affordable price. He realized that many Chinese immigrants in Hong Kong were lactose intolerant and he manufactured a soybean milk drink instead. However, Vitasoy was not an immediate success. On the first business day, only nine bottles were sold, at six cents each. Business grew very slowly. By the time the company ceased operations due to the Second World War in 1941, sales were recorded at only about 1,000 bottles a day. The company reopened in 1945 after the war was over. By 1950, sales grew to such an extent that a new factory was built in Aberdeen. In 1953, Vitasoy was further improved by sterilization, so that it no longer needed refrigeration, and business boomed again. By the mid-1950s, annual sales had reached 12 million bottles.

To keep up with the demand, another new plant was opened in Kwun Tong in 1962. By that time, Vitasoy attracted the attention of UNICEF, the United Nations Children's Fund, which endorsed the concept of a high-protein, vitamin-enriched soybean milk and encouraged developing nations to adopt it as a way of fighting malnutrition. In the 1960s, Vitasoy malt, the first line extension, was launched. Vitasoy gradually established itself as a household name in Hong Kong. Realizing the potential of modern packaging, the company took a giant step forward in 1975. It introduced the first Tetra Brik Aseptic packaging to Hong Kong and launched Vitasoy in this new package. The new packaging was enthusiastically received by consumers, and sales boomed to 4 million cases a year. During the late 1970s and early 1980s, the company expanded the business and penetrated overseas markets. Currently, Vitasoy is available in over twenty markets, including the United States, Canada, Europe, Papua New Guinea, Australia, and Southeast Asia. The company has opened subsidiary offices, appointed local distributors, and established local manufacturing in key markets. Exports now represent more than 20 percent of the group's total business (see www.vitasoy.com; http://en.wikipedia.org/wiki/Vitasoy).

Vitasoy's advertising and promotion strategies in a subjectivist lens

> [Y]ou're from Hong Kong when you drink this one [Vitasoy][8]

Vitasoy is the drink that is identified as distinctively Hong Kong (Cagape 2008). This chapter uses a subjectivist approach to interpret Vitasoy's promotion strategies. In particular, we investigate how Vitasoy's TV advertising makes sense to Hong Kong people so as to stimulate its consumption. If the promotion content does not make sense to Hongkongers,[9] it cannot convince them to buy at all. This approach requires us to know the cultural and social backgrounds of the story and/or people featured in the advertisements.

Early years: promotion of a "new" drink (1950s)

As mentioned previously, ground soybeans in a creamy drink is an age-old breakfast favorite in China. However, milk from cows is not so common in China. Especially when fresh cow milk is served cold in the morning, Chinese may not get used to it and suffer from slight diarrhea. After the Second World War, a lot of people from mainland China moved to settle in Hong Kong. They took Hong Kong as a temporary shelter, not a permanent home. Their national identity was essentially Chinese. At that time, they were strangers in the Territory and struggled for a living in the tiny British colony. With a stock of knowledge experienced from the mainland, they started to fill up their minds with lived experience in Hong Kong. It was against these economic and social backgrounds that Vitasoy came into being. In the early 1950s, many Hong Kong people suffered from malnutrition, in particular pellagra and beriberi diseases. They could not afford to consume cow milk. Lo wanted to provide people in Hong Kong with a nutritious soybean drink. However, Hong Kong people at that time doubted its effect. The reason was that Lo named it Vitasoy. In Chinese, the word means "milk with vitamin." So the soybean cream was interpreted by local people as 'milk'. As a result, Chinese people hesitated to buy this product when it appeared in the market. As Lo wrote in 1964, "we soon found that, even among us Chinese to whom the soybean was by no means new, there was a strong prejudice against soy milk. They not only did not believe its nutritional values, but they also thought it could cause diarrhea, indigestion, and stomach ache" (Shurtleff and Aoyagi 2010: 402). Encountering this misinterpretation, the aim of Lo's marketing strategy was to fit his product into consumers' stock of knowledge. His advertising is rather straightforward, focusing on the usefulness and effectiveness of the drink, with the simple slogan broadcast on Commercial Radio HK as follows:

> Vitasoy makes you taller
> Vitasoy makes you stronger
> Vitasoy makes you healthier and fitter!

After listening to this commercial, Hong Kong people with poor health conditions unlearned some of their past experience and received new knowledge. They were affected by Vitasoy's persuasive statement that the drink could make them stronger and healthier. The commercial slogan made much sense to them and Vitasoy gained initial recognition by the community. In other words, consumers began to share the same definition of the situation with Vitasoy's marketing team via intersubjective communication.

Vitasoy more than just a soft drink (1970s)

According to Mak and Chan (2013: 158), colonial Hong Kong witnessed "a collective struggle for survival in the post-war years, tremendous social instability in the 1960s, industrial take-off in the 1970s."[10] In particular, it experienced the Shek Kip Mei fire in 1953, riots in 1958 and 1966–67, and the Canton Trust Bank Run in 1966. However, the Territory recovered from misfortunes and achieved tremendous economic growth in the 1970s. Life in Hong Kong was getting better. Parents began to be very much concerned about the foods and drinks being consumed by their children. Unlike Western culture, which took raw vegetables (salad) as healthy and nutritious, traditional Chinese parents in Hong Kong thought that raw and cold foods/drinks were harmful to human health. During that time, soft drinks such as Coca-Cola, Schweppes (cream soda), 7-Up (lemon soda), Sunkist, and Green Spot (orange) were popular in Hong Kong. However, Hong Kong parents did not encourage their kids to drink too much of that kind of foreign beverage, because these drinks were cold, and in parents' view the ingredients might be harmful to health. Given the mentality of Hong Kong parents, Vitasoy implemented a marketing strategy which could kill two birds with one stone. On the one hand, Vitasoy needed to compete with the foreign soft drink. In doing so, it persuaded the community to buy the local drink. On the other hand, it attempted to convince Hong Kong parents that Vitasoy was not an ordinary beverage like the foreign one. It was a soybean milk drink which was good for health. In 1982, the company hired the advertising agent Miss Ji Wenfeng to create a famous advertising slogan on TV and billboards:

> Vitasoy is more than a soft drink!!

This catchy statement implied that Vitasoy was not another foreign beverage! It was a unique healthy drink too. So when parents selected drinks for their kids, they should buy Vitasoy. In short, Vitasoy promoted its product by making sense as much as possible with Chinese parents in Hong Kong.

Promoting a warm interpersonal relationship (1980s)

After three decades of economic development, children born during the post-war baby boom period became adults. They experienced childhood in the 1950s, adolescence in the 1960s and work experience in the 1970s. Following rapid economic growth in Hong Kong in the 1970s and 1980s, most of these people successfully established their family and career. The minds of these people were filled with life experience in Hong Kong for more than three decades. Interpreting advertising content would be very much affected by their personal growth experience. In particular, these people, while having lived and grown up in the colony for more than three decades, had gradually built up a sense of belonging and identity in the Territory. By the 1980s, Vitasoy had successfully established its brand as a healthy drink in Hong Kong. However, the company needed to continue to persuade Hong Kong people to buy the drink, which was no longer a new product then. What Vitasoy did was to evoke consumers' growth experience. Technically, the advertisement on TV at that time featured life in the 'good old days', including an old shop owner sitting at the front door of the traditional vendor store, young people playing in rock bands on the rooftops of residential buildings, mini soccer grounds between old and new buildings. The scene was accompanied by a slogan:

From childhood to the present, life [Vitasoy] is equally cute!

The aims of these images were to arouse Hong Kong people's collective memories. The success of this advertisement can be attested by consumers confessing their love for Vitasoy after watching the ad. The first testimonial said[11]:

Who did not drink Vitasoy during their school year? I remember that during deep winter days, the school cafeteria always kept bottles of Vitasoy inside a water-heated box. When I watched the TV advertising featuring a schoolgirl in sweater and a big scarf, drinking a bottle of hot Vitasoy in the schoolyard, the urge to drink a bottle of Vitasoy immediately comes to me.

The second testimony was from a Hongkonger who studied overseas. He said, "The commercial set off my homesickness, and I drove two hours for these [Vitasoy]."[12] The Vitasoy ads had successfully recalled much of the collective memories of Hong Kong people because the sharing of the same biography via Vitasoy's commercials was at work.

Experiencing grandfather's love in Vitasoy during homecoming (1993)

In Chinese literature, there is a well-known essay entitled "The Sight of Old Papa's Back," written by the renowned Chinese poet and essayist Mr. Zhu Ziqing (1898–1948). The essay portrays a father and son saying farewell at a railway station in Pukou (Jiangsu, China). The father wants to buy some tangerines for his 20-year-old son. The son watches his father climbing up the platform in a clumsy manner, echoing the true feelings between them. The following prose is extracted from the English translation of "The Sight of Old Papa's Back" by Zhu (1925):

> I said, "Dad, you might leave now." But he looked out of the window and said, "I'm going to buy you some tangerines. You just stay here. Don't move around." I caught sight of several vendors waiting for customers outside the railings beyond a platform. But to reach that platform would require crossing the railway track and doing some climbing up and down. That would be a strenuous job for father, who was fat. I wanted to do all that myself, but he stopped me, so I could do nothing but let him go. I watched him hobble towards the railway track in his black skullcap, black cloth mandarin jacket and dark blue cotton-padded cloth long gown. He had little trouble climbing down the railway track, but it was a lot more difficult for him to climb up that platform after crossing the railway track. His hands held on to the upper part of the platform, his legs huddled up and his corpulent body tipped slightly towards the left, obviously making an enormous exertion. While I was watching him from behind, tears gushed from my eyes. . . . The next moment when I looked out of the window again, father was already on the way back, holding bright red tangerines in both hands. In crossing the railway track, he first put the tangerines on the ground, climbed down slowly and then picked them up again. When he came near the train, I hurried out to help him by the hand. After boarding the train with me, he laid all the tangerines on my overcoat, and patting the dirt off his clothes, he looked somewhat relieved and said after a while, "I must be going now. Don't forget to write me from Beijing!" I gazed after his back retreating out of the carriage. After a few steps, he looked back at me and said, "Go back to your seat. Don't leave your things alone." I, however, did not go back to my seat until his figure was lost among crowds of people hurrying to and fro and no longer visible. My eyes were again wet with tears.

Most people in Hong Kong know this essay, since it was included in the textbook for high schools in Hong Kong. Zhu wrote in a very straightforward and concise style, in contrast to the popular "romantic butterfly" style at that time. This literary piece has become very much loved by all generations in Hong Kong.

In Vitasoy's TV advertising, the departure scene at the railway station is reproduced. However, the location is no longer Pukou. The original dad and 20-year-old son become granddad and grandchild. Benny Chan, a baby-faced Hong Kong actor and singer, plays the young boy in the TV ad, who migrates and lives overseas because his parents face a crisis of confidence regarding the transfer of sovereignty over Hong Kong to China in 1997.[13] During summer holiday, the young boy returns to his home village to see his granddad. The boy recalls many wonderful times during his childhood there, including climbing trees, catching fish, and fooling around in the green fields. Soon, the holiday is over and the teen has to leave the village. His granddad sees him off at the railway station. Before the whistle blows, the granddad crosses the railway tracks and climbs up and down the platform to buy Vitasoy (instead of tangerines) for his grandchild. As Hong Kong audiences watch this TV ad, they recall the essay they read in high school, and minds quickly link the content of the ad with family love and the kind Chinese father, who cares so much about his kid but never expresses his love in words. In other words, the TV ad and Hong Kong people share the same life experience or biography. The advertising captures the hearts of Hong Kong people. It wins the First Annual Most Popular TV Commercial Award in 1995.

"Stand by Me" (2009 and 2012)

From the 1980s to 2009, Hong Kong went through rains and storms, including the 1987 stock market disaster (Black Monday), confidence crises in 1982–84 triggered by the impending return of Hong Kong to China in 1997, and outbreak of bird flu in 1997 and 2003 and of SARS (severe acute respiratory syndrome) in 2003. After experiencing all of those misfortunes, Hong Kong people began to establish a local identity and recognized themselves as Hongkongers.[14] Vitasoy, born in the 1950s, also became a mature product, well known to Hong Kong citizens in the 2000s. Vitasoy, a truly Hong Kong drink, shares the same identity with Hong Kong people. As an age-old local drink, Vitasoy showed its support to Hong Kong people all the way in the ad. In 2009, it launched a TV commercial, "Stand by Me," emphasizing the long-term relationship between Vitasoy and Hong Kong people.[15] The lyrics, translated by the authors, are as follows:

> When I'm feeling bored, we date and you cheer me up,
> Laughter furnishes our months and years,
> We swap diaries and walk through the rain and storm, hand in hand,
> Funny things never end,
> With your sincerity, I never feel tired,
> We share dreams and joy from spring to winter.
> Stand by me!
> With your sincerity, I never feel tired,
> We share dreams and joy from spring to winter.
> Stand by me!
> Stand by me!

The TV ad starts with teenagers smiling and singing how Vitasoy has accompanied them through good times and bad. It features warm friendship among classmates, friends, soccer teammates, and band mates. The theme song emphasizes how Vitasoy, as their faithful friend, stands by them by repeating the refrain "stand by me." On the one hand, the repeated frequency of singing "stand by me," with a deep effect etched in viewers' hearts, attempts to reinforce the message that Vitasoy is their true friend. On the other hand, it attempts to impress Hong Kong people that Vitasoy will back them up all the way, despite rains and storms over the years.

In the advertisement, people are organized into different categories. According to the phenomenology, we tend to identify people differently and form impressions of others. Through this advertisement, audiences will classify these people according to the role construct. The construct was then related to the message that Vitasoy has been an indispensable part of their growth, hence establishing the significant friendship between Hong Kong people and the product.

In 2012, Vitasoy relaunched the advertisement "Stand by Me" with slightly different lyrics. The new version gave a familiar feeling to the audiences, as had the one in 2009. It refreshed Hong Kong audiences with cheerful and colorful images to bring out a pleasant atmosphere. However, the new video not only showed teens' and schoolkids' friendships, but also highlighted warm and sweet family relationships, with a mother holding her baby. This latest version targeted those people who had by then established families of their own. It reinforced the unbreakable tie between Vitasoy and Hong Kong people. The two "Stand by Me" TV commercials were extremely successful. According to the *Vitasoy Interim Report* (2009/2010: 7), they attract "over half a million online views."

Conclusion

After pointing out the weaknesses of the contemporary economic approach to advertising, this chapter explains the roles of advertising and promotion strategies from a subjectivist lens. In particular, it attempts to use a phenomenological approach to explain the persuasive power of advertising. It argues that when consumers watch an ad, they interpret the message conveyed in the promotion by their stock of knowledge accumulated from everyday life experience. If consumers do not understand the advertising content, we cannot expect them to accept and buy the product. In other words, the content of advertising has to make sense to consumers. Sensemaking implies subjective understanding. When consumers find that the advertising content make senses, then they and the advertising agent (on behalf of the product it promotes) share 'common sense', or share the same definition of the situation, which can be made possible only through intersubjective communication. The deeper the sharing of 'common sense', the better the chance that the product will be accepted by consumers. Since knowledge is obtained from everyday life experience and has history, in order to share the same biography with consumers, a successful piece of advertising requires the firm to know consumers' personal growth history, racial identity, culture, social and economic backgrounds, etc. The phenomenological approach to explain the persuasive power of advertising has been applied to understand the successful advertising campaign made by Vitasoy, a well-known soybean drink in Hong Kong. The analysis covers the new and mature Vitasoy. It concludes that Vitasoy has been extremely successful in promoting its soybean drink by linking the product with the biography of Hong Kong consumers. In the micro aspect, Vitasoy portrays itself as a longtime friend that has grown up with Hong Kong people, sharing everyday life experience with them. In the macro aspect, the campaign content of Vitasoy mirrors Hong Kong's economic and social development and hence witnesses the transformation of Hong Kong since the Second World War.

Notes

1 For an Austrian critique of the neoclassical analysis of advertising, see Kirzner (1973: 163–179) and Kirkpatrick (2007: 132–134).
2 For an account of the Austrian school of economics, see Yu and Shiu (2011).
3 Ignorance prevails when knowledge or information is available somewhere or is potentially discoverable, but some or all of the possible users have not yet acquired that knowledge. Uncertainty, however, results from the inherent inability of people to know exactly what will happen in the future (Robertson 1998).
4 Alderson and Sessions refer to "the remolding of demand." To them, *"Changing buying attitudes means supplying consumers with reasons for preferring the new product"* (cited in Penrose 1959/1995, p. 81; italics by Penrose).
5 For a phenomenological approach to advertising, see Nagel (2000).
6 In this chapter, we focus on TV advertising because it is still the most significant promotional vehicle in Hong Kong so far, despite the emergence of the Internet and social media.
7 Of course, it needs no further remark that full understanding may not necessarily lead to acceptance.
8 From Cagape (2008).
9 The term "Hongkonger" has recently been included in Oxford English Dictionary. For an account of the meaning of "Hongkonger" and its identity, see Chan (2013).
10 See also Chan (2013).
11 www.skyscrapercity.com/showthread.php?t=763826&page=4; retrieved 22 April 2014.
12 See note 10.
13 On 19 December 1984, China and the United Kingdom signed the Sino-British Joint Declaration to validate the transfer of sovereignty over Hong Kong to China in 1997. The declaration prompted massive emigration of Hongkongers, especially those in the middle class.
14 Otto Baurer in 1924 brought out the term "national communities of fate." He claimed that "a nation is a totality of men united through a community of fate into a community of character" (Shih 1995: 53).
15 The effect is similar to the club song of the Liverpool Football Club: "You'll Never Walk Alone" (originally sung by Gerry and the Pacemakers in 1963). Whenever the Liverpool team are in a downturn during the match, Liverpool's fans in the stadium will sing this song loudly. Like a miracle, the team can reverse the situation afterward.

References

Barzel, Yoram (1989) *An Economic Analysis of Property Rights*, Cambridge: Cambridge University Press.

Berger, P. and Berger, B. (1976) *Sociology: A Biographical Approach*, rev. ed., Middlesex: Penguin.

Cagape, Elmer W. (2008, July 12) "Vitasoy Black Eye," http://asiancorrespondent.com/16940/vitasoy-black-eye/; retrieved 4 April 2014.

Chan, Catherine S. (2013) "Narrating the Hong Kong Story: Deciphering Identity through Icons, Images and Trends," *World History Connected*, 10(1): 49 pars., http://worldhistoryconnected.press.illinois.edu/10.1/chan.html; retrieved 15 April 2015.

Cheung, S.N.S. (1983) "The Contractual Nature of the Firm," *Journal of Law and Economics*, 26(April): 386–405.

Kirkpatrick, Jerry (2007) *In Defense of Advertising: Arguments from Reason, Ethical Egoism, and Laissez-Faire Capitalism*, Claremont, CA: TLJ Books.

Kirzner, I. M. (1973) *Competition and Entrepreneurship*, Chicago: University of Chicago Press.

Kirzner, I. M. (1979) *Perception, Opportunity and Profit: Studies in the Theory of Entrepreneurship*, Chicago: University of Chicago Press.

Knight, Frank H. (1923/1936) "The Ethics of Competition," *Quarterly Journal of Economics*, 37: 579–624, reprinted in F. H. Knight, *The Ethics of Competition and Other Essays*, 2nd ed., New York: Harper, pp. 41–75.

Lancaster, Kelvin J. (1966) "A New Approach to Consumer Theory," *Journal of Political Economy*, 74: 132–157.

Mak, Ricardo K. S. and Chan, Catherine S. (2013) "Icons, Culture and Collective Identity of Postwar Hong Kong," *Intercultural Communication Studies*, XXII(1): 158–173.

Nagel, Christopher Paul (2000) "Truth in Advertising," in Michael T. Carroll and Eddie Tafoya (eds.) *Phenomenological Approaches to Popular Culture*, Bowling Green, OH: Bowling Green State University Popular Press.

O'Driscoll, G. P. Jr. and Rizzo, M. (1985) *The Economics of Time and Ignorance*, Oxford: Blackwell.

Penrose, Edith (1959/1995) *The Theory of the Growth of the Firm*, Oxford: Basil Blackwell.

Robertson, Paul L. (1998) "Information, Similar and Complementary Assets, and Innovation Policy," in B. J. Loasby and N. J. Foss (eds.) *Economic Organization, Capabilities and Coordination: Essays in Honor of G. B. Richardson*, London: Routledge.

Robertson, Paul L. and Yu, Tony Fu Lai (2001) "Firm Strategy, Innovation and Consumer Demand: A Market Process Approach," *Managerial and Decision Economics*, 22(4–5): 183–199.

Rogers, E. M. (1983) *Diffusion of Innovations*, 3rd ed., New York: The Free Press.

Schutz, A. (1962) *Collected Papers, V.1. The Problem of Social Reality*, The Hague: M. M. Hijhoff.

Shih, Cheng-Feng (1995) *National Identity and Taiwan Independence*, Taipei: Qian Wei Publisher. (Text in Chinese)

Shurtleff, William and Aoyagi, Akiko (2010) *History of Soybeans and Soyfoods in Southeast Asia*, Lafayette, CA: Soyinfo Center.

Taylor, S. A.; Celuch, H.; and Goodwin, S. (2004) "The Importance of Brand Equity to Customer Loyalty," *Journal of Product and Brand Management*, 13(4): 217–227.

Vitasoy Interim Report (2009/2010) Hong Kong: Vitasoy International Holding.

Weigert, A. J. (1981) *Sociology of Everyday Life*, New York: Longman.

Yu, Fu-Lai Tony and Shiu, Gary M. C. (2011) "A New Look at the Austrian School of Economics: Review and Prospects," *International Journal of Pluralism and Economic Education*, 2(2/June): 145–161.

Zhu, Ziqing (1925, October) "Sight of Old Papa's Back," translated by Zhang Peiji, May 1999, www.flickr.com/groups/back_sight/discuss/72157594238455524/; retrieved 22 April 2014.

7 Property rights and the failure of Chinese family business succession
The killing of Yung Kee's golden goose

Introduction

The dynamics of Chinese economies, including mainland China, Taiwan, and Hong Kong, are said to be built upon Chinese family businesses (Kao 1993; Yeung 1998). However, the Chinese family business, as an organization for coordinating economic activities, has its merits and demerits. On the one hand, using the Chinese way of management, the Chinese family business enjoys internal and external capabilities in the forms of flexibility and low communication costs (Yu 2001). On the other hand, the Chinese family business exhibits serious management disputes and infighting among family members when the business is passed on to the heirs by the founder,[1] often ending in bitter court feuds. Research on 250 companies controlled by Chinese families in Hong Kong, Taiwan, and Singapore by Fan (2012a) reveals that a steep decline of the stock value of these businesses can be related to a succession period beginning 60 months before the succession date and 50 months after the succession date. In Hong Kong, family business disputes in court have been rapidly increasing in recent years because of poor succession planning by the founders. In an extreme case, Mr. Li Po Chun, a wealthy Hong Kong businessman, died in 1964, and inheritance disputes over his estate continued until 2003, causing a significant waste of resources.

The succession disputes of some well-known Chinese family businesses in Hong Kong have been extensively reported and commented by mass media and newspaper journalists (for example, see *Businessweek* 2012; *China Daily* 2012; *South China Morning Post* 2012a, b; *Next Magazine* 2012a, b; *Ming Pao* 2012a, b, c, and d). However, these reports are descriptive in nature and lack analytical insights. There is also no dearth of academic research on the problems of Chinese family business succession from scholars in corporate governance (for example, see Lee and Li 2008; Fan 2012a, 2012b; Fan and Yu 2011; Fan and Zhang 2012; Zheng 2010; Zheng and Wong 2003, 2004). In particular, Zheng (2010) argues that if the Chinese family businesses can "equally take economic capital, human capital and network capital into account during succession, the chance of maintaining their business from one generation to the next will become higher." Fan et al. (2008) utilize the concept of specialized assets to explain the problems in family business succession in Asian emerging economies. Their study reveals that there is a tendency for entrepreneurial firms in Singapore, Taiwan, and Hong Kong to evolve into family owned and managed firms and that family ownership stays concentrated across generations of management. In their view, the lack of separation of ownership and control of the firms is largely due to the need to protect specialized assets, including the founder's ideology, reputation, or relationship with stakeholders. These assets are specific to the founder and hence difficult to divide, value, and/or transfer. Therefore, they are best kept within the family.

Despite vigorous quantitative analyses on East Asian family business succession conducted by scholars in corporate governance, these studies can only provide us with a general picture of problems in Chinese family business succession. While these works may be useful for broad interpretation, they are not entirely effective in understanding "why" and "how" (Yin 1994) an event happens. Hitherto, in-depth case studies on the causes of the disputes of Chinese family business succession in Hong Kong have been lacking. This chapter attempts to fill the gap, specifically adopting theories in economics and management that have been advanced in recent decades to reinterpret the succession problems in Chinese family businesses. It utilizes capabilities theories, property rights economics, and Neo-Confucianism to understand disputes in management and infighting among the members in a Chinese family business in Hong Kong. In particular, this chapter attempts to explain why Chinese family businesses in Hong Kong are able to excel under the leadership of their founders, but when the enterprises are passed on to the heirs, they exhibit a downfall. This chapter elucidates the phenomenon in Chinese family businesses that "wealth does not last three generations."

In this chapter, Yung Kee, a famous roast goose restaurant in Hong Kong, is used as an empirical case study for several reasons. First of all, Yung Kee is a legend in Hong Kong. It represents the efforts of a Chinese entrepreneur who single-handedly created a miracle in the food and catering industry. Secondly, the Yung Kee case is a prime example of how a successful Chinese family business in Hong Kong fell right after it was taken over by the second-generation heirs. From a harmonious team spirit in the founding period, Yung Kee turned into a showcase of full-scale and vigorously fought court battles among the heirs in Hong Kong. The rise and fall of Yung Kee has significant implications for Chinese family business succession.

In what follows, a theoretical framework which allows us to understand Chinese family business succession problems and estate disputes in Hong Kong will be presented. The sections that follow are the empirical analysis. Finally, policy recommendations on the succession of the Chinese family business will be given.

The Chinese family business as a unit of economic competition

A successful firm must consist of certain capabilities, or in a resource-based view, productive specialized assets. If these capabilities are inimitable, then the firm is said to possess a sustainable competitive advantage which allows it to earn economic rent (Barney 1991). Likewise, Chinese family businesses are said to possess some distinctive assets which allow them to compete in the market. Probably the most distinctive feature of a Chinese family enterprise is its Chinese way of business management. Chinese entrepreneurs in South East Asian regions in general and Hong Kong in particular manage their businesses like a family (Chau 1974; King 1987; Redding 1990; Zheng and Wong 2004). Specifically, Chau (1974) argues that manufacturing enterprises in Hong Kong in the 1960s and 1970s were principally Chinese family affairs. Wong (1988) creates the term "entrepreneurial familism" to describe the dynamics of the Chinese family business. In Wong's view (1988: 142–143), family is the basic unit of economic competition. Familism in practice extends to financial loans, management techniques, and marketing strategies. In a legal sense, the founder of the Chinese family business exclusively owns the firm. However, in Chinese entrepreneurs' mindset, the business belongs to the whole family, although some family members, usually the eldest son, may have stewardship of some resources. Without independent resources, members collectively work for the benefit of the family and the family relationship remains bounded (Redding 1990: 59).

Corporate governance in the Chinese family business

Team production brings about opportunistic behaviors and hence monitoring problems (Alchian and Demsetz 1972). The Chinese family business, as a team, is no exception. In this chapter, we argue that the Chinese family business, during its founding stage, tackles opportunistic behaviors by two measures, namely charismatic leadership of the founder and Chinese family values (rule). These two elements successfully reduce transaction costs and enhance dynamism in the Chinese family business. As the enterprise is passed on to the second generation, the loss of the charismatic entrepreneur, accompanied by changing social and family values, brings about governance problems to the Chinese family business. As a result, formal legal disputes replace family rules, resulting in heavy rent dissipation.

Sole ownership in the first generation of the Chinese family business

In the first generation, the Chinese family business is exclusively owned by the founder. In other words, property rights of the firm's assets are clearly defined. A complete property right implies that the founder-owner has the rights to own, use, and transfer the resources of the firm (Alchian and Demsetz 1972). Furthermore, the owner has the right to the income of the resources. He or she is the sole residual claimant (Alchian and Demsetz 1972). If the founder is diligent, profit (or residual) will be higher and the founder will enjoy a bigger return. However, sole ownership structure does not mean that there is no cheating problem in the firm. Team production in the Chinese family business involves the employment of the founder's sons, daughters, and close relatives. These de facto employees can behave opportunistically too. Some family members or black sheep in the family may shirk or even embezzle. The first-generation Chinese family business relies on the charismatic founder and traditional family values to handle opportunistic or cheating behavior.

The role of the charismatic entrepreneur in Chinese family business governance

This chapter argues that cheating or opportunistic behavior by employees in the first generation of the Chinese family business is not serious because of the authoritative image of the founder. The founders of Chinese family businesses in the early stage of Hong Kong's industrialization, such as Mr. Li Ka Shing and Mr. Fok Ying Tung, were charismatic entrepreneurs. Starting from nothing, they were able to identify profit opportunities and establish their business empires during Hong Kong's industrialization. Charismatic entrepreneurship is one of the most important assets in Chinese family businesses (Yu 2001). With a charismatic entrepreneur, the Chinese family businesses save a lot of monitoring costs in team production. As Witt (1998) argues:

> [A] persuasive business conception adopted by an employee may detract her/his attention in a self-reinforcing manner from non-compliance alternatives that actually exist. Hence if the entrepreneur can dominate the informal communication process within the firm so that elements of her/his conception become tacit cognitive commonalities among the firm members, this may enable the entrepreneur to get the employees cognitively involved into her/his endeavor.

Hence, when employees take the firm's problems as their own, they will be less likely to pursue opportunistic action. The development of a Chinese family firm relies heavily on the charismatic entrepreneur who creates a paternal image for his/her employees. Such leadership convinces employees to comply with the goals of the firm. Specifically, a Chinese family firm can reduce transaction costs in three ways. Firstly, family members identify very strongly with the organization's goals. If the key people in the company are all dedicated to the family's wealth accumulation, and if that is the hidden rationale behind much decision making, then a great deal of coordination is already taken care of. Secondly, motivation tends to be high, especially when extra effort is called for and the availability of an intensely dedicated set of executives in key positions has substantial value. Thirdly, as Redding (1990) points out, confidentiality of information is easier to guarantee.

In short, when employees feel that they are part of the family, they will be less likely to undertake opportunistic actions. Moreover, these employees may even engage in creative acts that are beneficial to the firm. Only if members consider themselves as outsiders will they exhibit opportunistic behaviors.

Traditional Chinese family values as a means to tackle problems in corporate governance

Even if cheating or opportunistic behaviors occur in the Chinese family business, the founder will exercise family rule instead of relying on the formal legal court system. In some situations, family rule is an effective way of solving the problems and saving transaction costs. As mentioned, the founder in the Chinese family enterprise manages his/her business in a "Chinese way," or more precisely, manages it like a family. A Chinese family firm is governed by paternalism. Chinese entrepreneurs take the position of "my staff is my family" (Redding 1990: 156). They exhibit a strong sense of responsibility towards employees that is not only economic but also moral. Chinese founders think that they have an obligation to look after their staff's welfare (Redding 1990: 61). If the staff misbehaves, the founder, who acts as a parent, has the obligation to teach the staff as children by family values. The founder uses traditional Confucian values, namely filial piety, 'face', and *renqing* to ensure that his/her heirs/staff live up to family expectations as well as conform to the goals of the family business (Redding 1990: 101).

- Filial piety is considered as the first virtue in Chinese culture. In Confucian philosophy, people should love, respect, and take care of their own parents and others' parents so as to bring good reputation to the family and ancestors. When people perform well in job duties, they will obtain material means of supporting parents and carrying out sacrifices to the ancestors. People should uphold fraternity and display sorrow for parents' sickness and death (Legge 1861).
- 'Face' is a reflection of personal dignity and reputation. It is applied to individuals, companies, and organizations. One can give and even boost face to others by a compliment. Public criticism and insult can cause a serious loss of face (i.e., reputation and social status). Therefore, people should not cause someone to lose face unless they really mean it. For this reason, minor issues are best handled in private (Kamnan 2012; Redding and Ng 1982).
- *Renqing* means humanity's feeling towards others. For Mencius, the master of Confucianism, *renqing* is "the reaction to the unbearable that is the root of humanity's feeling . . . which, itself, summarizes morality" (Jullien 1995). This feeling for humanity includes an obligation to it (Chen 1995). According to Hwang (1987), *renqing* encompasses three meanings:

  o as emotional responses in various situations of daily life. According to the *Book of Ritual*, "renqing consists of happiness, anger, sadness, fear, love, hatred and desire. All of them are acquired at birth."
  o as resources that an individual can present to another person as gifts during social exchange
  o as a set of social norms that an individual respects and allows him/her to get along well with other people. For instance, if a member violates a family rule and cheats, family rule will be applied and the wrongdoer will not be sent to the police.

In sum, in the first generation, with the charismatic founder and powerful family values, corporate governance in the Chinese family firm is effectively conducted.

Governance problems in the new generation of the Chinese family business

As the Chinese founder gets old, he or she has to pass on the business to the heirs. And yet, many Chinese founders follow their family tradition and do not want to see their business empire falling apart as a result of partition. It is quite common that "Chinese founders would want their offspring to stay together and lead the businesses they have founded. However, this is often 'wishful thinking' as family members . . . often want to sell the business and move on" (Fan 2012a). Some Chinese founders in olden days even passed away without making a will. This of course leads to court feuds among family members. This infighting will be even more complicated and severe if the founder had several wives or concubines, which was quite common in old Hong Kong.

Loss of the charismatic founder

As the founder passes away, his or her estate is usually passed on to the heirs in more or less equal shares, though some children may have marginally larger shares due to capabilities or affection from their father. As mentioned above, the charismatic founder is a source of centripetal force for the family members to work for the company. It should be reiterated that such force comes from the willingness of the staff to work for the company without the need of monitoring. If the charismatic founder passes away, such loyalty will disappear. Each offspring will attempt to promote his or her own welfare. The situation is just like the fall of the Roman Empire. Without a strong central authority, European landlords/kings expanded their powers and influences in the form of manor. Similarly, in the Chinese family business, after the founder passes away, heirs are free to pursue their own interest without paternal influence.

Changing social and family values

The fading of traditional Chinese culture and values is one of the reasons for internal disputes in the Chinese family business (Fan 2012a). As mentioned, in the first generation, corporate governance is enforced by family rule with a set of traditional Chinese values. In Hong Kong, however, old social values have been losing ground under the influence of British colonial rule and internationalization of the Territory. Taking the example of an influential Chaozhou rice importing company in the 1970s, the founder of the company took his staff as one family and paid much respect to the long-term old workers. When taking over the company after the father retired, the son showed little respect to the old workers and paid little attention to their opinions. As a result, two of his jobbers,[2] his sworn uncle and his father's sworn brother, left the firm unhappily (Zheng 2010).

Different perceptions and values between father and son is another cause of conflict (Levinson 1971; Handler 1990). Father and son grow up in very different generations. Generally, the father comes from a poor family. Poverty and lack of options forced him to leave school early, work at a young age, and mature earlier. The son, on the contrary, comes from a better-off environment. He does not need to worry about his salary (Menkhoff 1990; Cunningham and Ho 1994; Zheng 2010). Usually he studies abroad and obtains good academic qualifications.[3] The new generation learns foreign culture and defies traditional Chinese values their founders-dads imposed on them. Without traditional family rule as an enforcement mechanism, legal settlements gain ground. Disputes in business management move from "inside the family" to "outside the family."

Collective ownership in the second generation of the Chinese family business: the Chinese inheritance system

As mentioned above, the founder, embedded with traditional family values, is extremely reluctant to carry out partition among the heirs even when he/she becomes very old. Rather, the founder wants to keep the family business in unity and expects all children, especially sons, to work in harmony for the sake of the firm. Therefore, in Chinese society, a more or less equal inheritance system (Zheng 2010) is adopted in order to unify the heirs to work for the family empire, although the eldest son may become the managing board director and lead the company, if this son is considered capable and is loved by the founder. However, such practice ends in disaster in most cases.

Scholars (e.g., Wang 1977; Wolf 1981; Chen 1985; Chau 1986, 1991) point out that the coparcenary principle shortens the life of the family business, as it implies that male heirs have equal right to family property. By this principle, when the founder dies, his/her estate will be divided among the male heirs. If the founder has five sons, each son will get one fifth of the family business. If the founder has seven sons, each son will get only one seventh of the business share. The share will become even smaller in the next generation. In other words, family property and its business shares will get smaller and smaller after each partition (Zheng 2010). However, the eldest son, unlike the founder, encounters extreme difficulties in drawing all family members together. The keen competition among in-laws also worsens the family relationship. Freedman (1957, 1971) and Yeung (2000) conclude that the equal inheritance system impedes business growth by promoting fragmentation. In particular, Yeung (2000: 59) argues that "many Chinese family firms experience a downsizing effect when the family firm is broken down into separate business units, each headed by a son or a nephew."

Notwithstanding the argument above, these scholars do not elucidate Chinese family business succession from the perspective of property rights economics. We argue that collective ownership of property is a fatal factor of the Chinese inheritance system. If the property is divided among the offspring in more or less equal shares, it is difficult for the heirs to work towards the company's goal unselfishly before the fruit of teamwork is reaped. Such arrangement may work under the charismatic founder, with the effective enforcement of traditional family values. In other words, staff will not misbehave because they admire their charismatic leader. Furthermore, it is a Chinese value that offspring are told to work for the best of the family. However, when the founder passes away and the family values have changed, both enforcement mechanisms disappear. With collective ownership of the business, heirs will have the incentive to capture economic gain generated from the collectively owned property as much as possible, resulting in less total economic rent shared by all heirs. The methods to capture economic gains include arranging for the sons or daughters (third generation) to hold the important positions in the company, shirking during office hours, or even embezzlement, etc. As a result, the quality of the product or service will deteriorate. This adverse result is to be borne by all shareholders of the company.

In the old generation, when a staff member of the Chinese family enterprise misbehaved, the founder would exercise his/her authority and power to punish the heir by family rule. This saves a lot of legal expenses. After the founder passes away, the new generation forsakes the old family rule. They take the case to court for settlement whenever there is misbehavior. In many cases, court settlement can render higher costs than resolution by family rule. All parties lose in court battles. The summary of the whole theoretical framework is given in Figure 7.1.

In the mainstream neoclassical economic paradigm, a firm is portrayed as an economic unit making decisions regardless of its social environment. In other words, the neoclassical firm is "transhistoric" and "acultural" (Abolafia and Biggart 1992: 316–317). On the contrary, our model explains the behavior of the family firm in the Chinese cultural context. In particular, it integrates property rights economics, capabilities theories, and Neo-Confucianism to understand the fall of a Chinese family business in Hong Kong. This model is the first of its kind in corporate governance literature.

We shall use an in-depth case study to illustrate our theory. Data and materials in this study rely largely on secondary sources, including *60 Years of Yung Kee*

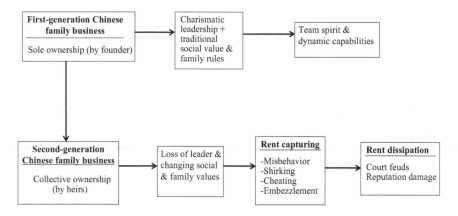

Figure 7.1 Chinese family business succession in Hong Kong

(the official publication of Yung Kee). As mentioned above, Yung Kee's legendary rise and court feuds have been extensively reported in newspapers and magazines such as *South China Morning Post, The Standard, China Daily, Next Magazine, Ming Pao, East Week Magazine*, and *Apple Daily*. Therefore, the reliability of the information from these newspapers and magazines can be checked against each other. In the next section, our model will be applied to understand the business succession of Yung Kee.

Yung Kee: from street food stall to a world-famous restaurant

Kam Shui-Fai (hereafter "Kam Senior"), the founder of Yung Kee Restaurant,[4] worked as an apprentice in a Chinese restaurant after a few years of education. He worked hard and learned secret skills of preparing roast meat. He then became a master of roast-flavored goose. Seven years after apprenticeship, he and his friends established an outdoor food stall called Yung Kee, near a ferry pier in Central, Hong Kong Island. In 1942, Kam Senior rented a unit in Wing Lok Street, Sheung Wan, at HK$4,000 (in 1939, Hong Kong dollar was pegged at HK$16 = 1 pound) and started Yung Kee Restaurant. After the restaurant was bombarded by the Japanese in World War II, Yung Kee was relocated in Pottinger Street, Central. With Kam Senior's leadership and reputation, Yung Kee became famous for tasty cuisine, roast meats, and good customer service. Local and international tourists, tycoons, and celebrities bought roast geese in Yung Kee and then shipped "Flying Roast Geese" around the world by air. In 1962, Yung Kee finally moved into the current premises in Wellington Street, Central. Kam Senior later acquired the adjacent four buildings and built the Yung Kee Building in 1978.

As early as 1968, Yung Kee was named by *Fortune* as one of the Top 15 Best Restaurants in the World and Top 20 Asia's Finest Restaurant by the Miele Guide (2008–2011). It was awarded one star in the "Bib Gourmand" section of the Michelin Guide (2008–2010). "Roast Goose" is acclaimed as the signature dish. Other awarded dishes include "Preserved Trotter with Soy Sauce," "Deep Fried Prawn with Mini Crab Roe," and "Steamed Melon with Black Seaweed." Kam Senior is regarded as an authoritative figure in Hong Kong's roast-flavored meat business.[5]

The core competence of Yung Kee: the world's famous roast goose cuisine

The core competence of Yung Kee lies in producing unique roast-flavored geese. Such capabilities or specialized assets could not be imitated by the founder's peers due to a secret recipe and a complicated process in processing geese. Starting from the selection of geese, Yung Kee only used top black maned geese from Conghua and Qingyuan (both in Guangdong) because the two places produced super quality geese. As baby geese were hatched out in the farm designated by Yung Kee, the best quality geese would be selected and raised in a special farm shack where a limited amount of exercise was allowed for the geese, so that their meat would not become tough. Goslings were only fed by grasses, leaves, and vegetables. Until they grew to 2.5 kg after 100 or 120 days, their meat would be tender with natural taste which was most suitable for roasting. Unlike today's goose farming, those geese supplied to Yung Kee had never been fed by synthetic forage. As a result of strict quality control, geese sold to Yung Kee were 20–30 percent more expensive than in the market.

Regarding seasoning ingredients, Yung Kee used secret family herbs, including anise, cumin, ginger, agaric, and 10- to 15-year-old dried tangerine peel from Xinhui (Guangdong). Furthermore, they did not use common "cloud ear" fungus but better quality "kitten ear" fungus as a side. Charcoal was also important in roasting geese. Yung Kee was the only restaurant in Hong Kong Island that could use charcoal briquettes for roasting. Charcoal briquettes needed to be stored in the right way. Other, inferior charcoal yielded excessive black smoke that ruined the taste of roast goose. Yung Kee used Nanyang charcoal, whose aroma perfectly matched goose meat. Also, this charcoal never yielded black smoke that could blacken roast goose. Instead, it gave a good aroma of charcoal. In short, under Kam Senior's leadership, Yung Kee was able to maintain its high quality roast geese through a complicated and picky process. Therefore, it is not surprising that the capabilities of Yung Kee could not be imitated by other restaurants in the market. In this way, Yung Kee, with a sustainable competitive advantage, earned economic rent from its famous golden roast goose.

Family business governance under Kam Senior

In the first generation of Yung Kee, the family business was exclusively owned by the founder Kam Senior. Kam Senior assigned the first son, Kam Kin-sing (or Kinsen Kam Kwan-sing), as the main shopkeeper, in charge of merchandizing, the kitchen, and cuisine design. The second son, Ronald Kam Kwan-lai, was responsible for finance, accounting, and renovation projects. The third son, Kam Kwan-ki, after successfully learning the skills of roasting geese from his father, was in charge of the roast-meats section of Yung Kee. With authoritative and charismatic leadership, and traditional Chinese family teaching, Kam Senior effectively managed and controlled Yung Kee, and the father-and-sons team created a miracle in the food and catering industry in Hong Kong.

Kam Senior as a charismatic leader

Kam Senior built up his image and leadership in three aspects, namely competence, work attitude, and interpersonal relationships. First of all, it is widely known that Kam Senior, with only a few years of education, single-handedly transformed Yung Kee from a street food stall into a world-famous restaurant. As a master of roast-flavored meat, Kam Senior's legendary roast goose is well known for succulent meat and crispy skin. He excelled at carving goose in three slices from head to chest and along the back. Roast goose was divided into two equal halves and ready to be served that only crispy skin was shown. Kam Senior was crowned as "King of Roast Goose" with culinary excellence. Throughout four decades, he built up the capabilities of Yung Kee, which was renowned a brand name of Hong Kong and worldwide reputation.

Secondly, Kam Senior was generally respected for his work attitude. Ever since being an apprentice, Kam Senior always enjoyed his work. He said, "my happiest moment is when I have the kitchen knife in my hand" (quoted in Kam 2002: 181). After his retirement in 1979, Kam Senior still went back to Yung Kee and helped in the kitchen during the peak lunch hour. He ensured the good reputation of Yung Kee with high quality dishes and good customer service.

Thirdly, Kam Senior treated all employees like his family members and looked after their welfare, including livelihood, sickness, and death (quoted in Kam 2002: 8). Each day, he and the Kams had lunch with managers to maintain their close relationship and, if necessary, give advice on innovative dishes of Yung Kee (Kam 2002: 35). Yung Kee was also famous for friendly and attentive customer service. Regardless of social class and ethnicity, Kam Senior fully understood the diet of each customer (Kam 2002: 70, 81–82, 183). He encouraged a good relationship between Yung Kee and customers. Outside Yung Kee, Kam Senior maintained a trustworthy personal relationship with old hands in wholesale, retail, and catering businesses. In short, all staff in the first generation of Yung Kee admired Kam Senior's skills and leadership. With a working environment like a family, it is hard to envisage that staff would cheat their boss.

Kam Senior: the sole ownership of Yung Kee

Under the charismatic leadership of Kam Senior, staff seldom misbehaved due to their admiration of the leader. Furthermore, in the 1970s and 1980s, Kam Senior owned 70 percent of Yung Kee, with absolute final say in the company. The remaining 30 percent was owned by three sons (*Next Magazine* 2012b). In this form of ownership, property rights of Yung Kee's assets were clearly defined. As the sole residual claimant of Yung Kee, if Kam Senior worked diligently, he was the one who exclusively claimed the profit (residual). However, there was still a chance that his staff (mostly his offspring and long-term employees) in Yung Kee might misbehave, shirk, or embezzle. On this, Kam Senior, as in other Chinese family businesses in Hong Kong, relied on traditional family rule to enforce the company's goal.

Traditional Chinese family values as an enforcement tool in Kam Senior's time

Using traditional Chinese family values such as filial piety, face, and *renqing*, Kam Senior effectively ensured that his children and employees would work for the company's goals. In particular, Kam Senior deeply influenced his two sons, Kinsen and Ronald, with Chinese family teaching. It is reported that the elder son, Kinsen, followed exactly what his father advised. To show filial piety to his father and maintain the good face (reputation) of Yung Kee, Kinsen behaved like his father and became a traditional hardworking Chinese businessman in charge of the family business.[6] Kinsen even dressed up in an old Chinese style gown as a means to resist the temptation of leisure enjoyment. The old style Chinese gown plays two roles. First, it is a reflection of Chinese culture, indicating that Kam Senior succeeded in educating his sons by traditional Chinese teaching. As a result, the sons followed traditional Chinese values in managing Yung Kee. Under the pressure of filial piety and face, his sons strove to maintain the family business well and would not ruin it. Secondly, dressing up in an old Chinese gown, Kinsen's friends regarded Kinsen as an old-fashioned man and did not want to invite him out for partying. However, Kinsen insisted that this was a right way to keep up with his father's expectation. It is also reported that the second son, Ronald, used Chinese family values and *renqing* to manage Yung Kee. In Kam Senior's time, though two sons disagreed on some business issues, the quarrels were kept behind closed doors and never disclosed to outsiders so that the good reputation of Yung Kee was maintained. Under Kam Senior's teaching and with the two sons working as a team, Yung Kee created a miracle in Hong Kong's food and catering industry (*East Week Magazine* 2010).

Succession of the Yung Kee enterprise

Kam Senior had four wives (four chambers) and eighteen children (eleven sons and seven daughters). According to traditional Chinese values, the estate would be equally shared by the four chambers. The first childless wife died shortly after the marriage. The fourth wife has no legal status. Hence, the estate would be shared by three chambers. Kam Senior allocated the Diamond Restaurant to the second chamber in 1938, Yung Kee to the third chamber. Mak Siu-Chun, the third wife, became the matriarch of Yung Kee. Mak had five children (for details, see *East Week Magazine* 2010; *Next Magazine* 2012b). She has two sons and two daughters, but one daughter died young. After Kam Senior died in 2004, four family members of the third chamber shared the inheritance of Yung Kee, valued at at least HK$1.5 billion, and had about HK$880 million in liquid assets (*South China Morning Post* 2012e) (1 USD = 7.8 HKD). According to Chinese tradition, sons should have larger shares, while daughters and wives are treated the same and have smaller shares. Kam Senior perceived that Yung Kee would be managed by the eldest son, Kinsen, and the second son, Ronald. Therefore, both of them received equal shares of 35 percent of Yung Kee (see Appendices 1 and 2). The rest, Kam's third wife (Mak Siu-chun), third son (Kam Kwan-ki), and young daughter (Kelly Kam Mei-ling) each received 10 percent of Yung Kee as living expenses. After Kwan-ki died in 2007, his 10 percent share was transferred to Ronald. In 2009, Yung Kee's matriarch, Mak, gave her own 10 percent share to Kinsen. Then, Kinsen and Ronald equally owned 45 percent shares of Yung Kee. In 2010, Kelly decided to give her 10 percent share to Ronald, giving him the majority stake of 55 percent of the company (see Appendix 2). After that, Kam's family infighting over Yung Kee began.

Corporate governance in the second generation of Yung Kee: loss of the influential leader and ineffective family ruling

In the old generation, when a staff member of the Chinese family enterprise misbehaves, the founder will exercise his/her authority and power to punish the wrongdoing heir by family rule. This saves a lot of legal expenses. After the death of the founder, the new generation, with overseas education, no longer sticks to the traditional family values. For example, in old Hong Kong, nephews respect their elder uncle (father's elder brother) as their father. However, this is not so in the new generation. It is reported that Kinsen was publicly humiliated by his nephew in front of ten employees (*South China Morning Post* 2012b; *Ming Pao* 2012c). As mentioned, face is significant in Chinese society. One should not tear down another person's face unless one means it. Public humiliation left no face to Kinsen. Without a way out, Kinsen turned to the court in a dogfight. In the inheritance disputes, Yvonne, the young daughter of Ronald, who graduated from an overseas university, also publicly criticized her grandmother in front of the mass media. In particular, Yvonne claimed "Grandma is deeply biased. . . . She values too much the Chinese tradition that the family wealth should be inherited by the oldest son. That is why she has been on my uncle's side" (*South China Morning Post* 2012c).

In sum, traditional Chinese family values and rule such as filial piety, face, and *renqing* play little role in resolving management disputes in Yung Kee today. Instead, family members have taken the disputes to the courts for settlement. As a result, heavy court cases will be conducted. In many cases, settlement by legal means render higher costs than family rule. All parties will lose in the battle of court cases.

Power struggle and rent dissipation under collective ownership rights

After the death of Kam Senior, there was a change in Yung Kee's shareholding (see Appendix 2). Notably, Yung Kee changed from sole ownership to collective ownership. Instead of one leader, there were two leaders in the company. From 2007, Ronald held the majority stake of 55 percent and Kinsen owned 45 percent of Yung Kee. Both brothers more or less equally shared power and responsibilities in Yung Kee, resulting in a power struggle. Each party pursued larger control of Yung Kee. While Kinsen attempted to handle Yung Kee's affairs by traditional family rule, Ronald wanted to manage Yung Kee in his own way. Specifically, Ronald took "unilateral and drastic steps" and dispossessed Kinsen's power in Yung Kee (*China Daily* 2012). Ronald further took over personnel arrangement duty, which Kinsen used to have charge of (*Ming Pao* 2012c). In 2011, Ronald changed marketing strategies without prior discussion with Kinsen. Furthermore, Kinsen required approval from the board of directors before taking an interview or placing a media promotion (ibid). In other words, he was no longer an exclusive spokesperson of Yung Kee. In addition, Kinsen was prevented from accessing financial information. He was denied access to Yung Kee's books and records. His demand to declare dividends at a board meeting was dismissed because Ronald reserved millions of dollars for renovation (*Ming Pao* 2012b). It is reported that

Ronald turned a blind eye whenever Kinsen was "humiliated" by Carrel, Ronald's first son (*South China Morning Post* 2012b).

Rent capturing: arrangement of siblings for major positions in the firm

As Yung Kee is more or less equally owned and controlled by two brothers, the attempt to capture economic benefits from Yung Kee is predicted. The simplest form of rent capturing was the arrangement of important positions for the children into Yung Kee, thereby increasing family influence and power in the company. In particular, Kevin Kam Shung-hin, the first son of Kinsen, was arranged to work in Yung Kee after finishing education in Canada in 1996. Despite being lazy and having no motivation to run Yung Kee, Kevin was promoted to assistant manager (*The Standard* 2012). Meanwhile, Ronald appointed his children, Carrel and Yvonne, as the director and alternate director (and chief financial officer), respectively. They were assigned "right at the top and took over" Yung Kee without any prior experience in the culinary industry (*China Daily* 2012). Subsequently, Ronald was successful in taking majority control on the board of directors. He also paid "excessive" wages to his family members. It is reported that the two sons of Kinsen were paid only a monthly wage of HK$17,500, while the two children of Ronald received a salary of HK$45,000 per month (*Ming Pao* 2012d).

Rent capturing: alleged embezzlement of Yung Kee's assets

Our theory argues that with the collective ownership of assets, family members behave in opportunistic ways, with an attempt to capture economic rent which is supposed to be shared by all members. Ronald was alleged to have embezzled Yung Kee's assets. It is reported that Ronald used Yung Kee's warehouse as his own company, CTE-Ease, a Chinese sausage company, without seeking approval from the managing board (*Ming Pao* 2012b). When Ronald was in charge of the renovation of Yung Kee, he delivered the contract to Design and Decoration Ltd., which was owned by his secretary (*Ming Pao* 2012a).

Rent dissipation: quality deterioration and damage to personal reputations

Long-term infighting among family members of Yung Kee, including power struggles, court disputes, mutual humiliations, etc., result in severe rent dissipation in the form of deterioration of food quality and damage to personal reputations.

Rent dissipation: deterioration in food quality

It is reported that the food quality of Yung Kee has significantly deteriorated in recent years. Office workers in Central complained about the service of Yung Kee, including poor customer service, a noisy environment; and more devastatingly, the roast goose, at HK$480, was overpriced due to its poor quality (*Next Maga-zine* 2012a).

A comment from Mr. Chau Yung-Kwai, an apprentice of Yung Kee 30 years ago and now the boss of a local food restaurant chain, is worth mentioning. He said that under Kam Senior's leadership, people and shop were united as one. The kitchen strictly controlled food quality. Goose dishes in Yung Kee had a special flavor which could not be obtained elsewhere. However, Yung Kee's roast goose could today no longer live up to its reputation. Chau concluded that even roast goose shops in Sham Tseng[7] were better than Yung Kee's (*Apple Daily* 2012).

The deterioration of food quality of Yung Kee can be officially evidenced from a professional gourmet guide. Yung Kee was honored with one star in the Michelin Guide (Hong Kong and Macau edition) in 2009 for three consecutive years. Unfortunately, it lost its star on 1 December 2011, and was placed only in the "Bib Gourmand" section of the Michelin Guide's 2012 edition (*South China Morning Post* 2012d; *Apple Daily* 2011).

Rent dissipation: court feuds and damage to personal reputations

Traditional family values and rule have lost their influence on the new generation in Hong Kong. Disputes in the family business are resolved in the courts, result-ing in heavy rent dissipation. In the case of Yung Kee, in 2010, Kinsen petitioned the court to have Yung Kee wound up unless Ronald bought his 45 percent stake or sold his own 55 percent share to him. The court heard that Kinsen was unfairly dispossessed of power in and control of the company, after Ronald gained the majority 55 percent stake in the business and arranged for his own son to be a director of the company. To let the family business move ahead, Kinsen applied for an order that his younger brother buy his shares in the company, or alterna-tively, he would buy Ronald's shares. Kinsen also claimed that in circumstances where he had been in a "quasi-partnership" with his younger brother, his shares should be sold for full value. The hearing was concluded in October 2012, 27 days after Kinsen unexpectedly died of illness (*Businessweek* 2012). The conclusion dismissed Kinsen's request because Yung Kee registered as an offshore company in the British Virgin Islands. Although both brothers agreed in principle that one brother should buy the other's shares, they could not agree on price. According to the HK$30 million lawsuit, the conclusion would hopefully assist Kam's family with an amicable solution "without the need for further recourse to the courts" (*Businessweek* 2012).

Personal reputations among family members were also severely damaged dur-ing a series of court disputes. On this, Bowers (2012) states:

> [W]hat is already clear is that the huge amount of publicity surrounding the family shareholder dispute is likely to have a long term negative impact upon the personal reputations of the family members involved and possibly upon the fortune of the family business – not to mention the irreparable damage to the personal relationships between all members of the family concerned.

The Chinese inheritance system, allowing a collective ownership of family business among heirs, leads to power struggling and rent capturing among family members. Severe rent dissipation ends up in loss for all shareholders.

Conclusions and discussions

This chapter utilizes capabilities theories, property rights economics, and Neo-Confucianism to understand management disputes and infighting among the members in Yung Kee, a famous Chinese family business in Hong Kong. This chapter has argued that the founder of Yung Kee was able to lead his offspring to create a dynamic enterprise via charismatic leadership and family rules embedded in traditional Chinese values. However, these two strategic assets disappeared following the passing away of the founder as well as the emergence of new social values. When the founder of Yung Kee passed the enterprise to his offspring using more or less the equal inheritance system, the traditional Chinese values were unable to enforce the leader's will to consolidate the strengths of second-generation family members to maintain the founder's business. Furthermore, when Yung Kee was owned by all family members, property rights of the firm were unclear. Without effective enforcement of traditional Chinese values and with collective ownership rights, some family members of Yung Kee had the incentive to capture the economic rent which was shared by all members. In other words, some family members behaved opportunistically in order to capture economic gains in the public domain. High monitoring and enforcement costs in the form of court battles and endless disputes followed. Rent dissipation occurred in the form of deterioration of the quality of the family business. Our study suggests that ownership structure and corporate culture are crucial elements for the survival of a Chinese family business.

So far, studies on Chinese family business succession in Hong Kong are mostly quantitative analyses. They may be useful for broad interpretation but are ineffective in understanding "why" and "how" the wealth of Chinese family businesses cannot last three generations. This chapter formulates a model integrating capabilities theories, property rights economics, and Neo-Confucianism to understand the rise and fall of a Chinese family business in Hong Kong. This new approach provides fruitful insights into Chinese family business succession. With minor modification, it can well explain Chinese family business succession in East Asia in general, and mainland China and Taiwan in particular.

The findings of this chapter also provide useful and practical advice to the founders of Chinese family businesses in planning to pass on their enterprises to the next generation. Chau (1991) compares the Chinese coparcenary system to the Japanese primogeniture system, a system of inheritance in which a single heir, usually the eldest male of the oldest branch in the family, gets the estate. He finds that the coparcenary inheritance system is "dysfunctional [and has] downward mobility and lack of corporate longevity," while the primogeniture system is "functional, assisting capital formation and corporate longevity." An important lesson to be learned from the Japanese system is that the estate is passed on to a single heir, hence avoiding collective ownership of the family business.

Chau's finding on the Japanese inheritance system is consistent with our property rights view adopted in this chapter. If the estate is exclusively owned by one heir, opportunistic behaviors such as shirking, misuse of assets, and cheating will be reduced. Along with this line of thinking, the founder of the Chinese family business should forsake the old thinking that the business is divided equally among family members to keep the enterprise in unity. Instead, he or she should follow the principle that the whole business should be given to one heir only. If the Chinese founder has several heirs, then the whole business should be given to one heir, perhaps compensating other heirs by cash of equal value.

Notes

1 Nearly a third of the members of the 2012 *Forbes* Hong Kong Rich List are 70 years old or beyond, and the succession of new leaders has to be settled sooner than later (Fan 2012a).
2 Jobber was an important position in the rice business in old Hong Kong.
3 Chinese parents are willing to spend on their children's higher education whenever they can afford to. Most founders in Hong Kong come from poor families and their educational levels are relatively low. They think that their children will be better off with higher educations. As a result, the second and third generations are well educated. Some of them obtain overseas academic degrees from institutions like Oxford, Cambridge, Yale, MIT, and Stanford (Postiglione 1999; Menkhoff 1990; Cunningham and Ho 1994; Zheng 2010).
4 In this chapter, the name "Yung Kee" means Yung Kee Holdings Ltd.
5 www.yungkee.com.hk/award/award-e.htm; retrieved 23 December 2012.
6 As will be argued below, Kinsen's traditional Chinese thinking brought a negative impact on the development of Yung Kee. Kinsen was unable to compromise with his nephews on new thinking and modern management style.
7 Several restaurants in Sham Tseng (New Territory, Hong Kong) are also well known for roast goose cuisine.

References

Abolafia, Mitchel and Biggart, Nicole (1992) "Competitive Systems: A Sociological View," in Paul Ekins and Manfred Max-Neef (eds.) *Real-Life Economics: Understanding Wealth Creation*, London: Routledge, pp. 315–323.

Alchian, Armen A. and Demsetz, Harold (1972) "Production, Information Costs, and Economic Organization," *American Economic Review*, 62(4): 777–795.

Apple Daily (2010, July 14) "Elder Brother Lost Court Case," http://hk.apple.nextmedia.com/news/art/20100714/14237656; retrieved 23 December 2012. (Text in Chinese)

Apple Daily (2011, December 2) "Yung Kee Relegated to Moderate Ranking," http://hk.apple.nextmedia.com/news/art/20111202/15855369; retrieved 30 January 2013.

Apple Daily (2012, November 1) "Roast Goose Legend Comes to the End," http://hk.apple.nextmedia.com/news/art/20121101/18054265; retrieved 26 December 2012. (Text in Chinese)

Barney, Jay (1991) "Firm Resources and Sustained Competitive Advantage," *Journal of Management*, 17(1): 99–120.

Bowers, Kevin (2012, March 13) "Message from the Court: Shareholder Beware!" Hong Kong Legal Community, http://law.lexisnexis.com/; retrieved 8 January 2013.

Businessweek (2012, October 31) "Roast Goose Family Fights as Asia Estate Battles Increase," www.businessweek.com/news/2012-10-31/roast-goose-family-feuds-amid-asia-estate-fights; retrieved 16 November 2012.

Chau, Sik Nin (1974) "Family Management in Hong Kong," in Lee Nehrt et al. (eds.) *Managerial Policy, Strategy and Planning for Southeast Asia*, Hong Kong: The Chinese University of Hong Kong, pp. 155–158.

Chau, Theodora Ting (1986) "The Second Generation Capitalists," in Y. C. Qi et al. (eds.) *The Ups and Downs of Hong Kong's Wealthy Families*, Hong Kong: North and South Journal Publisher, pp. 25–32. (Text in Chinese)

Chau, Theodora Ting (1991) "Approaches to Succession in East Asia Business Organizations," *Family Business Review*, 4(2/June): 161–180.

Chen, Min (1995) *Asian Management Systems: Chinese, Japanese and Korean Styles of Business*, London: Routledge.

Chen, Q. N. (1985) "Branch and Kin-Group: The Traditional Chinese Family System," *Study of Sinology*, 3(1): 127–148. (Text in Chinese)

China Daily (2012, January 31) "Elder Brother Exposes Track of Yung Kee Feud," www.chinadailyapac.com/article/elder-brother-exposes-track-yung-kee-feud; retrieved 25 December, 2012.

Cunningham, J. B. and Ho, J. (1994) "The Dynamics of Growth and Succession in Entrepreneurial Organization," *Journal of Enterprising Culture*, 2(1): 571–600.

East Week Magazine (2010, April 10) "5-Year Family Infighting and Breakup," http://eastweek.my-magazine.me/index.php?aid=6219; retrieved 26 December 2012. (Text in Chinese)

Fan, Joseph P. H. (2012a) "Chinese Businesses and Succession Planning," Insights-Articles, CUHK Business School, November 28.

Fan, Joseph P. H. (2012b) *Critical Generations: Out of the Succession Dilemma of Chinese Family Business*, Beijing: Dang Fang Publishers. (Text in Chinese)

Fan, Joseph P. H.; Jian, Ming; and Yeh, Yin-Hua (2008) "Family Firm Succession: The Roles of Specialized Assets and Transfer Costs," Second Singapore International Conference on Finance, National University of Singapore, July.

Fan, Joseph P. H. and Yu, Xin (2011) "Planning Family Governance and Avoid Family Infighting," *New Fortune*, February, pp. 84–88. (Text in Chinese)

Fan, Joseph P. H. and Zhang, Tian-Jian (2012) "Lessons from Chow Tai Fook and Yung Kee: Public Company and Family Business Succession," *New Fortune*, March, pp. 106–112. (Text in Chinese)

Freedman, M. (1957) *Chinese Family and Marriage in Singapore*, London: Her Majesty's Stationery Office.

Freedman, M. (1971) *Chinese Lineage and Society: Fukien and Kwangtung*, London: The Athlone Press.

Handler, W. (1990) "Succession in Family Firms: A Mutual Role Adjustment between Entrepreneur and Next-Generation Family Member," *Entrepreneurship Theory and Practice*, 15(1): 37–51.

Hwang, K. K. (1987) "Face and Favor: The Chinese Power Game," *American Journal of Sociology*, 92(4): 945–974.

Jullien, F. (1995) *Fonder la morale: Dialogue de Mencius avec un philosophe des Lumières*, Paris, Bernard Grasset. (Text in French; Chinese translation by Song Gang published by the Beijing University Press in 2005)

Kam, Kin-sing (2002) *60 Years of Yung Kee*, Hong Kong: Tong Wen Hui. (Text in Chinese)

Kamnan, O. (2012) "Hong Kong Culture," *Orient Expat: the Intelligent Community*, www. orientexpat.com/hong-kong-expat/culture; retrieved 26 December 2012.

Kao, John (1993) "The Worldwide Web of Chinese Business," *Harvard Business Review*, March-April, pp. 24–36.

King, Yeo-Chi (1987) "The Transformation of Confucianism in Post-Confucian Era: The Emergence of Rationalistic Traditionalism in Hong Kong," *Hong Kong Economic Journal Monthly*, 128(November): 54–62.

Lee, Jean and Li, Hong (2008) *Wealth Doesn't Last 3 Generations: How Family Businesses Can Maintain Prosperity*, Singapore: World Scientific.

Legge, James (1861) *The Classic of Filial Piety (Xiao Jing)*, http://ctext.org/xiao-jing; retrieved 26 December 2012.

Levinson, H. (1971) "Conflicts that Plague Family Business," *Harvard Business Review*, 49: 90–98.

Menkhoff, T. (1990) "Towards an Understanding of Chinese Entrepreneurship in Southeast Asia: Small Trading Firms in Singapore," *Working Papers #138*, Department of Sociology, University of Bielefeld.

Ming Pao (2012a, February 7) "Cheating: Ronald Alleged to Cover up Secretary Handles Renovation Projects in Yung Kee for 30 Years," http://news.hk.msn.com/local/article. aspx?cp-documentid=5825059; retrieved 25 December 2012. (Text in Chinese)

Ming Pao (2012b, February 8) "Kinsen Tries to Reconcile with Ronald," http://life.mingpao. com/cfm/dailynews3b.cfm?File=20120208/nalgm/gma2.txt; retrieved 20 December 2012. (Text in Chinese)

Ming Pao (2012c, February 9) "Yung Kee Family Infighting: Carrel Insults Uncle Kinsen in Public," http://news.sina.com.hk/news/20120209/-2-2572151/1.html; retrieved 25 December 2012. (Text in Chinese)

Ming Pao (2012d, February 9) "$2000 Pay Gap between Kam's Brothers," http://life.mingpao. com/cfm/dailynews3b.cfm?File=20120209/nalgo/goa2.txt; retrieved 27 December 2012. (Text in Chinese)

Next Magazine (2012a, October 25) "Kam Family Infighting: Mother Cries 'They Hound Elder Brother to Death' and Calls for Justice," http://hk.next.nextmedia.com/template/ next/art_main.php?iss_id=1181&sec_id=1000853&art_id=16702567; retrieved 14 November 2012. (Text in Chinese)

Next Magazine (2012b, November 8) "The 'Real' Eldest Son of Yung Kee: Happiness Lies in Contentment," issue 1183, http://hk.next.nextmedia.com/template/next/art_main. php?iss_id=1183&sec_id=1000853&art_id=16717884; retrieved 25 December 2012. (Text in Chinese)

Postiglione, G. (1999) *China's National Minority Education: Culture, Schooling and Development*, Hong Kong: Oxford University Press.

Redding, S. Gordon (1990) *The Spirit of Chinese Capitalism*, Berlin: De Gruyter.

Redding, S. Gordon and Ng, Michael (1982) "The Role of 'Face' in the Organizational Perceptions of Chinese Managers," *Organization Studies*, 3: 201–219.

South China Morning Post (2012a, February 2) "Yung Kee Brother 'Not a Partner in Eatery,'" www.scmp.com/article/991477/yung-kee-brother-not-partner-eatery; retrieved 5 December 2012.

South China Morning Post (2012b, February 9) "Yung Kee Brother 'Humiliated' by Family," www. scmp.com/article/.../yung-kee-brother-humiliated-family; retrieved 31 December 2012.

South China Morning Post (2012c, November 1) "Yung Kee Restaurant Dispute: What Next Kams' Golden Goose," www.scmp.com/news/hong-kong/article/1074054/yung-kee-restaurant-dispute-what-next-kams-golden-goose; retrieved 25 December 2012.

South China Morning Post (2012d, November 1) "Roasted Goose Helped Turn Kam Shui-fai into a Legend," www.scmp.com/news/hong-kong/article/1074053/roasted-goose-helped-turn-kam-shui-fai-legend; retrieved 30 January 2013.

South China Morning Post (2012e, October 31) "Petition in Yung Kee Family Feud Dismissed in Court," www.scmp.com/news/hong-kong/article/1073874/petition-yung-kee-family-feud-dismissed-court; retrieved 22 December 2012.

The Standard (2012, February 1) "Younger Brother Backed in Yung Kee Family Face-Off," www.thestandard.com.hk/news_print.asp?art_id=119279&sid=; retrieved 31 December 2012.

Wang, S. H. (1977) "Family Structure and Economic Development in Taiwan," *Bulletin of the Institute of Ethnology, Academic Sinica*, 44: 1–11.

Witt, Ulrich (1998) "Imagination and Leadership: The Neglected Dimension of the Evolutionary Theory of the Firm," *Journal of Economic Behavior and Organization*, 35(2): 161–177.

Wolf, A. P. (1981) "Domestic Organization," in E. D. Ahern and H. Gates (eds.) *The Anthropology of Taiwanese Society*, Stanford, CA: Stanford University Press.

Wong, Siu-Lun (1988) *Emigrant Entrepreneurs: Shanghai Industrialists in Hong Kong*, Hong Kong: Oxford University Press.

Yeung, Henry Wai Chung (1998) *Transnational Corporations and Business Networks: Hong Kong Firms in the ASEAN Region*, London: Routledge.

Yeung, Henry Wai Chung (2000) "Limits to the Growth of Family-Owned Business? The Case of Chinese Transnational Corporations from Hong Kong," *Family Business Review*, 13: 55–70.

Yin, Robert K. (1994) *Case Study Research: Design and Methods*, 2nd ed., London: Sage Publications.

Yu, Tony Fu Lai (2001) "The Chinese Family Business as a Strategic System: An Evolutionary Perspective," *International Journal of Entrepreneurial Behavior and Research*, 7(1): 22–40.

Yu, Tony Fu-Lai and Shiu, Gary M. C. (2011) "A New Look at the Austrian School of Economics: Review and Prospects," *International Journal of Pluralism and Economic Education*, 2(2/June): 145–161.

Zheng, Victor Wan Tai (2010) *Chinese Family Business and the Equal Inheritance System: Unravelling the Myth*, London: Routledge.

Zheng, Victor Wan Tai and Wong, Siu Lun (2003) "The Positive and Negative Sides of Family Conflicts on Family Business: Chaozhou Family Enterprises in Hong Kong," *Proceedings of the 7th World Chinese Entrepreneurs Convention: The Associated Chinese Chambers of Commerce and Industry of Malaysia*, pp. 415–424.

Zheng, Victor Wan Tai and Wong, Siu Lun (2004) *A Study of the Chinese Family Enterprise in Hong Kong*, Ming Pao Publishing Ltd. (Text in Chinese)

Appendix 7.1

Kam's family tree

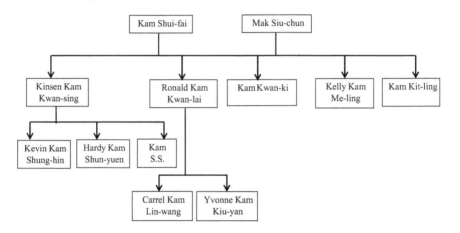

Source: Adapted from *Next Magazine* (2012a)

Appendix 7.2

Change in Yung Kee's shareholding

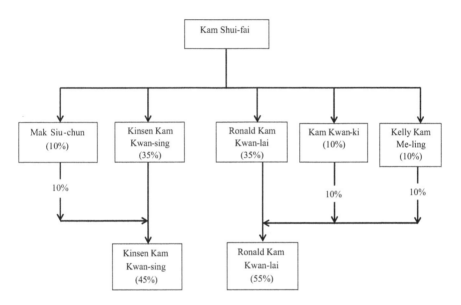

Source: Adapted from *Apple Daily* (2010)

8 An Austrian theory of competition and entrepreneurship

The supermarket war in Hong Kong

The neoclassical economic theory of market competition

The mainstream neoclassical economic theory of market competition has long been criticized (e.g., Hayek 1949: 92–106; Mises 1949/1966; Rothbard 1962/1993; Kirzner 1973: 7–9; High 1984/1985; Block et al. 2002). In particular, its assumptions associated with the perfect competition model do not depict the characteristics of the real world. When the assumptions are dropped, the neoclassical model of competition does not provide any useful conclusion about market behavior. Competition and production in the neoclassical paradigm is simply an exercise of choosing among known alternatives. The producer is assumed to be able to employ optimization techniques to reach a decision. In the neoclassical paradigm, there is no enterprising, clever strategy, innovation, or charisma and more seriously, no need for mutual information among individual participants in the market process (Baumol 1968: 68; Leibenstein 1968: 72; Kirzner 1985: 16). In essence, the mainstream neoclassical approach ignores knowledge and learning. Hayek (1949: 92) argues that "the theory of perfect competition has little claim to be called 'competition' at all, and that its conclusions are of little use as guides to policy." Based on the concept of perfect competition, mainstream neoclassical scholars condemn product differentiation, advertising, price discrimination, and innovation as "monopolistic" and thus as resource misallocation and socially undesirable (Armentano 1978: 96). Unfortunately, the model of perfect competition has often been used as the benchmark for policymaking, where policymakers maintain that it is the job of government to promote perfect competition. As a result, policymakers misuse the model as a normative benchmark in deciding what anti-monopoly actions should be taken. No wonder that "enthusiasm for perfect competition in theory and the support of monopoly in practice are . . . often found to live together" (Hayek 1949: 102).

During market competition, businesspeople formulate strategies in order to win. However, authors in analyzing firm strategy, notably Michael E. Porter (1980), largely follow the Structure-Conduct-Performance tradition.[1] Foss and Mahnke (2000) rightly point out that many of the shortcomings of traditional industrial organization concepts, such as homogeneous firms and decision makers, static and equilibrium analysis, with perfect competition as the yardstick for efficiency comparison, did in fact carry over to Porter's works. Economic models of strategy in neoclassical paradigms are generally static and equilibrium based and fail to cope with uncertainty (Foss et al. 1995).

The Austrian school of economics provides us with insight on market competition. However, its insights have seldom been applied in real world analysis. The aim of this chapter is to formulate a model of market competition and strategies based on the Austrian school of economics. This model will be applied to understand real world competition, namely the supermarket war in Hong Kong.

In what follows, an Austrian theory of market competition will be presented. This theory will be applied to understand the supermarket war in Hong Kong. In the next section, the development of supermarkets in Hong Kong is depicted. Then we present the pricing strategies and market power of the two supermarket giants in Hong Kong. The market power of the two giants is limited by the presence of substitute stores, which are able to sell cheaper products or provide better services than the two giants. The next section describes how the 759 Store, a new grocery and snack store, penetrates the supermarket networks by using new business strategies. The chapter concludes that without government restriction to entry, no firm can monopolize the market and abuse its market power. In a truly free open market, competition leads to discovery.

An Austrian theory of market competition

Austrian economics takes competition as a dynamic process involving change in knowledge and entrepreneurial learning (O'Driscoll and Rizzo 1985: 100). Unlike the perfect competition model, Austrian scholars argue that competition is a rivalrous process (Kirzner 2000: 225; Walker 2002). Each entrepreneur views all others as his or her enemies (Mises 1949/1966). In other words, there is a mutual awareness of market participants during competition (Kirzner 2000: 5).

A rivalrous process implies "the incentive of outstripping one's competitors in order to achieve market success" (Kirzner 2000: 225). Firms attempt to offer better products or service at a lower price than their competitors. Hence, entrepreneurs are on constant alert for opportunities (Kirzner 1973). They keep their eyes on the market trend, receive and interpret new information, and make new decisions. As Kirzner (2000: 227) puts it, "constantly looking over their shoulders, market participants are inspired alertly to notice and implement opportunities for offering superior options to the market." Because firms in the real world do not have perfect knowledge, they do not know what a successful competitive strategy is until they try it (Walker 2002). Hence, the competitive process involves entrepreneurial learning, knowledge interpretation, trial and error, and experimentation. As a result, new ways of doing things are discovered. Competition is a discovery process and is "important primarily as a discovery procedure whereby entrepreneurs constantly search for unexploited opportunities that can also be taken advantage of by others" (Hayek 2002: 18).

Due to the creativity of the human agent, the outcome of market competition is always a "surprise" (O'Driscoll and Rizzo 1985: 107). This is what Menger (1883/1985: 145) refers to as an unintended consequence of human action. Hayek

(2002: 10) rightly argues that "competition is important *only* because . . . its outcomes are unpredictable" (italics original).

Competition and monopoly power

During market competition, firms attempt to earn maximum profit by using their market power. Of course, they would like to be *the only seller* in the market if they could. "Only seller" means a single seller of any given good. In practice, it is very difficult for a firm to achieve the status of "only seller" in a market. On the one hand, a product offered for sale in the market by a firm always possesses some degrees of uniqueness. As Rothbard (1962/1993: 561–566) argues, "any difference (differentiation) in any two goods or resources and, more importantly, any consumer perceived difference in any two commodities or resources will make them unique (specific) goods." In subjectivist perspective, even "identical units" of some given stock might be regarded differently by potential users (Armentano 1978). Therefore, a firm always owns some degree of monopoly power.

On the other hand, in an open free market, no firm can be immunized from the competition itself. Though each firm possesses and sells some degree of unique products in the market, the entry into the market of similar goods or services is always possible (Kirzner 2000). Each firm can divert "the competitive, entrepreneurial process into other similar activities, employing other resources which create a 'turbulence' that surrounds and impinges upon the monopolist's, original activity" (Armentano 1978: 101). In conclusion, in a truly open market, no firm can abuse its market power. If a firm charges a higher price than it should, it can only do it temporarily. New firms can always move in and share the profit by charging lower prices with better service.

Finally, it is worth noting that the only source of monopoly comes from the government (O'Driscoll 1982: 189–214). Rothbard (1962/1993) and Armentano (1978) even take the property rights approach and focus on the many and varied ways in which governments create, foster, and maintain monopoly. For Armentano (1978: 108), a monopoly situation persists only if the government grants exclusive rights to a firm. Governmental monopoly or state restriction to entry "*always* restricts competition, *always* violates consumer (and producer) sovereignty, and *always* 'injures' consumer welfare" (italics original). Any anti-competitive legislation in the name of preserving market competition and protecting consumers' benefits can potentially lead to the opposite (negative) effect.

The development of supermarkets in Hong Kong

The first supermarket, Wellcome, was founded by three Chinese businessmen in Central in 1945. It sold imported liquor, confectionery, canned food, beverages, etc. In 1964, it was acquired by Jardine Matheson Holdings via the Dairy Farm International Group. It introduced the concept of the "self-service market." Customers did not require the assistance of the staff to get the products. They selected the products from the shelves and paid for them at the checkout counter. By the 1970s, there were around 30 supermarkets in Hong Kong. Most customers were expatriates from Britain, Commonwealth countries, and the United States, along with a small group of the local population who were familiar with the Western lifestyle (Ko 1981).

Most Hong Kong people at that time shopped at traditional stalls and hawkers. They bought rice in rice shops, oil in oil stores, and fresh vegetables and meats in wet markets. When the rice monopoly was abolished in 1974, supermarkets started to sell rice in sealed plastic bags cheaper than traditional rice shops (Gan 1995: 51). From the early 1970s, there was an expansion of the economy and a shortage in the labor force. More women started to work. As they did not have much time to do grocery shopping, they called for convenient shopping and fast preparation of home meals. From 1974 to 1985, "one-stop shopping" at supermarkets became a part of local culture (Ho 1999). The number of supermarkets increased to 200 stores by 1980 and to over 500 stores by 1990 (Williams 2007).

From the mid-1990s onward, hypermarkets were established. E-shopping and 24-hour supermarkets were also introduced. Different payment methods were allowed, such as cash, credit cards, smart cards, the Easy-Pay System, and vouchers. Reward points programs were implemented through membership schemes. In 2011, there were around 77 supermarkets in Hong Kong (Census and Statistics Department 2013). The two major supermarket chains, Wellcome and ParknShop, are owned by Hong Kong conglomerate companies. Wellcome is a member of Jardine Matheson Holdings and ParknShop is owned by the A. S. Watson Group under Hutchinson Whampoa Limited.[2] From 1993 to 2003, Wellcome and ParknShop increased the number of outlets by 29 percent (Consumer Council 2003a). In 2012, there were 305 and 257 Wellcome and ParknShop outlets, which represented 33.9 percent and 28.6 percent of the market share, respectively (Consumer Council 2013).

The market power and pricing strategies of the two giant supermarket chains

Wellcome and ParknShop occupy over 60 percent of the market share (see above). Hence, they enjoy strong market power in fixing product prices as well as bargaining power while dealing with manufacturers, suppliers, and agents. Given these advantages, there is no reason why they do not implement market strategies that can maximize their returns. It was reported that the two supermarket giants conduct price fixing, resale price maintenance, exclusive dealerships, tie-in sales, long-term supply contracts, incentive rebates, and collusive pricing (Consumer Council 1996, 2003b, 2013; Chinese University of Hong Kong 2007).[3] As a result, it is not surprising to find that some products, especially fast-moving consumer goods, are more expensive in the supermarkets than in other small retailers (e.g., Consumer Council 2003a; *South China Morning Post* 2012; *The Standard* 2013a).

Competing with rivals: predatory pricing

The two supermarket giants conduct predatory pricing to eliminate their rivals. Wellcome and ParknShop cut the prices as much as possible below cost and then increase the prices again, sometimes higher than before after rivals are removed.

In 1984, Wellcome and ParknShop introduced a big sale called an "anti-inflation scheme." They sold products cheaper than elsewhere. After the sale, more than 90 small supermarket outlets closed in two months (Gan 1995; Lee and Yeung 2005). In 1999, adMart, a Hong Kong direct marketing company, sold groceries below market prices through the Internet and phone orders and offered free delivery service. ParknShop reacted by reducing prices 10–50 percent (Tai 2002: 6). Encountering this, adMart sold parallel import goods but received customer complaints of poor quality (*Hong Kong Economic Journal* 2011); adMart eventually closed in 2000.

Enjoying special discount deals with suppliers

Possessing substantial market power, Wellcome and ParknShop ask for special discounts from suppliers that other retailers are not allowed to enjoy. In this way, supermarket giants lower some of their prices to attract customers. For instance, during the weekends, they offer discounts like "Red Hot Deals," "Buy Two Get One Free," and "Lowest Price Guarantee." Even though the advertised discounted price is a reduction in the normal retail price, the supermarket giants are able to obtain good profit margins because they obtain special discount deals from suppliers which other retail stores cannot enjoy. To prevent their rivals from reducing retail prices lower than theirs, the supermarket giants do not permit the suppliers to give the same discount deals to other shops. If suppliers violate their promise, the two giants will threaten not to sell their products in their chains (Consumer Council 1996, 2013; *Apple Daily* 2011b). For instance, Carrefour opened the first hypermarket in Hong Kong in 1996. It sold products at prices below those of Wellcome and ParknShop, but 22 suppliers refused to offer special discounts to Carrefour – only to the two giants (*Asia Times* 2003). Carrefour closed all four hypermarkets in 2000.

Slotting fees

Supermarkets decide the ways the products are displayed and when the products are removed from the shelves. For example, if a bottle of soft drink costs at HK$10, with an additional HK$2 for a slotting fee, each bottle will be sold at HK$15 in a supermarket where the profit margin is 20 percent (*Hong Kong Economic Journal* 2013b). It is reported that ParknShop charges a slotting fee of at least HK$1,500 for each product in one store (*Apple Daily* 2011c). There are also value-added fees for product packaging, advertising expenditure, store renovation, and remuneration (*Apple Daily* 2011c, 2013e; *The Standard* 2013b). As a result, it is no surprise that a supplier pays at least HK$200,000 of a product to the supermarket before making profit (*Apple Daily* 2013e). In recent years, the emergence of house brand products in major supermarkets raises another concern (Consumer Council 2013). Suppliers or manufacturers of branded products share product formulations and marketing strategies many months before the launching of the branded products. Supermarkets can change pricing, display-shelf allocation, and marketing strategies in favor of house brand products. Since both own-label products and branded products are so much alike and are substitutes, supermarkets have incentives to raise the prices of branded products, remove the branded products from the shelves, and launch house brand products.

Rebates from suppliers

Major supermarkets impose harsh trading terms on its suppliers. Suppliers give rebates to Wellcome and ParknShop. Flat rebates are given to the supermarkets based on the annual turnover. If sales exceed the agreed amount between super-markets and suppliers, incentive rebates will be offered. For a damaged goods allowance, suppliers are liable for damaged or unsold goods with a returned goods policy. They either reduce the prices for unsold goods or compensate supermarkets for damaged or unsold goods. A distribution allowance is charged for distributing the products from the warehouse to branch stores. To ensure cash flow, Wellcome and ParknShop settle payment to the suppliers over six months (Chew and Sun 2009). They make short delivery notice to keep inventory free. It is reported that ParknShop orders the stock at 9 a.m. and expects delivery by 3 p.m. on the same day (*The Standard* 2013b). Suppliers usually get the trucks ready all day long, and transport costs are 3 percent of their revenue (ibid).

The limit of market power

Even though the two supermarket giants attempt to maximize their profit by using various pricing tactics and business strategies, this does not mean that there is no limitation to the giants. As we have argued, if the market is truly open and free, no market participant will be able to abuse its market power. There are always substitutes in free market competition. In Hong Kong, there are many stores that compete with the two giants in certain ranges of products. These stores include limited-assortment grocery chains, convenience stores, local wet markets, and independent grocery retailers. These stores form a counterforce to limit the mar-ket power of the two giants so that the giants cannot charge higher prices, as they want. In other words, the two giants are constrained by market competition.

Limited-assortment grocery chains

Compared with large supermarket operators, limited-assortment grocery chain stores are located in local neighborhoods. They import products directly from for-eign suppliers to reduce transaction costs. For instance, the Kai Bo Food Super-market imports meat from South America, the United States, and Canada; seafood from Chile, Madagascar, Vietnam, and Norway; and fresh vegetables and fruit from mainland China (*Ming Pao* 2009). Other examples are the Dah Chong Hong (DCH) Food Mart, which focuses on the premium gourmet market, and Japanese confectionery chain stores such as Okashi Land and Aji Ichiban. These small gro-cery chain stores need not pay slotting fees or make exclusive deals with suppliers.

Convenience stores

Convenience stores operate 24 hours a day, 7 days a week. The two largest convenience stores are 7-Eleven, owned by the Dairy Farm, and Circle-K, owned by Fung Retailing (formerly Li & Fung Retailing). Convenience stores sell products which are usually bought for immediate or almost immediate consumption, such as beverages, confectioneries, etc. They also sell cup noodles and street foods such as fish balls and dim sum.

Local wet markets

Wet markets sell fresh fish, pork, beef, poultry, vegetables, and fruits. Before the emergence of supermarkets, Hong Kong people did their daily grocery shopping in wet markets. Even today, shopping in wet markets is an indispensable daily routine for many homemakers because Hong Kong people prefer fresh meats to frozen meats (Goldman et al. 1999; Consumer Council 2003b). Moreover, in wet markets, shopkeepers give warm and friendly service. They are enthusiastic to share information with customers on how to make great dishes with raw ingredients. In contrast, salespeople in supermarkets are as cool as vending machines. Their jobs are to organize the products and refill empty shelves, as well as facilitate the purchasing process (Choi 2010). Hence, wet markets are regarded as substitutes to supermarkets.

Independent grocery retailers

Independent grocery retailers are small family-owned businesses, including grocery shops, bakeries, and traditional drug stores.[4] They sell low-end grocery items in the neighborhood till late. They differentiate themselves from supermarket chains by forming a friendly relationship with the neighborhood (*Apple Daily* 2011d). In particular, drug stores are well known for their much lower prices for detergents, tissues, diapers, and health products. Most families buy these necessity goods from them. A summary of the competitive edges of the substitutes of the two supermarket giants is given in Table 8.1.

Table 8.1 Substitutes to the two supermarket giants

Substitutes to the two supermarket giants	Competitive edges
Limited-assortment grocery chains (e.g., Kai Bo Food Supermarket)	Lower prices for frozen meats, canned foods, and groceries
Convenience stores (7–11, Circle-K, VanGO)	24-hour operation, convenient locations
Local wet markets	Fresh fish, meats, and vegetables; friendly with neighborhood
Independent grocery retailers	Lower prices for detergents, tissues, diapers, and health products
Modern drug stores (e.g., Watsons, Mannings, Bonjour)	Professional advice on health care and medicine

Apart from the traditional wet markets, grocery retailers, and drug stores, there are also some newcomers which attempt to penetrate the retail market with new concepts. They intend to take the profit away from the well-established supermarket giants. One particular example is the 759 Store, which forms a threat to the two supermarket giants.

Enter the 759 Store[5]

The 759 Store was founded by the entrepreneur Mr. Lam Wai-chun (hereafter "Lam") in 2010. After working in the electronic component business for over 40 years, Lam closed his business in China and started a snack business in Hong Kong. Kirzner (1973: 39) argues that the role of entrepreneur "arises out of his alertness to hitherto unnoticed opportunities." Once the entrepreneur discovers the opportunity, he or she will exploit the profit margin by conducting arbitrageurship. Lam exemplifies Kirzner's theory of entrepreneurship. He attempted to fill in the market gap left by Wellcome and ParknShop. He exploited the price differentials, purchased products directly from foreign manufacturers, expanded the business in new markets, and adopted new marketing strategies. There are a total of 134 759 Stores in residential areas and railway stations in Hong Kong. From 2012 to 2013, 759 Stores' income increased 2.4 times to HK$810 million and operating profit increased 2.8 times to HK$11 million. Sales profit margin reached 31.4 percent (*Hong Kong Economic Journal* 2013d).

Exploiting price differentials

As mentioned above, the two supermarket giants cannot abuse their market power by selling at whatever prices they want. If the prices of the products are "too" high, new firms will move in to share the profit by exploiting price differentials. It is reported that the wholesale price of a unit of Japanese instant coffee was HK$3.42, but it was sold at HK$11 in Wellcome. Lam discovered that he was able to exploit price differentials by selling the coffee at HK$5.5 (*Apple Daily* 2013e). Similarly, for another brand of Japanese coffee, the 759 Store was able to sell it at a price 1.4 times lower than Wellcome and ParknShop (*Apple Daily* 2013d). Rice was a basic food in Hong Kong. The 759 Store was able to sell each bag of Vietnamese rice 25 percent lower than major supermarkets (*Apple Daily* 2013e). As a result, 400 bags of Vietnam rice were sold out in one day (*Ming Pao* 2013).

Since the 1980s, Japanese products have been well received by Hong Kong people.[6] Lam discovered that the wholesale prices from Japanese suppliers were 40–50 percent lower than the retail prices in supermarkets (*Hong Kong Economic Journal* 2013b). Lam then bypassed the middleman and bought goods directly from Japanese manufacturers. He established a dummy company in Japan and became a Japanese dealer. Hence, the 759 Store was able to import products directly from Japanese manufacturers by using bulk containers. As a result, the costs of his goods decreased between 16 and 20 percent (ibid). As the Japanese yen sharply depreciated in 2012, the costs of imported goods from Japan were further reduced. The 759 Store reduced the price of a pack of 5 Japanese instant noodles and Japanese instant coffee by 12 percent (*Apple Daily* 2013a). When people were enticed by cheaper Japanese food, the sales volume of Japanese snacks soared by 7–15 percent (*Hong Kong Economic Journal* 2013a). The 759 Store also imported Japanese groceries such as shampoo, toothpaste, and canned foods.

Competition is an endless dynamic process. As Korean culture went global, Lam started to sell Korean snacks and groceries. A pack of Korean cheese ramen (noodles) was about 38–70 percent cheaper in the 759 Store than in other supermarkets (*Apple Daily* 2013c).

By identifying profit opportunities and using the strategy of "small profit but quick turnover," the 759 Store was able to earn a gross profit of 37.5 percent, while the two supermarket giants earned gross profits ranging 40–50 percent on average (*Hong Kong Economic Journal* 2013b).[7] This means that new entrants are always possible, as long as the owners possess entrepreneurial minds.

Supermarket war: David versus Goliath

Like other supermarkets, the 759 Store has "recommended price agreements" on products with manufacturers and suppliers. In July 2011, Swire Coca-Cola HK Ltd. (hereafter "Swire"), the franchise of Coca-Cola in Hong Kong, increased the recommended wholesale price of the product from HK$2 to HK$2.2 and the market price from HK$2.7 to HK$3.0. The 759 Store saw that it could exploit the price discrepancy by selling Coke at a price lower than the major supermarket chains. Swire demanded the 759 Store to increase the price from HK$3.3 to HK$3.8 in August and October, respectively, of the same year. Lam refused to comply with the recommended retail prices set by Swire. As a result, Swire terminated business with the 759 Store. Similarly, the 759 Store was rejected for beverage supplies from other suppliers, such as the Four Seas Group and Vitasoy. Refusing to be controlled by huge chain stores (supermarkets and suppliers), the 759 Store introduced a "post–Coca-Cola" market strategy by importing soft drinks from Japan, Thailand, and Brazil (*Apple Daily* 2011a).

The Swire–759 Store event has brought a huge response from the community.[8] The case was widely reported in mass media, and the 759 Store was regarded by the community as "a store of conscience" against injustice. This brought huge publicity to the 759 Store. Since then, the 759 Store has been known to the community, and Lam took the opportunity to expand.

With this good public image, the 759 Store expanded into the Japanese snack market. Seeing this, major supermarkets and convenience stores reduced their prices of Japanese snack items too. When these counterparts reduced prices too much, Lam then moved into other products to avoid direct price wars with rivals (*Apple Daily* 2013b). It was like a guerrilla strategy. The 759 Store kept on exploring new products which revealed huge price differentials in the market. For example, it imported Chinese rice noodles and pork luncheon meat, chilled and frozen food, oil, condiments, and fresh vegetables. It opened Japanese-style mini-markets in residential areas. Furthermore, it utilized a membership system to promote sales and built up customer loyalty. Consumers were given membership the first time they visited the shop. The membership offered 10 percent off an in-store purchase anytime. On the weekends and other specific days/period, members were given extra discounts (*Hong Kong Economic Journal* 2013c). When customers believed they could buy cheaper in the 759 Store than in the giant supermarket chains, they would continue to shop at the 759 Store and become routine customers.

In short, with entrepreneurial spirit, Lam created the 759 Store and a brand new shopping experience to compete with the two supermarket giants in Hong Kong. From the establishment of the first store in 2010, the number of 759 Stores expanded into 163 branches. The 759 Store exercises as a force to limit the supermarket giants' market power. The story of the 759 Store testifies that without any government entry restriction, under a truly open free market, no firm can abuse its market power. With entrepreneurial spirit and by providing better service at cheaper prices, firms with new and better ways of doing things can always eliminate inefficient firms. The phenomenon is consistent with Hayek's argument that "competition is a discovery process."

Conclusion

This chapter has applied the Austrian theory of market competition to interpret the supermarket war in Hong Kong. It focuses on the market process in which groceries and retail stores are fully aware of their rivals. In the dynamic competitive process, entrepreneurs or shop owners are active, creative, and strategic. To achieve business success, they explore new alternatives and invent new methods with an incentive to outperform others. The process involves entrepreneurial learning, knowledge acquisition, trial and error, and experimentation. As a result of competition, new ideas and discoveries in supermarket businesses emerge and bring "surprises" to the market. This chapter concludes that in a free open market without government entry restriction, supermarkets or grocery stores cannot abuse market power by charging unreasonable "high" prices for their products. If they do, new entrants or rivals can always join in and take profit away by providing better but cheaper service to customers. The confrontation between two supermarket giants in Hong Kong, namely ParknShop and Wellcome, and a new entrant, namely the 759 Store, testifies to the Austrian theory of market competition.

Notes

1 The neoclassical theory of market competition adopts the Structure-Conduct-Performance paradigm (SCP) put forward by Edward Mason (1939) and his student Joe S. Bain (1951, 1956); F. M. Scherer (1970; and with D. Ross 1990).
2 In 2013, it was reported that Hutchinson Whampoa decided to sell the ParknShop chain (*Wall Street Journal* 2013).
3 Whether these tactics are harmful or beneficial to the societies is still controversial, and we do not intend to discuss that here.
4 Modern drug stores such as Watsons, Mannings, and Bonjour are chain stores owned by giant retailers.

5 The 759 Store originated from the stock code of its mother company, CEC International Holdings, in the Hong Kong Stock Exchange. In Chinese, the 759 Store is called 759 Oshin House. *Oshin* is a famous Japanese television drama in the 1980s. The story was based on a biography of a Japanese woman who overcame hardships during her lifetime.

6 With the philosophy of Kaizen ("continuous improvement"), Japanese goods were acclaimed for quality control, design, and marketing. Hong Kong people, especially the young and women, were willing to buy Japanese goods at higher prices.

7 For popular products, supermarkets earned gross profits of 60–100 percent (*Apple Daily* 2013f).

8 A group of Hong Kong students called in social media for a boycott of Swire Coca-Cola Hong Kong's drinks. As a result, more than 77,000 people signed up in the first three days (*South China Morning Post* 2011).

References

Apple Daily (2011a, October 27) "Swire Coca-Cola HK Ltd Demands to Increase the Price from HK$2.7 to HK$3.8 and Terminates Business with 759 Store," http://hk.apple.nextmedia.com/news/art/20111027/15745056; retrieved 20 August 2013. (Text in Chinese)

Apple Daily (2011b, November 14) "Demand Compensation from the Suppliers: ParknShop Reveals Their Power," http://hk.apple.nextmedia.com/news/art/20111114/15798567; retrieved 11 September 2013. (Text in Chinese)

Apple Daily (2011c, November 15) "Senior Management Makes Money in Many Ways: How ParknShop Exploits the Suppliers," http://hk.apple.nextmedia.com/news/art/20111115/15802206; retrieved 6 September 2013. (Text in Chinese)

Apple Daily (2011d, November 24) "Supermarket Giant Rips off the Lower Class: ParknShop Opens a Frozen Food Store in the Street Market and Local People Must Boycott," http://hk.apple.nextmedia.com/news/art/20111124/15830345; retrieved 11 September 2013. (Text in Chinese)

Apple Daily (2013a, February 7) "Yen Falls Sharply in 5 Months, Hong Kong People Rush to Buy Japanese Goods," http://hk.apple.nextmedia.com/news/art/20130207/18159338; retrieved 22 October 2013. (Text in Chinese)

Apple Daily (2013b, May 10) "Rapid Expansion: 759 Stores Takes over ParknShop's Shop Tenancy," http://hk.apple.nextmedia.com/news/art/20130510/18255161; retrieved 9 September 2013. (Text in Chinese)

Apple Daily (2013c, May 12) "759 Store Fights Back by offering 30% Discount and Sells Chinese Rice Noodles," http://hk.apple.nextmedia.com/news/art/20130512/18257246; retrieved 9 September 2013. (Text in Chinese)

Apple Daily (2013d, May 13) "759 Store Competes with Supermarkets by Entering Non-staple Food Market such as Sauteed Fish with Black Beans," http://hk.apple.nextmedia.com/news/art/20130513/18258250; retrieved 26 October 2013. (Text in Chinese)

Apple Daily (2013e, May 20) "759 Store Sells Rice at 26% Cheaper than Supermarkets," http://hk.apple.nextmedia.com/news/art/20130520/18265665; retrieved 9 September 2013. (Text in Chinese)

Apple Daily (2013f, May 20) "When Rivals Are in Trouble, Housewives Applause," http://hk.apple.nextmedia.com/news/art/20130520/18265667; retrieved 9 September 2013. (Text in Chinese)

Armentano, D. T. (1978) "A Critique of Neoclassical and Austrian Monopoly Theory," in Louis M. Spadaro (ed.) *New Directions in Austrian Economics*, Kansas City, MO: Sheed Andrews and McMeel, pp. 94–110.

Asia Times (2003) "The 'Freest Economies in the World,'" www.atimes.com/atimes/Asian_Economy/EG12Dk01.html; retrieved 11 September 2013.

Bain, Joe S. (1951) "Relation of Profit Rate to Concentration: American Manufacturing, 1936–1940," *Quarterly Journal of Economics*, 65(3): 293–324.

Bain, Joe S. (1956) *Barriers to New Competition: Their Character and Consequences in Manufacturing*, Cambridge, MA: Harvard University Press.

Baumol, W. J. (1968) "Entrepreneurship in Economic Theory," *American Economic Review Papers and Proceedings*, 58: 64–71.

Block, Walter; Barnett, William II; and Wood, Stuart (2002) "Austrian Economics, Neoclassical Economics, Marketing and Finance," *Quarterly Journal of Austrian Economics*, 5(2/Summer): 51–66.

Census and Statistics Department (2013) *Key Statistics on Business Performance and Operating Characteristics of the Import/Export, Wholesale and Retail Trades, and Accommodation and Food Services Sectors in 2011*, Hong Kong: Census and Statistics Department.

Chew, Matthew M. and Sun, Lai Ngun (2009) "Retailer-Supplier Relationship in Hong Kong: Asymmetry, Power Play, and Supply-Chain Management," *International Journal of Business and Management*, 4(8): 3–10.

Chinese University of Hong Kong (2007) "Press Releases: CUHK Marketing Department Survey on Hong Kong's Retailing Industry Reveals that Unfair Practices Generally Exist in Supplier/Retailer Relationship," www.cpr.cuhk.edu.hk/en/press_detail.php?1=1&id=710; retrieved 13 September 2013.

Choi, Jackson (2010, November 3) "Shopping Experience at Wet Market vs Supermarket," http://jacksonchoi.com/archives/307; retrieved 21 January 2014.

Consumer Council (1996) *Competition Policy: The Key to Hong Kong's Future Economic Success*, Hong Kong: Consumer Council.

Consumer Council (2003a) "Competition in the Foodstuffs and Household Necessities Retailing Sector," www.consumer.org.hk/website/ws_en/competition_issues/competition_studies/20030811supermkt.html; retrieved 5 September 2013.

Consumer Council (2003b) "Press Release: Wet Markets Are in Danger of Gradual Decline Which Could Have Serious Implications to Consumers in the Competitive Choices of Foodstuffs and Household Necessities in General and Fresh Produce in Particular," www.consumer.org.hk/website/ws_en/news/press_releases/WetMarkets20030811. html; retrieved 12 September 2013.

Consumer Council (2013) *Grocery Market Study: Market Power of Supermarket Chains under Scrutiny*, Hong Kong: Hong Kong Consumer Council.

Foss, N. J.; Knudsen, C.; and Montgomery, C. A. (1995) "An Exploration of Common Ground: Integrating Evolutionary and Strategic Theories of the Firm," in C. A. Montgomery (ed.) *Resource-Based and Evolutionary Theories of the Firm: Towards a Synthesis*, Boston: Kluwer, pp. 1–17.

Foss, Nicolai and Mahnke, Volker (2000) "Strategy Research and the Market Process Perspective," in Jackie Krafft (ed.) *The Process of Competition*, Cheltenham: Edward Elgar, pp. 117–142.

Gan, Changqiu (1995) *Supermarkets in Hong Kong: A New Trend of Retailing*, Hong Kong: Commercial Press. (Text in Chinese)

Goldman, Arieh; Krider, Robert; and Ramaswami, S. (1999) "The Persistent Competitive Advantage of Traditional Food Retailers in Asia: Wet Markets' Continued Dominance in Hong Kong," *Journal of Macromarketing*, 19(2): 126–139.

Hayek, F. A. (1949) "The Meaning of Competition," in *Individualism and Economic Order*, London: Routledge.

Hayek, F. A. (2002) "Competition as a Discovery Procedure," *Quarterly Journal of Austrian Economics*, 5(3/Fall): 9–23.

High, Jack (1984/1985) "Bork's Paradox: Static vs. Dynamic Efficiency in Antitrust Analysis," *Contemporary Policy Issues*, 3: 21–34.

Ho, Suk-Ching (1999) "Supermarkets in Hong Kong – in Search of an Eventual State?" *Journal of International Consumer Marketing*, 12(1): 73–89.

Hong Kong Economic Journal (2011, November 4) "Agents Maximize the Profit. Anti-Monopoly Specialist Calls for Not Selling Coca-Cola," www.hkej.com/template/daily news/jsp/detail.jsp?dnews_id=3243&cat-id=2&title_id=468920; retrieved 20 August 2013. (Text in Chinese)

Hong Kong Economic Journal (2013a, April 15) "Good Business in Japanese Snack Shops," www.hkej.com/template/dailynews/jsp/detail.jsp?dnews_id=3672&cat_id= 1&title_id=588909; retrieved 20 August 2013. (Text in Chinese).

Hong Kong Economic Journal (2013b, August 5) "759 Store's Boss Exercises 'Small Businesses against Large Enterprises' Strategy," www.hkej.com/template/dailynews/jsp/ detail.jsp?dnews_id=3775&cat_id=2&title_id=617484; retrieved 9 September 2013. (Text in Chinese)

Hong Kong Economic Journal (2013c, August 20) "The Boss of 759 Store Depicts a New Era after Hutchison Whampoa Sells ParknShop," www.hkej.com/template/dailynews/ jsp/detail.jsp?dnews_id=3788&cat_id=9&title_id= 621190&txtSearch; retrieved 20 August 2013. (Text in Chinese)

Hong Kong Economic Journal (2013d, July 30) "Looking into the Operation of ParknShop' from 759 Side," www.hkej.com/template/dailynews/jsp/detail.jsp?dnews_id= 3770&cat_id=4&title_id=616126&txtSearch; retrieved 20 August 2013. (Text in Chinese)

Kirzner, I. M. (1973) *Competition and Entrepreneurship*, Chicago: University of Chicago Press.

Kirzner, I. M. (1985) *Discovery and the Capitalist Process*, Chicago: University of Chicago Press.

Kirzner, I. M. (2000) *The Driving Force of the Market: Essays in Austrian Economics*, London: Routledge.

Ko, K. K. (1981, May 11) "Development of Retailing in Hong Kong: Part One," *Hong Kong Economic Weekly*, pp. 14–15.

Lee, Shu-Kam and Yeung, Wai-Man (2005) *The Impact of the Conglomerate on Market Economy: The Case of the Supermarkets in Hong Kong*, Hong Kong: Hong Kong Shue Yan College.

Leibenstein, H. (1968) "Entrepreneurship and Development," *American Economic Review*, 58: 72–83.

Mason, E. (1939) "Price and Production Policies of Large-Scale Enterprise," *American Economic Review*, 29(1): 61–74.

Menger, Carl (1883/1985) *Investigations into the Method of the Social Sciences with Special Reference to Economics*, New York: NYU Press.

Ming Pao (2009, October 8) "Kai Bo Combines the Supermarket Functions with Wet Market to Avoid Direct Confrontation with Supermarket Giants," www.mpfinance. com/htm/Finance/20091008/News/fz_fza1.htm; retrieved 14 October 2013. (Text in Chinese)

Ming Pao (2013, May 25) "759 Store Sells Sauteed Fish with Black Beans at Cheaper Price Tomorrow," http://life.mingpao.com/cfm/dailynews3b.cfm?File=20130525/nalgo/gol1. txt; retrieved 9 September 2013. (Text in Chinese)

Mises, Ludwig von (1949/1966) *Human Action: A Treatise on Economics*, Chicago: Henry Regnery.

O'Driscoll, G. P. Jr (1982) "Monopoly in Theory and Practice," in I. M. Kirzner (ed.) *Method, Process, and Austrian Economics*, Lexington, MA: Lexington Books, pp. 189–213.

O'Driscoll, G. P. Jr. and Rizzo, M. (1985) *The Economics of Time and Ignorance*, Oxford: Blackwell.

Porter M. E. (1980) *Competitive Strategy: Techniques for Analyzing Industries and Competitors*, New York: Free Press.

Rothbard, Murray N. (1962/1993) *Man, Economy, and State*, Auburn, AL: Mises Institute.

Scherer, F. (1970) *Industrial Market Structure and Economic Performance*, Boston, MA: Houghton Mifflin.

Scherer, F. and Ross, D. (1990) *Industrial Market Structure and Economic Performance*, 3rd ed., Boston, MA: Houghton Mifflin.

South China Morning Post (2011, December 6) "Fizzy Drink's Price Sparks Debate," www.scmp.com/article/986981/fizzy-drinks-price-sparks-debate; retrieved 17 December 2013.

South China Morning Post (2012, April 12) "Fix Is on Supermarket Shelves, Study Suggests," www.scmp.com/article/998034/fix-supermarket-shelves-study-suggests; retrieved 5 September 2013.

Tai, Susan H. C. (2002) "Supermarket Cyber Storm: Where adMart Went Wrong," *Asian Case Research Journal*, 6(1): 1–13.

The Standard (2013a, April 16) "Supermarkets Told to Give Shoppers a Break," www.the standard.com.hk/news_detail.asp?pp_cat=30&art_id=132877&sid=39484482&con_type=1; retrieved 5 September 2013.

The Standard (2013b, August 26) "Suppliers Fear Being Squeezed," www.thestandard.com.hk/news_detail.asp?pp_cat=30&art_id=136853&sid=40230959&con_type=1; retrieved 24 September 2013.

Walker, Deborah (2002) "Austrian Economics," *Concise Encyclopedia of Economics*, www.econlib.org/library/Enc1/AustrianEconomics.html; retrieved 7 January 2014.

Wall Street Journal (2013, July 20) "Hutchison Whampoa Confirms Plans to Sell Hong Kong Grocery Chain," http://online.wsj.com/article/SB10001424127887324448104578616930593671260.html; retrieved 7 October 2013.

Williams, M. (2007) "The Supermarket Sector in China and Hong Kong: A Tale of Two Systems," *Competition Law Review*, 3(2): 251–268.

9 The co-evolution of culture and technology

The oyster sauce empire of Lee Kum Kee

Introduction

> Building a cultural bridge between East and West with our sauce products.
>
> Lee Kum Kee's vision[1]

Hong Kong is a Chinese society. Soy sauce is an important ingredient in preparing Cantonese cuisine. After a century of development, four big Chinese companies emerged in Hong Kong's soy sauce market, namely Lee Kum Kee (oyster sauce), Pat Chun (sweetened vinegar and soy sauce), Tung Chun (soy sauce), and Amoy (soy sauce). Competition in the soy sauce market, both local and overseas, is keen. In particular, Amoy is the major competitor of Lee Kum Kee in soy sauce. This paper examines how Lee Kum Kee, a traditional sauce brewer, has evolved into a global manufacturer. It will argue that Lee Kum Kee is able to adapt to the rapidly changing economy in two major areas, namely culture and technology. Successful adaptation to the changing Chinese culture and new technologies in the sauce processing industry allow the company to occupy a major market in the world.[2] In what follows, we shall examine the roles that technology and culture play in strategic management, followed by a discussion of methodology. The background of Lee Kum Kee is given in the next section. Then the empirical analysis of the relationship between Chinese culture and technology in the business strategies of Lee Kum Kee will be presented. The last section is the conclusion.

The roles of culture and technology in business strategy formulation

This paper argues that culture and technology influencing each other imposes impacts on business strategy formulation and adoption. First, the role of culture on technology adoption is considered. Culture is defined by Mitchell (2000: 4) as "a set of learned core values, beliefs, standards, knowledge, morals, laws and behaviours shared by individuals and societies that determines how an individual acts, feels and views oneself and others." In the management of technology literature, scholars have developed a "Technology Adoption Model" (Davis 1989) to explain how users come to accept and adopt a technology. The model suggests that when users are presented with a new technology, two major factors influence their decision about how and when they will use it, namely "perceived usefulness" and "perceived ease-of-use." Davis (1989: 320) defines "perceived usefulness" as "the degree to which a person believes that using a particular system would enhance his or her job performance" and "perceived ease-of-use" as "the degree to which a person believes that using a particular system would be free from effort." The original TAM is conceived largely as a framework for explaining decision making by an individual person. However, much of human behavior is not best characterized by an individual acting in isolation. Venkatesh et al. (2003) argue that where the "basic concept underlying user acceptance models" is highlighted, it is explicitly stated that decisions and usage are initiated by "individual reactions to using information technology" (Venkatesh et al. 2003: 427). Bagozzi (2007) suggests considering group, cultural, or social aspects of technology acceptance. Ward and Kennedy (1999) examine the effect of culture on technology. They define sociocultural aspects of technology as "the ability to fit in to acquire culturally appropriate skills and to negotiate interactive aspects of the host environment" (Ward and Kennedy 1999: 660). They identify a list of encounters and issues that may be relevant to sociocultural adjustment. A brief sample of their 29-item scale includes "making friends," "using the transport system," "going shopping," "dealing with unsatisfactory service," "getting used to the local food/ finding food you enjoy," "dealing with people in authority," and "understanding the locals' world view" (Ward and Kennedy 1999: 663).

We can further argue that business strategies are formulated according to the entrepreneurs' stocks of knowledge, which in turn are based on their everyday life experiences. Since everyday life experience is culturally based, culture affects entrepreneurs' decisions on the adoption of new technology. Culture can impede or facilitate the adoption of new technology. For example, during the late Ch'ing dynasty, the economy of imperial China was predominantly agricultural and the society was generally closed to the outside world. Cultural triumphalism and moral superiority made China a reluctant improver and bad learner (Landes 1999: 336). As a result, foreign science, astrology, and technologies were regarded by Chinese officials and mandarins as miseries, absurdities, and evils and therefore should be warded off (Guo 1986: 34). Unlike China, Japan's ancestors came from several countries. Different cultures were subsequently "remixed" in Japan to fit local needs and tastes. Hence, Japanese did not reject foreign technologies. Instead, during the Meiji period, Japanese actively learned foreign technologies. The government employed more than 3,000 foreign experts in science, engineering, the army, navy, and English language. It also dispatched many Japanese students to Europe and America to learn foreign technologies. The willingness to learn and adopt new technologies is a key factor for latecomers to compete successfully in the global market.

On the other hand, technology can change the traditional mindset of people in general and organizational culture in particular. New technology and novel events bring about conflicts of knowledge in entrepreneurs' minds. Two results may occur. The entrepreneur either resists the new technology and events by condemning them as vice or deviance or adapts to them by modifying his/her ways of thinking. Those entrepreneurs who resist new ideas do not catch up with the changing world and are doomed to fail. A reason why businesspeople refuse to change is inertia. Resistance to change is fundamentally associated with mentality and thinking. In other words, agents see things in a certain way and expect things to be worked out in a certain way. Once incoming information is organized into a (mental) pattern, then a habit develops. The entrepreneur simply interprets the incoming event routinely. Resistance to change means that his or her thinking is locked up in the old concept and culture (deBono 1992: 17). Given new technology, most entrepreneurs will learn to adopt new methods by trial and error and experimentation. Encountering uncertainty, they will cope with their knowledge deficiency by creating temporary expectations which serve as "knowledge surrogates" (White 1977: 80). These knowledge surrogates, if they work, will be adopted and routinized as a rule of thumb, resulting in cultural evolution.

An interpretative method by storytelling and case study

We adopt the interpretative approach to explain the business success of a Chinese family firm.[3] According to Buchanan and Bryman (2007: 486), an interpretative discourse "regards sense-making individuals as engaged participants, as co-creators of social structures, using ethnographic and hermeneutic methods to establish local meanings grounded in social and organizational practices." The interpretative approach means that it is preferable to use storytelling in empirical analysis.[4] Storytelling via case studies allows a deep understanding of the issues over time. Yin (1994: 9) argues that the case study is a preferable empirical strategy "when a 'how' and 'why' question is being asked about a contemporary set of events over which the investigator has little control or no control."[5] Data and materials in this study rely largely on secondary sources, including the Lee Kum Kee website, newspapers, magazines, and trade journals. In the next section, we shall examine the extent to which business strategies of Lee Kum Kee are influenced by the changes in culture and technology.

Background of Lee Kum Kee

Lee Kum Kee has been a Chinese family business in the sauce industry for 125 years. Mr. Lee Kum-sheung invented oyster sauce and established the Lee Kum Kee Oyster Oil Workshop in Nanshui, Guangdong, China in 1888. Unfortunately, the factory was destroyed by fire in 1902. Lee then moved to Macau and continued his business. After he died in 1920, his three sons inherited Lee Kum Kee.[6] After Lee Shiu-tang, the second son of Senior Lee, expanded oyster sauce production to Hong Kong in 1932, Lee Kum Kee became a renowned Chinese family enterprise. During the 1970s, Lee Man-tat, the eldest son of Lee Shiu-tang, took over the company. In the 1980s, the fourth generation of the Lees joined Lee Kum Kee after graduating from universities in the United States.[7] Taking advantage of the Closer Economic Partnership Arrangement (CEPA)[8] signed between mainland China and Hong Kong in 2003, Lee Kum Kee expanded into mainland China's traditional health service and herbal markets because these areas obtain a lot of benefits from CEPA (Cabrillac 2004: 6). Specifically, the company collaborates with Southern Medical University in China to develop Chinese natural and herbal foods (Wu and Du 2004). Nowadays, Lee Kum Kee produces over 220 different sauces and condiments serving over 100 countries and regions around the world. Its annual revenue amounted to HK$1 billion (*South China Morning Post* 2003). In 2012, there were more than 8,000 staff in mainland China, North America, Europe, and Southeast Asia (*South China Morning Post* 2012a). The headquarters of the company is in Hong Kong. There are five production plants – in Hong Kong, Xinhui, Huangpu, Malaysia, and Los Angeles. In 2009, Lee Kum Kee produced 24,000 bottles of sauces each hour.[9] The plant in Xinhui is equipped with 2,000 soy sauce fermentation tanks, each of which holds 60 tons in capacity (ibid). Lee Kum Kee met stringent international food quality and safety standards. It achieved ISO9002 and ISO9001:2008 certifications. All factories were accredited by HACCP in food safety.[10] After sauces passed ISO and HACCP quality control, they were put in a fully automated production cycle and packed in bottles for sale. Each product was analyzed for freshness, viscosity, and salinity. Food organoleptic tests were conducted to ensure natural sauce flavor. By automatic production and scientific tests, Lee Kum Kee increased productivity, food quality, and safety.

Lee Kum Kee, being run by the fourth generation, has transformed from a traditional Chinese sauce producer to a modern global food product leader. It won many awards in products, management, and social responsibility.[11] Lee Kum Kee gained the following awards (Lee Kum Kee 2010):

- Most Favorable Enterprise with Good Credibility in 2008
- Most Favorable Hong Kong Brands in 2008
- Trusted Brand – Gold Medal in 2010
- Most Favorite Brand in the Sauce and Condiment Industry in 2011
- Greater Chain Sauce Manufacturer Brand Award in 2009
- The Grocer UK Food and Drink Gold Award for Double Deluxe Soy in 2010.

Pertaining to corporate social responsibility, Lee Kum Kee was presented "Best Employer in China and Best Employer in Asia" (2007), "Corporate Award" (2008), "China Charity Award – Most Caring Charity Individual Award" (2008), and "The Second Outstanding CSR Enterprise Award" (2013). It was named as the "Caring Company" for 11 consecutive years. As claimed by Lee Kum Kee, "wherever there are people, there are Lee Kum Kee products."[12]

Impact of culture on Lee Kum Kee's production, trade practice, corporate governance, and branding

Cultural characteristics have been found to be related to the implementation of advanced manufacturing technologies (McDermott and Stock 1999). In this section, we shall examine the impact of culture on Lee Kum Kee's operation in four

major areas, namely oyster sauce production, trade practice, corporate governance, and marketing strategies.

Oyster sauce production in the traditional Chinese way

China has a long history of culinary skills. There is a popular saying that "fashion
is in Europe, living is in America, but eating is in China" (Lin 2000). However,
Chinese people in general are not concerned with nutrition as much as their European counterparts. Instead, Chinese people are more concerned with the food's
texture, flavor, color, and aroma. Cooking foods with proper sauce is very important in Chinese tradition. As Confucius said, "do not eat if food is not served with
proper sauce." Therefore, Chinese cuisine is sauce oriented. A right sauce makes
the perfect harmony of aroma and taste of food. Soy sauce came into being in
China sometime between the 3rd and 5th centuries. However, oyster sauce did
not appear in China till Lee Kum-sheung's innovation. In traditional Chinese wisdom, "if people live by the hillside, then they eat whatever can be found in the
wood. If people live by the sea, then they eat whatever can be found in the water."
People in South China coastal areas relied on fisheries. In particular, Nanshui
(Guangdong, China) was suitable for oyster farming. Back in the 1880s, people in
Nanshui had already been familiar with the skills of cooking fresh oysters in brine
and then turned them into dried oysters so that they could sell preserved oysters
in the market. Lee Kum-sheung owned one of these small workshops. His skills
inherited from his parents were native and naïve. The invention of oyster sauce
by Lee Kum-sheung is often described as purely by chance. However, it may be
more correct to say that the discovery of oyster sauce was associated with Chinese
culture. One day in 1888, Lee cooked oysters in a Chinese big wok and attempted
to turn them into dried oysters. He forgot to remove the big wok from the wood
fire and left oyster soup in the wok on a dying fire. In the next morning, he discovered that the broth had become a rich dark brown sauce with a strong natural
oyster aroma, and hence the birth of oyster sauce. Without scientific research or
modern food processing techniques, Lee, with his entrepreneurial spirit, manufactured and sold his unique oyster sauce to fellow villagers in ceramic jars. He
received encouraging feedback from customers. Lee initiated a cultural sauce in
China. When Lee Kum Kee moved to Macau, oyster sauce manufacturing was
still native and labor intensive, although food processing techniques in the West
had improved tremendously. By the 1970s, the recipe of making oyster sauce in
Lee Kum Kee remained unchanged. One kilogram of oyster sauce was made of 10
kilograms of oysters. Fresh oyster spats were placed in a cultch and then moved
to oyster farms for growing. Immediately after the harvest, fresh oysters were
cleaned and fermented in barrels. Oyster extract was flavored with soy sauce, salt,
sugar, and cornstarch (*ChinaPress* 2010).

Impact of Chinese culture on trade practice and selling style

Lee Kum Kee advocated the concept of "considering others' interests" (*Si Li Ji
Jen*). Based on the Confucian teaching of 'Jen',[13] Senior Lee, the founder, thought

that entrepreneurs who pursued profits should also consider the interests of other people. Lee was regarded as a role model of integrity, honesty, and doing good for society (Zou 2010: 59–60). For instance, when customers were unable to pay back loans, Lee wrote off all credits after the Chinese New Year. He did not want to increase the financial burden of the customers.

Lee Man-tat followed the same traditional Chinese values as his grandfather. During the mid-1980s, a Malaysian factory produced oyster sauce using a trademark logo which made out to be Lee Kum Kee's Panda brand (Zou 2010: 75). Lee Kum Kee filed a trademark infringement lawsuit against the Malaysian factory and the related 18 supermarkets selling the product. Lee Kum Kee won the court battle. The supermarkets were ordered to pay compensation to Lee Kum Kee. Instead of taking the compensation, Lee Kum Kee proposed to the 18 supermarkets that they sell authentic Lee Kum Kee products in their stores. The supermarkets were stunned by the proposal but later glad to sell Lee Kum Kee's products. As consumers bought authentic Lee Kum Kee products in these 18 supermarkets, the supermarkets increased their profits. Lee Kum Kee expanded the market in Malaysia. In this way, it is consistent with the Chinese saying that "what benefits yourself also benefits your trading partner."

Cultural impact on corporate governance

The first three generations of Lee Kum Kee received little formal education and they managed the family business in a very traditional way. They followed their ancestors' teachings, namely Confucianism and paternalism. They managed their enterprise like a family (Redding 1990). The first three generations of Lee Kum Kee's bosses exhibited a strong sense of responsibility towards employees that was not only economic but also moral. They felt that they had an obligation to look after their staffs' welfare (Redding 1990: 61). If a member of the staff misbehaved, they had the obligation to teach the staff member as a child by family rules. They used traditional Confucian values, namely filial piety, face, and *renqing* to ensure their that heirs/staff lived up to family expectations as well as conformed to the goals of the family business (Redding 1990: 101). The company also relied on blood relationship to promote and stimulate the staff's incentive to work for the company (Zheng and Chow 2013).

When Lee Kum Kee was managed by the fourth generation, the company still kept the virtue of Chinese values with a modification of business management. Both Eddy and Sammy Lee, the two sons of Lee Man-tat, joined Lee Kum Kee after graduating from university in the United States. They designed a new family business management by mixing the good of traditional family values with modern culture.

The traditional family value that "family is more important than oneself" permeated Lee Kum Kee's fourth generation's management. However, for the sake of family business continuity, Sammy Lee and his siblings formulated the new management model in Lee Kum Kee. The new Family Constitution was made to be valid to the fourth generation and beyond. It advocated the principle of "'We' is larger than 'I.'" It stated "3 don'ts," i.e., don't get divorced, don't marry too late, and don't take a concubine. Only those with a consanguinous relationship to the Lee family had the right to inherit shares of the Lee Kum Kee business (Li et al. 2011: 53). Family shareholders could only make an internal transfer of shares within the family in case of a withdrawal. The Family Constitution maintained the core traditional Chinese family values generation after generation.

Branding the products in Chinese style

In the early years, without any foreign marketing concept, selling oyster sauce was governed by traditional Chinese culture. At that time, business trust relied on the name of the shop. Hence, if a signboard was painted in a golden color, it would reflect the goodwill of the shop (Yim and Mark 2005: 65). Lee Kum Kee was a traditional Chinese workshop which sold oyster sauce and groceries. Lee Kum-sheung named his shop Lee Kum Kee.[14] At the very beginning, a wooden signboard was hung outside the workshop. This brand name went through 125 years, and Lee's oyster sauce is a famous cultural food in China. A company logo is not only a symbol, but also represents the firm's determination to build a familiar brand of sauces around the globe (Slater 1999: 60).

On the old label of the Lee Kum Kee oyster sauce bottle, a traditional Chinese woman held a "dim sum"[15] made by oyster sauce with a pair of chopsticks. Another label showed mother and son rowing a sampan after collecting fresh oysters. Both labels reflected Chinese culture and lifestyle.

After US president Richard Nixon was presented with a panda as a gift by the Chinese government in 1972, sinomania arose in the United States. Lee Kum Kee introduced a new Panda oyster sauce which was cheaper than the prototype. After the Panda brand was established, Lee Kum Kee expanded its markets in the United States, Europe, and Southeast Asia. To meet the demands of consumers in different markets, it created different kinds of oyster sauce, including premium, Choy Sun ("God of Wealth"), oyster sauce with dried scallops, and vegetarian oyster-flavored sauce. It was the beginning of Lee Kum Kee's innovation of new products for different cultures in local and international markets. Thus, Yim and Mak (2005: 70) argue that it was the segmentation strategy that contributed to the business success of Lee Kum Kee.

In the late 1980s, the company attempted to go global. Its logo revealed a red cultural bridge between the East and West.[16] Lee Kum Kee promoted Chinese and Western food cultures in international markets. In the 1990s, Lee Kum Kee's trademark plaque represented a golden traditional Chinese window frame to symbolize Chinese heritage and the guarantee of premium quality. Living in a high pressure environment, people pursued good health and high quality of life. Traditional Chinese medicine became an alternative regimen. Lee Kum Kee developed a new health product brand and replaced the new logo with a green cultural bridge with a piece of leaf. When Lee Kum Kee penetrated the international market, it insisted on using the Chinese brand name to distinguish it as a modern globally trusted Chinese family business. It delivered the brand as a premium quality product with authentic food flavor.

Technological change, organizational culture, and family business management

In the last section, we examine the impact of culture on Lee Kum Kee's production, selling practice, corporate governance, and branding. In this section, we shall examine the impact of technological change on the mindset of Lee Kum Kee's successors as well as on its organizational culture.

Impact of technological change on corporate governance

As mentioned in the last paragraph, unlike the early generations of Lee Kum Kee, younger members of the fourth and fifth generations received good formal educations in overseas universities. They learned new management skills there. In particular, they visited foreign family businesses in Switzerland, England, the United States, Japan, etc. The new generation respected traditional Chinese values of pragmatism, integrity, and conscientiousness. Yet, they encouraged innovative thinking and promoted meritocracy, flexibility, and individualism in the organization.

Yeung (2000) argues that venturing into foreign markets has become an effective means for Chinese family firms to expand beyond the limits of domestic markets and traditional management practices. Implementing international business strategies enables Chinese family firms to transform family members into a modern international corporate team, provides a training ground for the heir to become the leader in the future, and consolidates effective personal and business networks. Yeung's argument also holds true for Lee Kum Kee. Unlike in the old generation, family affairs were separated from the business in the fourth generation. Using new management concepts overseas, Lee Kum Kee was transformed from a Chinese family business to a modern Western-style business. As Eddy Lee claimed, "we separate the non-business part from that of the family and make sure business belongs to the business" (quoted in Hong Kong Institute of Certified Public Accountants 2012: 18).[17]

Regarding business succession planning, Lee Kum Kee cultivated the right environment for the next generation. The company motivated the fifth generation to participate in the business via learning and development (Li et al. 2011: 55). If young members joined Lee Kum Kee, they were required to work outside the company for three to five years (Federation of Hong Kong Industries 2008: 18). They faced the same recruitment procedures as those that were applied to non-family employees. Once joining Lee Kum Kee, they were treated like other employees. Such an innovative mechanism "not only promotes and safeguards mutual trust among family members, but also serves as the key to ensure the continuity of the family, and provides the impetus for the sustainability of the business" (Lee Kum Kee 2012: 14).

Furthermore, the old Chinese family way of hiring staff gave way to new thinking in human resources management. The limit of family size implies that as a family firm expands, it has to rely on non-family members and recruit staff from outside (Tsang 2001: 91). Lee Kum Kee attempted to "promote employees to management and recruit specialists from outside – just like other companies" (*Businessweek* 2002). In 2005, it appointed two external non-executive board directors, Dr. Fong Ching Eddy and Mr. Sze Cho-cheung Michael. It recruited Dr. Lui Songtien Stephen as chief executive and Mr. George Tsang as chief operating officer, followed by Mr. Daniel Saw as the chief operating officer from 2009 to 2012. The company advocates Chuang Tze's principle of "the usefulness of uselessness."[18] That is to say, "all men know the uses of the useful, but no one knows the uses of the useless." Lee Kum Kee adopted an innovative "autopilot" leadership model to promote mutual trust and enhance the effectiveness of the company (Lee Kum Kee 2009: 3). Employees were empowered with decision-making authority and freedom of action. The managers facilitated a platform for the team to achieve. A five-year plan was implemented. In consumer-oriented human resource management, employees who coordinated with consumers, suppliers, and distributors were the most important component and the managers at ground level. With the empowerment of the employees and managers, Lee Kum Kee provided the best quality and service to the clients.

Technology and human resource management

Garg and Ma (2005: 268) argue that in the past, Chinese family firms "would use few motivational techniques to enhance work ethics, higher quality products and customer service." Now the new generations focus on global markets and move away from collective family systems. In contrast to traditional top-down Chinese family businesses, employees in Lee Kum Kee were encouraged to put themselves in other's shoes, care about other's feeling, and demonstrate a helicopter view (Li 2007). Utilizing a quantitative technique, a Happiness Index was formulated as a communication tool. Managers were concerned with job satisfaction and motivation of all staff. Employees always did well for the business when working happily. Good staff members were rewarded while consultation sessions or punitive actions were given to those who underperformed or committed an offense. Moreover, Lee Kum Kee equipped the staff with training programs. In 2007, it organized 41 in-house training programs and 32 external training programs (Zou 2010: 174–175). Study trips were offered for long-term employees. Staff members were also given opportunities to rotate jobs in different departments or transfer overseas (*South China Morning Post* 2012a). Lee Kum Kee presented its products to employees at traditional Chinese festivals, including Chinese New Year, the Dragon Boat Festival, and the Mid-Autumn Festival. On Founder's Day, the Lees, local staff, and representatives from overseas branches met and shared views. Outdoor activities were organized throughout the year (see Zou 2010: 143).

Impact of technological change on product development

As is widely known in the wine industry, XO Cognac represents supreme luxury and premium quality. During the 1980s, there was an emergence of the middle class in Hong Kong. Lee Kum Kee derived the XO concept from the wine industry to launch XO sauce in 1992.[19] XO sauce was made of conpoy (dried scallop), small dried shrimp, Chinese ham, flatfish, dried shallot, chili, and garlic (Yim and Mak 2005: 65). When XO sauce was popular in local families and the food industry, Lee Kum Kee modified the product into premium XO sauce with abalone, seafood XO sauce, olive oil XO sauce, and truffle XO sauce. David Lee, from the fourth generation of Lee Kum Kee, said, "we are a very old company, but we recognise that our consumers are changing, so we continually develop the new products to reflect this" (quoted in *South China Morning Post* 2012b). When Chinese families cooked steamed fish at home, Lee Kum Kee modified traditional soy sauce into seasoned soy sauce for seafood to "simplify the cooking and make, say, fish taste good. Unless, of course, you buy bad fish" (*South China Morning Post* 2012b). Families used the new soy sauce and cooked steamed fish the same as Chinese restaurants. Meanwhile, young middle class people prepared and ate more of their meals at home. They demanded food at "convenience and better quality at affordable prices" and a healthy diet in the hustle and bustle of life (*South China Morning Post* 2003). Lee Kum Kee developed preservative-free sauces and salt-reduced soy sauce. It also produced single-use sauce packets, convenience meal sauce, menu-oriented sauce, cooking and dipping sauce, and chicken bouillon powder.

As communication facilities improved, Lee Kum Kee was able to develop new sauces with varieties of tastes for consumers around the globe. In mainland China, Chinese cuisine is characterized by "south sweet, north salty, east hot, and west sour." The tastes of people who live in different places are different. Lee Kum Kee manufactured Guilin chili sauce, Chiu Chow chili sauce, sauce for spicy tofu, etc. For the international market, Lee Kum Kee understood and met consumers' dietary needs around the globe. It launched Japanese teriyaki sauce, Korean barbecue sauce, Mahsuri oyster sauce, Malaysian satay sauce, Thai Sriracha chili sauce, etc. It broke with traditional packaging in small glass bottles and introduced a toothpaste-like tube with an inverted vertical design for its renowned oyster sauce. The modern tube's flow control valve made the oyster sauce dispense safely and conveniently. It created "different packaging and tastes to suit different markets, so a chili product in Japan will come in smaller bottles and be sweeter and less thick, for instance, than it would be in Hong Kong" (Eddy Lee, quoted in *South China Morning Post* (2012b). Lee Kum Kee gained profit and reputation by product innovation.

Using foreign technology, Lee Kum Kee developed a traditional Chinese way of health preservation. For instance, it worked with Southern Medical University in China and developed the traditional Chinese health care brand Infinitus. Lee Kum Kee also collaborated with the Hong Kong University of Science and Technology and Tsinghua University (China) to conduct research on traditional Chinese medicine. By research and development, Lee Kum Kee adopted foreign technology to modernize traditional health products and an herbal regimen around the world (Wu and Du 2004).

Technological change and marketing strategies

Unlike the first three generations, who promoted business in a traditional Chinese way, the fourth generation of Lee Kum Kee borrowed foreign consumer-oriented marketing strategies which focused on affection and product quality. It created many slogans, including "Where there are Chinese people, there are Lee Kum Kee products," "Where there are people, there are Lee Kum Kee products," "Promotes Chinese cuisine worldwide," "Advocating the premium Chinese health regime."[20] Advertisements showed that Lee Kum Kee sauces flavored foods with affection, including family love and friendship. Between the 1970s and 1980s, Lee Kum Kee invited Hong Kong's famous singers and soap-opera stars to feature in advertisements. Advertising campaigns were presented on trams, trains, and motorcycles. To promote the brand in the international market, Lee Kum Kee organized food expos, seminars, exchange programs, chef certification programs, and cooking competitions around the world (Zou 2010: 49–52; *Ming Pao* 2010). Lee Kum Kee joined cooking television shows and produced DVDs featuring world-famous chefs (e.g., Martin Yan) who presented Chinese cuisine and fusion foods with its products. It took part in international activities, including international dragon boat tournaments, and charity activities. It was also appointed as the official sponsor of Disneyland Hong Kong, the Beijing Olympic Games 2008, and the Shanghai World Expo 2010. At the Mid-Autumn Festival 2011, it made a giant lantern sculpture in Hong Kong that set a Guinness world record.

When there was no computer and Internet in the 1970s, Lee Kum Kee sold Panda brand products to foreign firms which distributed them to grocery wholesalers, retailers, and restaurants (*Ming Pao* 2010). However, these firms demanded high profit margins and commission rebates. Lee Kum Kee decided to make open accounts with wholesalers. To enhance export competitiveness, it extended credit until the products were sold out. By the late 1990s, electronic communication had facilitated a new platform for business-customer relations. Lee Kum Kee adopted global networking to integrate interdepartmental communication, global coordination, and customer relations management. It enhanced technological capabilities beyond national borders via the Internet and online social networking services. It developed e-commerce to access historical and real-time data for production, distribution, marketing, financial management, and customer service. It also designed a user-friendly corporate website to provide the latest information on the company, products, cooking recipes, health tips, etc. Online shopping and food videos were delivered via the Internet, Facebook, blog, iPhone, and Android applications. As a result of interactive digital communication, Lee Kum Kee enhanced customer relations, consumers' level of knowledge of the brand, and a sense of community among local and overseas Chinese.

Conclusion

This paper has attempted to examine the roles of technology and culture in the business success of Lee Kum Kee, a well-known oyster sauce manufacturer in

Hong Kong. In the first part, this paper examined the impact of culture on Lee Kum Kee's operation in four major areas, namely oyster sauce production, trade practice, corporate governance, and marketing strategies. Firstly, in product innovation, the invention of oyster sauce by Lee Kum-sheung is often described as being purely by chance. However, this study has revealed that the discovery of oyster sauce was largely associated with Chinese culture. Without scientific research or modern food processing techniques, the entrepreneurial founder manufactured and sold his cultural sauce in South China. Secondly, in trade practice, based on the Confucian teaching of 'Jen', Lee Kum Kee advocated the concept of "considering others' interests" (*Si Li Ji Jen*) in doing business, and the founder, Lee Kum-sheung, was regarded as a role model of integrity, honesty, and doing good for society. Thirdly, inside the firm, Lee Kum Kee managed the company according to ancestral teachings with Confucianism and paternalism. The senior management exhibited a strong sense of responsibility towards employees that was not only economic but also moral. They used traditional Confucian values, namely filial piety, face, and *renqing* to ensure that their heirs/staff lived up to family expectations as well as conformed to the goals of the family business. Fourthly, in product branding, Lee Kum Kee successfully adopted designs enriched with Chinese culture such as "a pair of chopsticks," "a sampan loaded with fresh oysters," as well as a "panda" to market its products. In the late 1980s, the company designed a new logo revealing a red cultural bridge between the East and West in an attempt to catch up with the globalization wave.

In the second part of this paper, we also examined the impact of technological change on the mindset of Lee Kum Kee's successors as well as on the organizational culture. Regarding the impact of technology on management, unlike in the old generation, family affairs were separated from the business in the fourth generation. Lee Kum Kee was gradually transformed from a traditional Chinese family business to a Western-style corporation. In terms of human resource management, in contrast to traditional top-down Chinese family businesses, employees were encouraged to put themselves in other's shoes, care about other's feelings, and demonstrate a helicopter view. A scientific method, namely a Happiness Index, was formulated as a communication tool. Managers were concerned with job satisfaction and motivation of all staff. Good staff members were rewarded, while consultation sessions or punitive actions were given to those who underperformed or committed an offense. In 2007, Lee Kum Kee organized 41 in-house training programs and 32 external training programs. On product management, deriving the XO concept from the wine industry, Lee Kum Kee launched XO sauce in 1992. When XO sauce was popular in Hong Kong's families and food industry, Lee Kum Kee modified the product into a premium XO sauce with abalone, seafood XO sauce, olive oil XO sauce, and truffle XO sauce. In marketing, unlike the first three generations, who promoted business in a traditional way, the fourth generation of Lee Kum Kee borrowed foreign consumer-oriented marketing strategies which focused on affection and product quality. It created many slogans to reinforce its product in peoples' minds. Lee Kum Kee sauces were flavored with affection, family love, and friendship. Lee Kum Kee invited celebrities to feature in advertisements. To promote the brand in international market, Lee Kum Kee organized food expos, seminars, exchange programs, chef certification programs, and cooking competitions around the world. This paper concludes that Lee Kum Kee has been able to assimilate the best of Chinese and foreign cultures in order to compete in the global market. Combining Chinese and foreign cultures with new technology, Lee Kum Kee has successfully transformed into a Chinese multinational corporation.

Notes

1 From Lee Kum Kee's homepage: Milestones 1988, http://hk-kitchen.lkk.com/en/AboutLKK/MileStonePage#; retrieved 17 July 2013.
2 From an illustration of how a Chinese family business in Taiwan evolves into a leader in the global market, see Chen (2010).
3 For a discussion of economics as an interpretative science, see Yu and Shiu (2011: 150).
4 For storytelling as an economic methodology, see McCloskey (1990).
5 Unlike Yin (1994) who uses the case study to test *a priori* theory, Eisenhardt (1989, 1991) uses it more to promote theory building and argues that propositions can be developed (and tested) during data collection, rather than prior to it. Since the aim of a case study is to obtain a rich understanding of the cases in all their complexities, insights gained during data collection can be used to inform the theory (Crosthwaite et al. 1997). For a further discussion of this issue, see Dyer and Wilkins (1991).
6 Lee Kum-sheung had three sons. The eldest son, Lee Shiu-wing, died young. Lee Shiu-tang, the second son, was responsible for marketing in Lee Kum Kee. Young Lee Shiu-nam was in charge of product quality and production procedures.
7 Lee Kum Kee is managed by the fourth generation of the Lees. They are Eddy Lee, David Lee, Charlie Lee, Sammy Lee, and Elizabeth Mok. For the details of the succession of Lee Kum Kee, see Lee and Li (2008) and Li et al. (2011).
8 China's Closer Economic Partnership Arrangement (CEPA) with Hong Kong was signed on 29 June 2003 with the aims of promoting joint economic prosperity and development and facilitating the economic links between China, Hong Kong, and other countries. Its main content lies in elimination of tariff and non-tariff barriers applying to goods trade and reducing bilateral restrictions on service trade. Under the agreement, Hong Kong maintains its current zero tariff policy towards goods imported from the mainland, with a progressive tariff elimination for goods imported by China from Hong Kong. China agrees to introduce zero tariffs for a list of specific goods. Furthermore, all goods have to meet CEPA rules of origin. To acquire Hong Kong origin, a good must have 30 percent value added in Hong Kong (Cabrillac 2004; Antkiewicz and Whalley 2005).
9 www.hktdc.com/sourcing/hk_company_directory.htm?companyid=1X02ZK57; retrieved 16 July 2013.
10 HACCP is known as Hazard Analysis and Critical Control Point.
11 http://hk-kitchen.lkk.com/en/AboutLKK/achievement; retrieved 15 July 2013.
12 "Where there are people, there are Lee Kum Kee products" (Lee Kum Kee 2012).
13 *Jen* refers to humanity, humaneness, benevolence, compassion, love for fellow beings or co-humanity (the last term is translated by Peter Boodberg. See Tu (1997: 9).
14 In Chinese, "Kee" means shop.
15 A traditional Chinese breakfast includes dim sum and Chinese tea.
16 For Lee Kum Kee's logo, see http://hk-kitchen.lkk.com/en/AboutLKK/MileStonePage#; retrieved 18 July 2013.
17 It was reported that the new generations manage their big family using foreign concepts. The Family Council was formed to implement family rules. A regular family meeting

was held in each quarter of the year for four days. Matters concerning business operations were excluded. In addition, members were designated to different departmental activities in the family, i.e., Family Business, Family Investment, Family Foundation, Family Office, and Family Learning and Development Centre. They changed the roles every two years. The Family Assembly was constituted by all family members of the third to fifth generations of Lee Kum Kee. It organized family activities to encourage open communication, mutual trust, and understanding (Lee Kum Kee 2012).

18 Chuang Tze is an ancient Chinese philosopher. For translation of his work, see Graham (1981: 75).

19 XO means extra old. XO sauce originated in Hong Kong's Peninsula Hotel in the early 1980s. It was initially served to the customers in high-end Cantonese restaurants.

20 http://hk-kitchen.lkk.com/en/AboutLKK/MileStonePage#; retrieved 18 July 2013.

References

Antkiewicz, A. and Whalley, J. (2005) "China's New Regional Trade Agreements," *The World Economy*, 28(10): 1539–1557.

Bagozzi, R. P. (2007) "The Legacy of the Technology Acceptance Model and a Proposal for a Paradigm Shift," *Journal of the Association for Information Systems*, 8(4): 244–254.

Buchanan, D. A. and Bryman, A. (2007) "Contextualizing Methods Choice in Organizational Research," *Organizational Research Methods*, 10(3): 483–501.

Businessweek (2002) "SAP 30th Anniversary Leadership Series: Lee Kum Kee," www.businessweek.com/adsections/2002/sap/lkk.htm; retrieved 24 January 2013.

Cabrillac, B. (2004) "A Bilateral Trade Agreement between Hong Kong and China: CEPA," *China Perspectives*, 54(July-August): 39–47.

Chen, Simon Chien-Yuan (2010) "Dimensions of Taiwanese Entrepreneurship: Lessons from the World's Top Producer of Touch Fasteners," *Global Business Review*, 11(3/October): 333–345.

ChinaPress (2010) "The Legend of Lee Kum Kee," http://series888.blogspot.hk/2011/03/blog-post_26.html; retrieved 1 August 2013.

Crosthwaite, Jim; MacLeod, Neil; and Malcolm, Bill (1997) "Case Studies: Theory and Practice in Natural Resource Management," paper submitted for the Proceedings of the Australian Association for Social Research Conference, February, Charles Stuart University, Wagga Wagga.

Davis, F. D. (1989) "Perceived Usefulness, Perceived Ease of Use, and User Acceptance of Information Technology," *MIS Quarterly*, 13(3): 319–340.

deBono, Edward (1992) *Serious Creativity*, New York: Harper Business.

Dyer, W. Gibb Jr. and Wilkins, Alan L. (1991) "Better Stories, Not Better Constructs, to Generate Better Theory: A Rejoinder to Eisenhardt," *Academy of Management Review*, 16(3/July): 613–619.

Eisenhardt, Kathleen M. (1989) "Building Theories from Case Study Research," *Academy of Management Review*, 14(4): 532–550.

Eisenhardt, Kathleen M. (1991) "Better Stories and Better Constructs: The Case for Rigor and Comparative Logic," *Academy of Management Review*, 16(3): 620–627.

Federation of Hong Kong Industries (2008) "Passing on the Legacy: Family Business Succession," *Hong Kong Industrialist*, May: 14–19.

Garg, R. K. and Ma, J. (2005) "Benchmarking Culture and Performance in Chinese Organizations," *Benchmarking: An International Journal*, 12(3): 260–274.

Graham, A. C. (1981) *Chuang-Tzu: The Seven Inner Chapters and Other Writings from the Book Chuang-Tzu*, London: Allen & Unwin.

Guo, Ting Yi (1986) *Jin Dai Zhong-guo Shi Gang* [The Recent History of China], Hong Kong: The Chinese University Press (vol. 1, 19th century; vol. 2, 20th century). (Text in Chinese)

Hong Kong Institute of Certified Public Accountants (2012) "Family Affairs," *A-Plus: Driving Business Success*, 9(8): 14–18.

Landes, David (1999) *The Wealth and Poverty of Nations*, New York: W. W. Norton.

Lee Kum Kee (2009) *Corporate Link*, 44 (June), http://korea.lkk.com/sites/default/files/corporate/hk/media_center/LKK44_final.pdf; retrieved 31 January 2013.

Lee Kum Kee (2010) *Corporate Link*, 26 (April), http://hk-kitchen.lkk.com/sites/default/files/corporate/hk/media_center/LKK%2046-final.pdf; retrieved 16 July 2013.

Lee Kum Kee (2012) *Corporate Link*, 56 (October), http://hk-kitchen.lkk.com/sites/hk/Corplink55_FINAL.pdf; retrieved 30 June 2013.

Lee, Jean and Li, Hong (2008) *Wealth Doesn't Last 3 Generations: How Family Businesses Can Maintain Prosperity*, Singapore: World Scientific Publishing.

Li, Huisen (2007) *The Power of Si Li Ji Ren: Nine Rules of Success*, Beijing: China Youth Press.

Li, Xinchun; Zhu Hang, Chen; Wenting; and Fu, Mimi (2011) "Lee Kum Kee Corp. Ltd (HK): 120 Years and Going Strong," in Kevin Au, Justin B. Craig, and Kavil Ramachandran (eds.) *Family Enterprise in the Asia Pacific: Exploring Transgeneration Entrepreneurship in Family Firms*, Cheltenham, UK: Edward Elgar, pp. 40–59.

Lin, Kathy (2000) "Chinese Food Cultural Profile," *EthnoMed*, http://ethnomed.org/clinical/nutrition/chinese_food_cultural_profile; retrieved on 4 September 2013.

McCloskey, D. (1990) "Storytelling in Economics," in C. Nash (ed.) *Narrative in Culture: The Use of Storytelling in the Science, Philosophy and Literature*, London: Routledge, pp. 5–22.

McDermott, C. M. and Stock, G. N. (1999) "Organizational Culture and Advanced Manufacturing Technology Implementation," *Journal of Operations Management*, 17(5): 521–533.

Ming Pao (2010, August 12) "Lee Kum Kee Keeps Constant Entrepreneurship: From Sauces to Herbal Health Products," www.mpfinance.com/htm/Finance/20100812/News/fz_fza1.htm; retrieved 1 August 2013. (Text in Chinese)

Mitchell, Charles (2000) *A Short Course in International Business Culture*, 3rd ed., Novato, CA: World Trade Press.

Redding, S. Gordon (1990) *The Spirit of Chinese Capitalism*, Berlin: De Gruyter.

Slater, Joanna (1999) "Spreading the Sauce," *Far Eastern Economic Review*, 162(20): 60–61.

South China Morning Post (2003, March 18) "Lee Family Still Flavours Veteran Sauce Maker," www.scmp.com/article/409656/lee-family-still-flavours-veteran-sauce-maker; retrieved 16 July 2013.

South China Morning Post (2012a, July 21) "Team Recipes at Lee Kum Kee," www.scmp.com/article/1007339/team-recipes-lee-kum-kee; retrieved 23 January 2013.

South China Morning Post (2012b, July 16) "LKK Reveals Recipe for Success," www.scmp.com/article/176143/lkk-reveals-recipe-success; retrieved 24 April 2013.

Tsang, E. W. (2001) "Internationalizing the Family Firm: a Case Study of a Chinese Family Business," *Journal of Small Business Management*, 39(1):88–93.

Tu, Weiming (1997) "Chinese Philosophy: A Synoptic View," in E. Deutsch and R. Bontekoe (eds.) *A Companion to World Philosophies*, Oxford: Basil Blackwell, pp. 3–23.

Venkatesh, V.; Morris, M. G.; Davis, G. B.; and Davis, F. D. (2003) "User Acceptance of Information Technology: Toward a Unified View," *MIS Quarterly*, 27(3/September): 425–478.

Ward, C. and Kennedy, A. (1999) "The Measurement of Sociocultural Adaptation," *International Journal of Intercultural Relations*, 23(4): 659–677.

White, L. H. (1977) "Uncertainty and Entrepreneurial Expectation in Economic Theory," unpublished Senior Honours Thesis, Harvard College, March 31.

Wu, Shang Qing and Du, Qing Yun (2004) "Southern Lee Kum Kee Recreates Miracle," *China Economic Weekly*, 271(38): 13–20. (Text in Chinese)

Yeung, Henry W. C. (2000) "Limits to the Growth of Family-Owned Business? The Case of Chinese Transnational Corporations from Hong Kong," *Family Business Review*, 13(1): 55–70.

Yim, Bennet and Mak, Vincent (2005) "Lee Kum Kee: Old Company, Modern Marketing Strategy," in Ali Farhoomand (ed.) *Small Business Management and Entrepreneurship in Hong Kong: A Casebook*, Hong Kong: Hong Kong University Press, pp. 63–73.

Yin, Robert K. (1994) *Case Study Research: Design and Methods*, 2nd ed., London: Sage Publications.

Yu, Tony Fu-Lai and Shiu, Gary M. C. (2011) "A New Look at the Austrian School of Economics: Review and Prospects," *International Journal of Pluralism and Economic Education*, 2(2/June): 145–161.

Zheng, Victor and Chow, Man Kong (2013) *A Study on Chinese Family Enterprises Succession*, Beijing: Dang Fang Publishers. (Text in Chinese)

Zou, Guangwen (2010) *The Road to Build up National Company's Brand: The Case of Lee Kum Kee, Hong Kong*, Hong Kong: Hong Kong Economic Times. (Text in Chinese)

10 African entrepreneurs and international coordination in petty businesses

The case of low-end mobile phone sourcing in Hong Kong

Introduction

The success of many multinational corporations from economically advanced countries, such as Walmart (USA), Tesco (UK), H&M (Sweden), Aldi (Germany), AEON (Japan), and Li & Fung (Hong Kong), is well known. Through sourcing and merchandising all over the world, they not only earn impressive profits each year, but also significantly contribute to international trade and global well-being. However, global markets do not accommodate only multinational giants. There are also millions of small entrepreneurs all over the world who are involved in petty businesses which the multinationals do not bother to go into. These small entrepreneurs survive by identifying opportunities and exploiting narrow profit margins. Through careful economic calculation, they buy goods in one part of the globe and sell them in the other part. Their self-interest activities also enhance global well-being. In this chapter, we introduce the contribution of African entrepreneurs to world trade. It begins with an Austrian perspective of international entrepreneurship and global coordination. This framework is illustrated by African entrepreneurs who source Shenzhen-made mobile phones in Hong Kong and sell them in Africa. By arbitraging price differentials, they earn pure entrepreneurial profit. A detailed case study of the global coordination of a Tanzanian entrepreneur is accounted in the next section. This chapter concludes that as a result of the effort of African entrepreneurs, low-end mobile phones manufactured in Shenzhen are shipped to Hong Kong and consumed by people in Tanzania, bringing benefits to all parties concerned. The case study fully illustrates the principle of the "invisible hand" in global markets.

Solo entrepreneurship and global coordination: a theoretical framework

Entrepreneurship appears in many forms in practice. In technology management, it can be Schumpeterian/revolutionary (Schumpeter 1934/1961) or imitative/ followership (Baumol 1988). It can be necessity-driven entrepreneurship (such as corner shops) or opportunity-driven entrepreneurship (such as Bill Gates's Microsoft) (Reynolds et al. 2002). It can also be corporate entrepreneurship in multinational giants such as Sir William Jardine, the founder of Jardine, Matheson & Co. or solo entrepreneurship involving carrying parallel goods across the border. This chapter deals with solo entrepreneurship in low-end commodities. Specifically, it attempts to explain how solo African entrepreneurs operate in petty businesses and single-handedly coordinate resources in the world's low-end markets by utilizing Hong Kong as a knowledge hub. This chapter argues that knowledge is dispersed all over the world and each individual is ignorant, possessing only a tiny bit of information. This fact provides an opportunity for international entrepreneurs to assimilate knowledge, coordinate resources, and reap narrow profit margins in world markets. With self-interest and careful economic calculation, these small entrepreneurs succeed in arbitraging price discrepancies between Africa and Asia. Furthermore, running around the globe as a one-man band, small entrepreneur-owners enjoy flexibility in the capital structure and are able to quickly respond to the rapidly changing condition in global markets.

Scattered knowledge in the global market

Assuming two individuals, Yul and Meiling, living in Africa and Hong Kong, respectively, each possesses a unique stock of knowledge and subjectively assesses incoming events every day. Assume further that Yul, who lives in rural Africa, would like to buy a secondhand mobile phone which can do the basic job of communication. However, he does not know where and how he can obtain a cheap mobile phone. On the other hand, Meiling in Hong Kong knows that she can purchase a large quantity of old-model mobile phones from China because she has connections in Shenzhen. Though she wants to make some money for her living, she does not know that many Africans such as Yul want to buy those old-model phones. The *economic problem* is that these two people do not know each other. Obviously, in this case, international trade cannot be carried out because both lack the knowledge required for trade. According to the subjectivist theory of knowledge (Kirzner 1979: 137–153), to these two persons, the opportunity for them simply does not exist.[1] Given the fact that each individual is ignorant and knowledge is dispersed over the globe (Hayek 1945), how can trade between Yul and Meiling be possible so that both parties can be better off? This is the "knowledge problem" in the Austrian school of economics. Rather than saying that economic problems are "allocation of resources" problems, as argued by mainstream neoclassical economists, Hayek (1945) argues that economic problems are coordination problems. More specifically, Hayek asks how the preferences and desires of millions of people in the world can be coordinated. Adam Smith (1776) argues in terms of the "invisible hand" in the market. For Smith, self-interest is the foundation of exchange and can lead to welfare gain for traders. However, Smith does not explain how this can be done in the real world.

In the Yul and Meiling case, even if the two persons accidentally discover that both have the intention to trade, the international transaction may not be carried out because both parties' thinking and actions are socially embedded. Their minds are governed by a set of habits, traditions, institutions, norms, customs, and legal rules which make them follow without being asked. Knowledge is taken for granted and socially constructed (Berger and Luckmann 1966). Each trading party, with different cultures and values, will accordingly interpret the social world differently. Specifically, it takes a lot of effort to find out if the trading partner is trustworthy. Hence, knowing your trading parties, learning, and testing foreign markets by trial and error are the main elements in international trade. However, such important elements are missing in the neoclassical economic paradigm.

The issues of culture and knowledge make the further justification for the role of middleman in international trade. To be sure, the role of middleman is well documented in the mainstream price and transaction costs theories (for example, see Casson 1982; Reekie 1984). However, in a human agency perspective, a middleman is more than just a person who links both parties together. The middleman, in our case, is also an entrepreneur as well as a knowledge creator. He or she transmits knowledge and performs entrepreneurial discovery, and hence raises the well-being of trading parties (see below).

The role of the entrepreneur: coordination and arbitrageurship

International entrepreneurs are global knowledge brokers who transmit, assimilate, and create knowledge around the world. They attempt to coordinate economic activities for profits. In Mises' words (1949: 328):

> The driving force of the market process is provided neither by the consumers nor by the owners of the means of production – land, capital goods, and labor – but by the promoting and speculating entrepreneurs. These are people intent upon profiting by taking advantage of differences in prices. Quicker of apprehension and farther-sighted than other men, they look around for sources of profit. They buy where and when they deem prices too low, and they sell where and when they deem prices too high. They approach the owners of the factors of production, and their competition sends the prices of these factors up to the limit corresponding to their anticipation of the future prices of the products. They approach the consumers, and their competition forces prices of consumers' goods down to the point at which the whole supply can be sold. Profit-seeking speculation is the driving force of the market as it is the driving force of production.

Israel M. Kirzner adds further insight into Hayek's and Mises' arguments. Using Kirzner's (1973) groundbreaking work, we argue that the role of international entrepreneurs lies in their abilities to identify global profit opportunities. They discover and exploit global opportunities according to their hunches. Profit opportunities in the world market come in three ways, namely the recognition of mismatches of plans, the introduction of new opportunities, and the uncertainty of the future (Martin 2007: 6). An international entrepreneur is able to integrate "innumerable scraps of existing information that are present in scattered form" throughout the world (Kirzner 1985: 162). The international coordination process is thus "the systematic plan changes generated by the flow of market information released by market participation – that is, by the testing of plans in the market" (Kirzner 1973: 10). Increased coordination means that entrepreneurs' plans are made more compatible (Martin 2007: 4).

The entrepreneur as an arbitrageur

In the case of Yul and Meiling, we further assume that another African, Uti, practices as a middleman. Uti discovers that there is an opportunity in the international market. He knows that plenty of people in Africa need secondhand mobile phones and that such goods are available at the affordable prices to Africans in small stores in Hong Kong. After some searching, he contacts Meiling, who is able to sell China-made low-end mobile phones to him. He then buys phones from Meiling and sells them to African people, including Yul. As a consequence of Uti's entrepreneurial action, all three parties gain. This is essentially the case of Kirznerian entrepreneurship (Kirzner 1973) which conducts arbitrageurship.[2] In Uti's case, he conducts global arbitrageurship. Moreover, in the process of arbitrage activities, knowledge is transmitted, created, and further utilized or assimilated, opening more opportunities in the world markets.

Creation of knowledge[3]

According to de Soto (1995: 234–237), there are at least three significant implications due to Uti's entrepreneurial arbitrageurship.

Firstly, by performing as a middleman, entrepreneur Uti creates new information which did not exist before. An entrepreneurial action implies a creation of information which takes place in the agent's mind. In our case, information is created by Uti. Moreover, as soon as Uti enters into the international transaction with Yul and Meiling, new information is created in their minds as well. As a result of Uti's action, Yul in Africa becomes aware that the resource that he lacks is available in another part of the world. Hence, Yul will take a new action that he did not consider before. On the other hand, Meiling in Hong Kong becomes aware that she can buy mobile phones in China and sell them to African businesspeople at a good price too. Therefore, Meiling also takes a new action previously not taken, such as stock up on more secondhand mobile phones for buyers. In short, Uti's entrepreneurial action gives rise to a chain of new knowledge in the world market.

Secondly, entrepreneurial creation of knowledge implies a simultaneous transmission of knowledge in the global market. Knowledge transmission means that people learn from others and create new knowledge in their minds as a result. In our example, new ideas have been created in the minds of both Yul and Meiling as a result of Uti's entrepreneurial action: (1) Yul now may proceed to pursue his desired goal which could not be attained before; (2) Meiling now realizes that her link to China's mobile phone market is useful. It can be conceived that in general, through the price signal, the knowledge (received by both Yul and Meiling) will be spread to the entire global community in the market process.

Thirdly, through learning, trading parties revise their plans, formulate new expectations (Lachmann 1956), and make economic judgments (Knight 1921) of the new situation. Hence, economizing of resources or, more precisely, coordination of actors' expectations or plans will be possible. In our case, as a result of Uti's entrepreneurial action, both Yul and Meiling will revise their plans in accordance with the new messages they receive. In particular, Yul, now having the resource (a secondhand mobile phone) at his disposal, can attain his end and undertake action that he did not take previously. On the other hand, Meiling takes action in Hong Kong and China in order to earn more money. Therefore, all trading parties in the market learn, revise plans, and accordingly modify action; thereby economic coordination is made possible. More importantly, the parties each adjust to the world market in the best possible way without knowing that they are actually learning. As Schutz and Luckmann (1989: 8) note, "one learns both to 'adjust' one's own conduct appropriately to the goal of action and also to improve one's interpretation of the conduct of others." This interactive market process, a simple and effective way of coordinating economic activities and improving human welfare, is precisely Adam Smith's concept of the "invisible hand."

Economic calculation of the solo entrepreneur

Global connection was made possible by Uti's entrepreneurship through self-interest and economic calculation. On self-interest, Smith (1776: 354) contends that in the market, the individual "intends only his own gain, and he is, in this, as in many other cases, led by an invisible hand to promote an end which was not part of his intention. Nor is it always the worse for the society that it was no part of it. By pursuing his own interest he frequently promotes that of the society more effectually than when he really intends to promote it."

Taking care of his or her own interest, the entrepreneurial agent needs to do economic calculation carefully before implementing a trading plan. Menger (1871/2007: 160), the founder of the Austrian school of economics, argues that one of the entrepreneurial activities is "economic calculation – all the various computations that must be made if a production process is to be efficient (provided that it is economic in other respects)."

Mises (1949) adds that in the market process, entrepreneurs discover discrepancy between current factor prices and future product prices and exploit it for their own advantages. More importantly, every single step of entrepreneurial activities is subject to scrutiny by economic calculation. As Mises (1949: 210–211) notes:

> The task which acting man wants to achieve by economic calculation is to establish the outcome of acting by contrasting input and output. Economic calculation is either an estimate of the expected outcome of future action or the establishment of the outcome of past action. But the latter does not serve merely historical and didactic aims. Its practical meaning is to show how much one is free to consume without impairing the future capacity to

produce. It is with regard to this problem that the fundamental notions of economic calculation – capital and income, profit and loss, spending and saving, cost and yield – are developed.

For Mises (1949: 229–230), "monetary calculation is the guiding star of action under the social system of division of labor. It is the compass of the man embarking upon production. He calculates in order to distinguish the remunerative lines of production from the unprofitable ones. . . . Monetary calculation is the main vehicle of planning and acting in the social setting of a society of free enterprise directed and controlled by the market and prices." More importantly, resources can be efficiently allocated via the entrepreneur's economic calculation.

Uti, just like any entrepreneur, responds to profit incentive. Though he can identify the potential opportunity in the market, he needs to do careful economic calculation before implementing his profit plan. For Uti, a profit (or a loss) is simply the difference between the total revenue earned by selling mobile phones in Africa and the total cost of buying them in another part of the globe. The costs of providing secondhand mobile phones in Africa may include:

1. The price of low-end phones paid to Meiling in Hong Kong. For this, he shops around and searches for the best price. This information is not free but costly.
2. Airfare, food, accommodations, and miscellaneous consumption in Hong Kong. In particular, it is well known that hotel prices in Hong Kong are expensive. Uti may also hear from his African friends that the living standard in Hong Kong is quite high. Therefore, Uti prepares to stay in a cheap hostel in Hong Kong.
3. The cost of shipping the goods back to Africa. It also involves customs duties, insurance, etc.
4. Uti's own labor, including sweat and toil, brain energy, and anxiety.[4]

Given all these costs, Uti estimates the prices of his mobile phones to be sold in Africa. This job is not easy because economic conditions change rapidly each day. Fixing a good price requires economic judgment. Other selling expenses may include transactions with his fellow Africans, etc. After balancing the estimated costs and revenues of providing low-end mobile phones in Africa, if Uti finds that there is a profit, then he will proceed with his business plan. Uti, as a middleman-entrepreneur, earns profits only by correctly anticipating the future conditions. As Mises (1949: 664–665) said, "the ultimate source of profits is always the foresight of future conditions. Those who succeeded better than others in anticipating future events and in adjusting their activities to the future state of the market, reap profits because they are in a position to satisfy the most urgent needs of the public." In the following sections, we shall apply this framework to understand how African entrepreneurs coordinate economic activities globally via the Hong Kong hub.

African entrepreneurs as international coordinators: the Shenzhen–Hong Kong–Africa connection

In one part of the globe, China is able to produce low-end mobile phones at relatively low costs. In the other part of the globe, many low-income African nations have a huge demand for low-end mobile phones, including old-model or secondhand items. There exists a demand and supply gap for the product. African entrepreneurs identify this profit opportunity. They come to Hong Kong to buy China-made or -used mobile phones and ship them back to Africa for profit, thus acting as international coordinators. We analyze the demand for and supply of low-end mobile phones in the following sections.

Mobile phone usage in Africa

Since GSM (Global System for Mobile Communications) was introduced in the 1990s, mobile phone coverage has expanded in Africa. The percentage of the African population who accessed mobile phone coverage increased from 10 percent in 1999 to over 60 percent in 2008. Mobile phone subscriptions increased from 16 million in 2000 to 376 million in 2008 (Aker and Mbiti 2010). More people in Africa are eager to buy mobile phones.

African people are unable to produce mobile phones due to low technological capabilities, institutional constraints, and poor infrastructure. In particular, the cost of producing mobile phones in Nigeria is very high due to corruption and frequent electricity blackouts. With average low income, most African people cannot afford to buy quality original mobile phones from advanced nations. China is a major supplier of low-end mobile phones to the developing countries of Africa. A Nigerian phone trader once remarked, "not many people in my country can afford original products from Europe and America. There is no way we can produce things in Nigeria as cheaply as China can" (Yang 2012: 167). African people turn to China for low-end mobile phones.

Mobile phone production in Shenzhen, China[5]

After its entry into the World Trade Organization in 2001, China has emerged as the world's manufacturing powerhouse. China is the world's largest mobile phone supplier.[6] In 2011, 880 million (around 80 percent of) mobile phones in the world were made in China and sold at US$33.3 on average (*Hong Kong Economic Journal* 2012). In particular, G'Five, based in Shenzhen, is the tenth largest mobile phone manufacturer in the world. It sold more than 5 million mobile phones in the second quarter of 2010.[7]

China is a fast and smart learner in making mobile phones. Factories in China produce quality branded phones, as well as "parallel" and "shanzhai" phones.[8] Lin (2011: 21) estimates that shanzhai phones are 80 percent of the phones manufactured in China. They are known as China-made phones or China-made knock-offs. Almost half of shanzhai phones are produced in the region of the Pearl

River Delta, Guangdong (Zhu and Shi 2010). In Shenzhen, there are 4,000 shanzhai enterprises making mobile phones, 4,000–5,000 mobile phone accessory suppliers, and many phone retailers (Reuters 2010).

China-made shanzhai phones include copycat, refurbished, and branded phones. Copycat phones are known as sheer imitations, clones, or Triple-A. Some phones replicate branded phones with unofficial logos such as "Nokla," "Sansung," "Hip-phone," "Sany Erickson." They are high-quality fake phones as good as the prototypes at cheaper prices. For example, Samsung's "Anycall" becomes "Anycat," selling for 20 percent of each genuine Anycall (Hu et al. 2011). Some fake phones have printed branded logos even though the brand does not have such a product, such as LV phone. The refurbished cellphones, *fanbanji*, have famous brand names but are not authentic after replacing unofficial components and accessories. In Huaqiangbei, Shenzhen, people engage in recycling mobile phones. They replace old plastic cases or batteries of secondhand mobile phones with copies, and the original circuit boards with cheap Mediatek chips. As new components are usually illegal and substandard, the refurbished phones may last for a few months only or leave consumers susceptible to accident (*The Sun* 2013). Tianyu Communication Equipment Co. Ltd. is regarded as the king of shanzhai phones. The company modifies mobile phones with special features. K-touch is well known for dual-SIM support, ultraviolet lights used for detecting counterfeit banknotes, and batteryless technology. Shanzhai phones made in China are targeted for low-income groups in general and emerging economies such as those of Africa and Latin America in particular. Custer (2012) reports that shanzhai mobile phone makers in China grab a huge chunk of the East African mobile phone market. It accounts for about 50 percent of the cell phones across East Africa.

From Shenzhen to Hong Kong

Shanzhai phones made in Shenzhen have rapidly caught up with the latest original brand models. For example, in 2010, when iPhone 4 was launched and sold at HK$14,000 in Hong Kong, the shanzhai iPhone 4 had already been produced and sold in Shenzhen from HK$200 to HK$680 (*Hong Kong Economic Journal* 2010). Like the prototype, the shanzhai iPhone4 included Bluetooth, Wi-Fi, GPS, and other features.

Since Shenzhen is situated next to Hong Kong, businesspeople in Hong Kong can directly buy the latest shanzhai phones in Shenzhen. In particular, mobile phone stall owners in Sham Shui Po[9] go to Shenzhen by 45-minute train and procure Shenzhen-made shanzhai iPhone 4s. They return to Hong Kong and sell the product at HK$950–999 (ibid). The Shenzhen-made shanzhai phones are even covered by a one-month carry-in warranty. Customers can also return defective shanzhai iPhone 4s to the manufacturer in Huaqiangbei, Shenzhen within 14 days. Some Hong Kong phone merchants refurbish these returned phones with cheap components/parts.[10] It is reported that 60 percent of mobile phones sold in Chungking Mansions[11] are 14-day phones (Mathews 2011: 117). They are the favorites of African buyers.

From Hong Kong to Africa

Low-end mobile phones manufactured in China end up in the hands of African households. How can this be possible? Obviously, quality branded mobile phones made in China are shipped and sold to rich African consumers by the multinational giants. However, the low-end shanzhai mobile phones are not the big corporations' targets due to small profit margins in the business. These petty businesses are handled by African entrepreneurs who come to Hong Kong as one-man bands. Borrowing money from families, friends, and even strangers, they source low-end mobile phones in Hong Kong, Shenzhen, and Guangzhou and sell them in Africa. Bringing small amounts of economic capital with them, they return home with low-end mobile phones in their suitcases (Bertoncelo and Bredeloup 2007; Bodomo 2007, 2010; Mathews 2011). It is estimated that 20 percent of mobile phones used in sub-Saharan Africa pass through Chungking Mansions in Hong Kong (Mathews 2011: 106). A Nigerian trader once noted, "China is there for large scale, for the big fish, not the small fish. The small fish will stay in Hong Kong – they need Hong Kong" (Mathews 2012: 211).

Chungking Mansions: an international bazaar and a miniature of the global market

Though African entrepreneurs can source low-end mobile phones worldwide, they choose to come to Hong Kong because it is a very convenient entrepot or international logistic hub. Hong Kong is renowned for the Mart of East Asia. Since the territory was founded by British traders in the 19th century, it has grown as "a city of middlemen" (Chau 1993: 23). As a gateway to China, entrepreneurs around the world come to seek their fortunes in Hong Kong. International merchants specialize in east-west trades. They regard Hong Kong as a new "treasure island."

After China's entry into the World Trade Organization, many African entrepreneurs, mostly from Nigeria, Ghana, and Tanzania, fly to Hong Kong to engage in China trade (*China Daily* 2010a). Hong Kong, a safe, reliable, and accessible place, opens to people all over the world. People from many African countries, such as Algeria, Tanzania, and Kenya, are granted visa-free entry to Hong Kong from 14 to 90 days. Traders from African countries for which a visa is required, like Nigeria and Ghana, apply for business visas by a letter of recommendation from a Hong Kong company hiring Hong Kong agents, or by passport from another country which is granted easier access to Hong Kong (Mathews 2011: 167).

Unlike those foreign CEO or taipans in Hong Kong with highly paid salaries or commissions, African entrepreneurs are solo traders who make frequent trips to Hong Kong to grasp profit opportunities. They travel three or more times a year and stay in the territory from one week to three months, with an attempt to reap narrow profit margins.

African entrepreneurs, once arrived at Hong Kong, build up or join a business network there. They live and gather in Chungking Mansions, where English is used as the lingua franca. A phone trader from Kenya said he traveled to Hong

Kong eight times a year and stayed in Chungking Mansions because it was "convenient and safe" (*Financial Times* 2009). It is reported that around 2,000 African traders stay in Chungking Mansions on any given night, live there, and shop for weeks at a time (Mathews 2012: 208). There are plenty of cheap guesthouses, restaurants, retail and wholesale businesses, foreign exchange offices, etc. Inside a building, African entrepreneurs exchange business information in informal ways. A Ghanaian phone trader noted, "I meet Africans here [Chungking Mansions] with whom I can discuss business or swap contacts. I live in Hong Kong and I buy while based here. I listen to my friends in destination countries such as Ghana and Jamaica and, when they tell me the price for what I have is good, I ship them over" (*China Daily* 2010b). Another trader from Ghana said, "When I come to Hong Kong I want to stay in Chungking Mansions, an area with lots of Africans. This is the heart of Hong Kong; this is where the action is. Here you meet people who are your type, and you can get lots of information" (Mathews 2011: 141–142). They also keep up information on the markets in Africa and Hong Kong by Internet and social media. They access an Internet connection through free Wi-Fi service in guesthouses or surrounding Internet cafes where cheap rates are offered.

African entrepreneurs exhibit a high degree of flexibility in doing business and a streetwise way of doing things. Many petty trade business is made by verbal deals or handwritten receipts that are kept off the books and accepted by cash on delivery. African phone traders bear the risk of being cheated. Some mobile phones purchased from local suppliers may not correspond to description. Some phone suppliers do not comply with the order but mix the phones with substandard products such as refurbished phones. As an African phone buyer complained, "the phones for sale in Chungking Mansions: the outsides look good, Sony and other brands, but the inside of many of them is rubbish. . . . I think 80 percent of the mobile phone stores in Chungking Mansions cheat customers sometimes" (Mathews 2011: 113). Therefore, African entrepreneurs know that they have to be careful in the mobile phone trade. They check products one by one and take photographs or video of every step. They pack the mobile phones in marked boxes with security wires and get on vans to go to the airport.

Mobile phones from Shenzhen ending up in Africa

After comparing mobile phone prices in Chungking Mansions, Sham Shui Po, and Mongkok,[12] African entrepreneurs may end up buying Shenzhen-made phones from stores in Hong Kong at around HK$200 each and sell them at about HK$1,000 in Africa.[13] As most phones weigh between 130 and 140 grams, African traders can pack 6–7 phones per kilogram, or even more of Shenzhen-made phones. In total, they can carry around 200–250 phones within 30 kilograms of checked baggage allowance or add several hundreds more if they pay extra baggage allowance with frequent flyer points or bargain for unused baggage quotas of fellow traders.

Customs in African countries is a problem too. High customs duties and corruption are common in Africa (e.g., Mathews 2011, 2012; Awumbila et al. 2011).

As hundreds of shanzhai cloned phones are packed in luggage, African entrepreneurs are subject to confiscation and prosecution by customs officials. When they are prosecuted, their defense is that they had no idea the products were copies (Mathews and Yang 2012). Lacking connections with government officials and the support of big companies or patrons, African traders are prone to be exploited by border officials. To get their products through customs, traders pay off officials or claim that their relatives work in the government. A West African phone trader said:

> If I pay customs, I may lose everything. I can't pay it all. If you buy a hundred mobile phones, you must pay fifty as tax. It's better to give the customs person two mobile phones as a present instead. You have to be illegal; you have no choice. It's the only possible way. I have a friend, his father is a minister in the government. Everything he buys he pays no taxes. He can do that because his father works in the government. When someone is a minister's son, nobody can touch him. . . . Sometimes customs comes to my shop and says, "Oh, how much did this phone cost?" because they want money. You cannot stop them. If you don't give them money, they bother you. So you pay them off. . . . When you come back, they want to check everything. They always want money. Better to give them a present.
>
> (Mathews 2011: 138)

Case study: a Tanzanian entrepreneur engaging in the low-end mobile phone trade in Chungking Mansions, Hong Kong[14]

In Tanzania, mobile telephony has been observed as the fastest growing information and communication technology, with five mobile providers in 2006. The mobile tele-density in the country increased from almost zero to five between 1993 and 2006. Increase in mobile phone usage is said to be attributed to the liberalization of telecommunication markets, user-friendliness of the phones, the need for basic literacy in using the phones, prepayment modes, and usage of local languages in communication (Sife et al. 2010: 1–2). In 2011, Tanzania had 56 mobile phone subscriptions per 100 inhabitants. This is an almost threefold increase within four years. Mobile phone usage in Tanzania is no longer confined to urban areas, but also to remote or isolated rural areas. In particular, in 2010, more than one third of rural households owned a cell phone, up from 17 percent in 2007. In 2010–11, average household spending on telecommunication in Tanzania was even higher than on health care (World Bank 2013). With such a fast growing mobile phone usage phenomenon, how and where do Tanzanian people in general and those people in the poor rural regions in particular obtain their mobile phones? The answer stems from the profit-seeking efforts of Tanzanian entrepreneurs. This is illustrated by Mr. Ramadhan Myolele, a 38-year-old entrepreneur from Morogoro in Tanzania.

Ramadhan Myolele: a Tanzanian entrepreneur

Ramadhan Myolele owned two stores in Tanzania, involving wholesaling and retailing businesses in consumer appliances. Previously, he bought electronics products in Dubai. He heard stories from other African traders that there were many cheap mobile phones available for sales in Chungking Mansions in Hong Kong. The models ranged from simple Nokia models to Shenzhen-made shanzhai phones. Myolele also heard that their African peers could earn good money by reselling the low-end mobile phones purchased in Hong Kong to people in Tanzania. For example:

- A phone trader from Dar es Salaam, Tanzania, stayed in Hong Kong for three days and bought 820 phones, both authentic and copies, at Chungking Mansions. After deducting air fare and other expenses, he earned US$400 in one trip (Mathews and Yang 2012: 103).
- Mickey from Nigeria bought Shenzhen-made KGtel 8520, modeled on the BlackBerry 8520, in Chungking Mansions (*Think Africa Press* 2013). The KGtel 8520 lacked a trackpad and could not connect to the BlackBerry Messenger services. Yet, it had a torch and dual-SIM support. It was sold at US$15 in Chungking Mansions but the BlackBerry 8520 sold at US$250. Mickey bought 600 pieces of KGtel 8520 and sold them for triple the price in Nigeria. For his expenditure of US$9,000, he could earn US$27,000. Deducting the expenses of travel, daily expenditure, and customs duty, there was a profit of around US$15,000. In some African countries with less supply and higher selling prices, profit margins would be wider.

With this information, Myolele decided to fly to Hong Kong in 2005 for a trial. He intended to buy low-end mobile phones in Hong Kong and sell them in Tanzania. In other words, he intended to perform arbitrageurship. As Myolele claimed in confidence, "I can understand which is required to sell there, and which is required to sell somewhere else."

Once Myolele landed in Hong Kong, he checked into a guesthouse in Chungking Mansions with a daily rent as low as US$13 (Mathews 2011: 16). Though Chungking Mansions is located in Tsim Sha Tsui, one of the most expensive urban areas in Hong Kong, the building accommodates many cheap hostels or guesthouses for backpackers. Many visitors in the building are businesspeople from Africa, the Middle East, and South Asia. Chungking Mansions is the "unofficial African quarter of Hong Kong" (CNN 2011). The complex is also known as the "centre of low-end globalization" (Mathews 2011). Businesses inside the building are regarded as the "best example of globalization in action" (*Time* 2007). Though the guestroom had only a single bed, small bedside cabinet, TV, and free Wi-Fi service, it was good enough for Myolele to do his business. Myolele believed that "if you want to be a big boss, you must be fit in each and every place." After checking in, he immediately ran out to the street to collect trade information. He was told that African traders gathered in front of the 7–11 store next to Chungking Mansions. Myolele first shared a fist bump with fellow traders and greeted them with his African tone, "Hey, what you know, brother?" Then he tried to behave as a member of the "in-group." While the old hand traders talked about good stalls and bad stalls in Hong Kong, Myolele carefully listened and learned. Being a newcomer in the mobile phone trade, he was extremely careful to avoid being cheated. For each gathering, Myolele acquired plenty of trade information, which was utterly important for his survival in the business:

- A Pakistani phone merchant sold a camera phone that he got for HK$30 to Tanzanians for HK$300 (Mathews 2011: 113).
- Rizwan Buff, a phone retailer in Chungking Mansions, said, "Before, Africans were buying phones for HK$60 (US$7), now they're paying HK$500 (US$64)" (*Quartz* 2013).
- A genuine Samsung Galaxy S1 sold for around US$142, while a Shenzhen-made copycat sold for around half that price (*Quartz* 2013).
- A Pakistani phone merchant in Chungking Mansions proudly reported that "they change the phone's housing. They refab [refabricate] it, then sell it to you as if it were a brand-new phone. You don't know this. But we know" (Mathews 2011: 113).
- Some phone dealers replace original batteries (around HK$300) in 14-day phones with Shenzhen-made copy batteries (around HK$11) and sell the originals separately (*The Sun* 2013). Since copy batteries may work as well as original batteries, customers may not know the authenticity of batteries.

Of course, Myolele needed to explore the mobile phone trade himself. The next morning, Myolele checked prices of different mobile phone models inside the Chungking Mansions shopping complex. Trade was busy there. Transnational middlemen in low-end businesses move around inside the building. Apart from mobile phones, there were also clothing, runners, home appliances, and all sorts of African and South Asian food stores, etc.

Since not many Tanzanians could afford luxurious goods, Myolele did not bother with new brand phone models. He told the mobile phone stall owners, "I'm just taking Chinese models, different types of Chinese models." What a surprise to Myolele that Shenzhen-made multi-function phones even had special features for African consumers, including voice changer, non-stop ringtone, and a voice recorder. Yet, none of the phones in the glass counter had price stickers. Myolele was familiar with these models and haggled with phone stall owners over the prices.

After several visits and intense bargaining, Myolele made a deal with Ibrahim Zidwemba from Burkina Faso, West Africa, who owned a phone stall on the first-floor mezzanine of Chungking Mansions. Myolele spent $28,000 on mobile phones. He also hired Wagala Investments to carry on and check in his luggage on the return flight. After he packed hundreds of phones in big suitcases, a South Asian coolie drove him to the airport by van. Two days later, Myolele's mobile phones appeared in the streets of Dar es Salaam. Like other African traders,

Myolele could sell phones from Chungking Mansions for double or even triple the price and earn a profit in his hometown. As Myolele concluded, "Yes the business is very good, I went to buy here [Hong Kong] and I sell there [Dar es Salaam], and I get a profit compared to when I go and buy somewhere else, that's why I proceed to buy in Hong Kong" (BBC 2013).

Conclusion

This chapter uses an Austrian perspective of entrepreneurship and global coordination to understand how African entrepreneurs survive on small profit by engaging in petty businesses in Hong Kong. Unlike the multinational giants which earn profit through sourcing worldwide, African entrepreneurs survive by identifying opportunities in petty businesses and exploiting small profit margins. Through careful economic calculation, they buy Shenzhen-made shanzhai mobile phones in Hong Kong and sell them in Africa. By arbitraging price differentials, they earn pure entrepreneurial profit. This chapter concludes that the African entrepreneurs, through self-interest, benefit low-end mobile phone makers in China, retailers in Chungking Mansions, Hong Kong, and most importantly, low-income African households in rural areas.

Notes

1 The subjectivist approach does not stress knowledge itself, but rather what people know about knowledge. This approach focuses on the kind of knowledge about which people know nothing at all. It follows that "things about which men are completely ignorant are things that simply do not exist" (Kirzner 1979: 138).
2 White (1976: 4) argues that Kirzner does not distinguish arbitrageurship from entrepreneurship.
3 Adopted from de Soto (1995). Using simple stick figures as an illustration, de Soto demonstrates the essence of the Austrian entrepreneurial process.
4 This is called "normal profit" in economics textbooks.
5 Shenzhen is situated immediately north of Hong Kong.
6 www.gartner.com/newsroom/id/1372013; retrieved 23 June 2014.
7 See note 6.
8 In Chinese, the term "shanzhai" can refer to activities such as imitation, cloning, copying, or manufacturing of pirate, counterfeit, or fake goods.
9 Apliu Street in Sham Shiu Po is a famous shopping area of cheap electronics products.
10 These returned defective phones are called 14-day phones.
11 Chungking Mansions is located in the business district in Kowloon, Hong Kong. For details of Chungking Mansions, see below.
12 Mongkok, located at the Kowloon side of Hong Kong, is another busy commercial and entertainment district.
13 https://groups.google.com/forum/#!msg/yotu/TkUykdt2djc/vvRfgPvedsMJ; retrieved 11 July 2014.
14 Adapted from BBC 2013.

References

Aker, Jenny C. and Mbiti, Isaac M. (2010) "Mobile Phones and Economic Development in Africa," *Journal of Economic Perspectives*, 24(3): 207–232.

Awumbila, M.; Quartey, P.; Manuh, T.; Bosiakoh, T.; and Tagoe, C. (2011) *Changing Mobility Patterns and Livelihood Dynamics in Africa: The Case of Transnational Ghanaian Traders*, Legon, Accra: University of Ghana.

Baumol, W. J. (1988) "Is Entrepreneurship Always Productive?," in H. Leibenstein and D. Ray (eds.) *Entrepreneurship and Economic Development*, New York: United Nations, pp. 85–94.

BBC (2013, October 11) "A One-Stop Shop in Hong Kong for African Traders with China," www.bbc.com/news/business-24494174; retrieved 21 April 2014.

Berger, Peter L. and Luckmann, Thomas (1966) *The Social Construction of Reality: A Treatise in the Sociology of Knowledge*, Harmondsworth: Penguin.

Bertoncelo, Brigitte and Bredeloup, Sylvie (2007) "The Emergence of New African 'Trading Posts' in Hong Kong and Guangzhou," *China Perspective*, 218: 94–105.

Bodomo, Adams (2007) "An Emerging African-Chinese Community in Hong Kong: The Case of Tsim Sha Tsui's Chungking Mansions," in Kwesi Kwaa Prah (ed.) *Afro-Chinese Relations: Past, Present and Future*, Cape Town: The Centre for Advanced Studies in African Societies, pp. 367–389.

Bodomo, Adams (2010) "The African Trading Community in Guangzhou: An Emerging Bridge for Africa-China Relations," *China Quarterly*, 2(3): 693–707.

Casson, Mark (1982) *The Entrepreneur: An Economic Theory*, Oxford: Blackwell.

Chau, L.L.C. (1993) *Hong Kong: A Unique Case of Development*, Washington DC: A World Bank Publication.

China Daily (2010a, July 6) "The Pride, Passion and Purpose of HK's Africans," www.chinadaily.com.cn/hkedition/2010-07/06/content_10067689.htm; retrieved 30 June 2014.

China Daily (2010b, December 10) "Market Movers," www.chinadaily.com.cn/hkedition/2010-12/10/content_11680498.htm; retrieved 21 April 2014.

CNN (2011, February 4) "China, Hip-hop and the New Sudan," http://edition.cnn.com/2011/WORLD/africa/02/02/sudan.jal/; retrieved 31 July 2014.

Custer, C. (2012, December 19) "Chinese Mobile Phones Hold a Big Chunk of East African Market, but That's Not a Good Thing," TECHINASIA, www.techinasia.com/chinese-mobile-phones-hold-big-chunk-east-african-market-good/; retrieved 22 July 2014.

de Soto, J. H. (1995) "Entrepreneurship and the Economic Analysis of Socialism," in Meijer Gerrit (ed.) *New Perspectives on Austrian Economics*, London: Routledge, pp. 228–253.

Financial Times (2009) "The Numbers Game," www.ft.com/intl/cms/s/0/39cc88b2-ef36–11dd-bbb5–0000779fd2ac.html#axzz2zaM8LNTy; retrieved 22 April 2014.

Hayek, F. A. (1945) "The Use of Knowledge in the Society," *American Economic Review*, 35: 519–530.

Hong Kong Economic Journal (2010, June 28) "Shanzhai iPhone 4 Found in Hong Kong, Value Chain Worth over a Million Dollars," www.hkej.com/template/dailynews/jsp/detail.jsp?dnews_id=2536&cat_id=1&title_id=315277; retrieved 3 June 2014. (Text in Chinese)

Hong Kong Economic Journal (2012, October 24) "1 Billion Smartphone Exports with Net Profit Ratio Less than 1 Percent," www.hkej.com/template/dailynews/jsp/detail_print.jsp?dnews_id=3539&cat_id=3&title_id=551825; retrieved 15 July 2014. (Text in Chinese)

Hu, Jin-Li; Wan, Hsiang-Tzu; and Zhu, Hang (2011) "The Business Model of a Shanzhai Mobile Phone Firm in China," *Australian Journal of Business and Management Research*, 1(3): 52–62.

Kirzner, I. M. (1973) *Competition and Entrepreneurship*, Chicago: University of Chicago Press.

Kirzner, I. M. (1979) *Perception, Opportunity, and Profit*, Chicago: University of Chicago Press.

Kirzner, I. M. (1985) *Discovery and the Capitalist Process*, Chicago: University of Chicago Press.

Knight, Frank (1921) *Risk, Profit and Uncertainty*, Boston: Houghton Mifflin Company.

Lachmann, L. M. (1956) *Capital and Its Structure*, Kansas City, MO: Sheed Andrews and McMeel.

Lin, Yi-Chieh Jessica (2011) *Fake Stuff: China and the Rise of Counterfeit Goods*, New York and London: Routledge.

Martin, Adam (2007) "Mises, Kirzner and Knight on Uncertainty and Entrepreneurship: A Synthesis," working paper, http://adamgmartin.com/Site/Working%20Papers/B1F9899F-6D08-43B9-A8A7-E2B6FA0644EC.html; retrieved 25 February 2008.

Mathews, Gordon (2011) *Ghetto at the Center of the World: Chungking Mansions, Hong Kong*, Chicago and London: University of Chicago Press.

Mathews, Gordon (2012) "African Traders in Chungking Mansions, Hong Kong," in David W. Haines, Keiko Yamanaka, and Shinji Yamashita (eds.) *Wind over Water: Migration in an East Asian Context*, New York: Berghahn Books, pp. 208–218.

Mathews, Gordon and Yang, Yang (2012) "How Africans Pursue Low-End Globalization in Hong Kong and Mainland China," *Journal of Current Chinese Affairs*, 2: 95–120.

Menger, Carl (1871/2007) *Principles of Economics*, Auburn, AL: Mises Institute.

Mises, Ludwig v. (1949) *Human Action*, 3rd ed., Chicago: Contemporary Books.

Quartz (2013, May 4) "Hong Kong's Counterfeit Mobile Hub Loses Ground to Cheap Phones on the Mainland," http://qz.com/79768/photos-hong-kongs-counterfeit-cell-phone-hub-is-losing-ground-to-cheap-phones-on-the-mainland/; retrieved 20 April 2014.

Reekie, W. Duncan (1984) *Markets, Entrepreneurs, and Liberty: An Austrian View of Capitalism*, Brighton, Sussex: Wheatsheaf Books.

Reuters (2010, August 11) " 'Made in Shenzhen': A Hidden Empire of Mobile Phones," http://cn.reuters.com/article/wtNews/idCNCHINA-4750020110811; retrieved 22 April 2014.

Reynolds, P. D.; Camp, M.; Bygrave, W. D.; Autio, E.; and Hay, M. (2002) *Global Entrepreneurship Monitor, 2001 Executive Report*, Babson College, London Business School, and Kauffman Foundation.

Schumpeter, J. A. (1934/1961) *The Theory of Economic Development*, New York: Oxford University Press.

Schutz, A. and Luckmann, T. (1989) *The Structures of the Life World*, Vol. II, Evanston, IL: Northwestern University Press.

Sife, Alfred Said; Kiondo, Elizabeth; and Lyimo-Macha, Joyce G. (2010) "Contribution of Mobile Phones to Rural Livelihoods and Poverty," *Electronic Journal on Information Systems in Developing Countries*, 42(3): 1–15.

Smith, Adam (1776) *An Inquiry into the Nature and Causes of the Wealth of Nations*, New York: Modern Library Classics.

The Sun (2013, October 18) "Triple-A Phones Prone to Explode," http://the-sun.on.cc/cnt/news/20131018/00410_020.html; retrieved 10 June 2014.

Think Africa Press (2013, May 2) "Hong Kong Calling: How China's Cheap Phones Make Their Way to Africa," http://thinkafricapress.com/development/hong-kong-calling-cheap-chinese-phones-make-way-africa; retrieved 21 April 2014.

Time (2007, May 7) "The Best of Asia," www.time.com/time/specials/packages/completelist/0,29569,1614524,00.html; retrieved 23 August 2011.

White, L. H. (1976) "Entrepreneurship, Imagination and the Question of Equilibrium," in S. Littlechild (ed.) *Austrian Economics*, Vol. III, 1990, Aldershot: Edward Elgar, pp. 87–104.

World Bank (2013) *World Development Indicators 2013*, Washington DC: World Bank, https://openknowledge.worldbank.org/handle/10986/13191; retrieved on 20 April 2015.

Yang, Yang (2012) "African Traders in Guangzhou: Routes, Reasons, Profits, Dreams," in Gordon Mathews, Gustavo Lins Ribeiro, and Carlos Aba Vega (eds.) *Globalization from Below: The World's Other Economy*, London: Routledge, pp. 154–170.

Zhu, Sheng and Shi, Yongjiang (2010) "Shanzhai Manufacturing – an Alternative Innovation Phenomenon in China: Its Value Chain and Implications for Chinese Science and Technology Policies," *Journal of Science and Technology Policy in China*, 1(1): 29–49.

Index